Inequality and Stratification: Class, Color, and Gender

Second Edition

Robert A. Rothman

University of Delaware

Prentice Hall, Englewood Cliffs, New Jersey 07632

Library of Congress Cataloging-in-Publication Data

Rothman, Robert A.
    Inequality & stratification : class, color, and gender / Robert A.
Rothman. -- 2nd ed.
      p.   cm.
    Rev. ed. of: Inequality and stratification in the United States.
c 1978.
    Includes bibliographical references (p.   ) and indexes.
    ISBN 0-13-457375-7
    1. United States--Social conditions. 2. Equality--United States.
3. Social structure. 4. Social classes--United States. 5. Social
status--United States. 6. Minorities--United States. I. Rothman,
Robert A.,   Inequality and stratification in the United
States. II. Title. III. Title: Inequality and stratification.
HN57.R577 1992
305'.0973--dc20
                92-2542
                CIP

To Nancy:
For Everything

Acquisitions editor: Alison Reeves
Production editor: Elaine Lynch
Copy editor: Mary Louise Byrd
Editorial assistant: Diane Peirano
Cover design: Patricia Kelly
Pre-press buyer: Kelly Behr
Manufacturing buyer: Mary Ann Gloriande

© 1993, 1978 by Prentice-Hall, Inc.
A Simon & Schuster Company
Englewood Cliffs, New Jersey 07632

The first edition of this book was published, by Prentice Hall, with the title
Inequality and Stratification in the United States.

Printed in the United States of America

10 9 8 7 6 5 4 3 2

ISBN 0-13-457375-7

Prentice-Hall International (UK) Limited, *London*
Prentice-Hall of Australia Pty. Limited, *Sydney*
Prentice-Hall Canada Inc., *Toronto*
Prentice-Hall Hispanoamericana, S.A., *Mexico*
Prentice-Hall of India Private Limited, *New Delhi*
Prentice-Hall of Japan, Inc., *Tokyo*
Simon & Schuster Asia Pte. Ltd., *Singapore*
Editora Prentice-Hall do Brasil, Ltda., *Rio de Janeiro*

Contents

Preface
to the Second Edition

The study of social class has been a central theme in sociology since its origins in the nineteenth century. Much has changed since the first edition of this book was written in the mid-1970s, but no development has been more salient than recognition that considerations of color and gender are central to a full appreciation of the composition and dynamics of class systems. Although this perspective was addressed in the first edition, the recent outpouring of fresh conceptualizations and new research has resulted in a significant reorganization and reorientation of the whole volume in an attempt to include a systematic consideration of the interaction among class, color, and gender.

Consequently, the preparation of this version demanded broader change and revitalization than is usually required for the preparation of a second edition. The book has been retitled to reflect the new emphasis. In fact, it can more actually be described as a new book rather than a revision. Although the American experience remains as the central emphasis, the scope has been broadened to elaborate other historical and contemporary forms of social stratification.

One thing that has not changed is the central pedagogical thrust. This edition, like the original, is intended to provide the fundamentals of social stratification for undergraduates in a concise and readable format. Consequently, it may be used in two ways, either as a basic text for courses in stratification or as one component of courses such as introduction to sociology, social problems, race and minorities, or gender studies.

Any book that attempts to lay out the fundamentals of an area as complex and broad as stratification cannot elaborate all the areas of debate and controversy. Therefore, more advanced students are directed to the material contained in the Bibliography and Additional Readings sections for the resources needed to explore these issues in more depth and detail.

This book has benefited from the ideas and comments of countless friends and colleagues, and from the supportive advice of the following, who served as reviewers for the publisher: Norval D. Glenn, University of Texas, Austin and George F. Stine, Millersville University, Pennsylvania.

Robert A. Rothman

Part One

The Nature
of
Inequality and Stratification

Structural inequalities based on position in the economic system (class) and ascribed statuses (color and gender) shape the rewards and opportunities of all members of industrial societies. The effects are most pronounced in the distribution of economic rewards, social judgments and evaluations, and access to political power but extend to most facets of modern life. Chapter 1 develops concepts and perspectives basic to an understanding of sociological perspectives on inequality and stratification. Chapter 2 reviews three major theoretical conceptualizations and interpretations of the origins of class systems that inform current theory and research. Chapter 3 develops models of four recurring forms of stratification—slave, caste, estate, and class— each of which has contemporary relevance, either characterizing a current society or having enduring consequences for understanding stratification in the United States in the 1990s.

Chapter 1
Structural Inequality and Social Stratification

STRUCTURAL INEQUALITY: An Introduction and Overview

Differences—sometimes vast differences—in wealth, material possessions, power, prestige, and access to simple creature comforts are readily
apparent to anyone in modern industrial societies. Inequalities in the
distribution of financial resources are among the most readily evident and
easy to document. Some people enjoy immense inherited wealth that allows
them to indulge extravagant lifestyles. Wealthy American heiress Doris
Duke, for example, feels it necessary to fly her two pet camels with her on
her annual trip to her vacation home in Hawaii (Clancy, 1988). Industrial
societies also contain millions of people whose daily lives are a struggle
against economic hardship. One child in five in America grows up in
"poverty." Hundreds of thousands of homeless are compelled to wander the
streets and fill the shelters of Los Angles, London, and Moscow. Many
others are denied fundamental necessities. It is believed, for example, that
each year 250,000 people are turned away from hospitals in the United
States because they are too poor to pay (Ansberry, 1988). Between such
extremes are smaller gradations of monetary inequality, often measured
by the size of homes people live in, the kind of cars people drive, or the
quality of the schools their children attend.

Probably the most important contribution that sociology can make to
the analysis of social inequality is to emphasize that inequality is patterned rather than random. Many of the most significant rewards, resources, privileges, and opportunities are distributed at least in part on
the basis of social position or membership in socially defined categories.
This is referred to as *structural inequality*. In industrial societies, social
class (position in the economic system, defined by occupation for the vast
majority of people), color or minority status (race and ethnicity), and
gender are among the three most salient social categories in understanding
the distribution of inequality.

CLASS, COLOR, AND GENDER: Basic Concepts

The analysis developed here centers on the concept of social stratification as it has traditionally been used in sociology to denote the division of industrial societies into broad, economically grounded classes. This will entail an examination of the origins and arrangement of classes and the economic, social, and political inequities associated with class position. An integral part of the analysis involves systematically exploring the ways that color and gender modify or amplify the ramifications of class. The implications of color and gender permeate most facets of social life in industrial societies but such a comprehensive undertaking is beyond the scope of this volume. Rather, the more narrowly defined intent is to focus on the convergence of class, color, and gender.

Three specific areas are emphasized. The first deals with the effects of class, color, and gender on attainments and mobility within the class system. This approach builds on the well-documented observation that children of blue-collar parents, members of minority groups, and women are often under represented among the upper middle class and over represented at lower levels of the class system, and proceeds to explore the social and educational arrangements that work to the disadvantage of these groups.

Next are the differences among people at the same level in the class system for there are many situations in which considerations of color or gender apparently overwhelm class considerations. For example, the over-all gender gap that separates women's and men's earnings is much greater in some working class occupations than others. In addition, although some African Americans have attained upper middle class status they continue to confront segregation in the housing market and discrimination in the job market.

Third is influence of color and gender on how social class position is perceived and experienced. For example, it appears that there are gender differences in the perceptions of the stratification system as well as variations in the manner in which women and men at different class levels interpret and cope with the demands of dual-career family life.

Therefore, it is evident that a full understanding of the dynamics of inequality requires a consideration of the interaction of class, color, and gender. Each of these three basic concepts requires clarification at the outset.

Social Class

For the purposes of this analysis, *social classes* are defined as those people who occupy a similar location in the economic system (i.e., the social organization of production and distribution) in industrial societies.[1] Position in the economic system includes two major considerations, the type of work people do and the ownership and control of resources. For most people, except for those at the higher and lower levels of the stratification system, occupation is the most convenient single measure of social class. The lines separating classes are, admittedly, not always clearly demarcated, and the position of some occupations is more complex than others. For example, the position of agricultural workers, the self-employed, and small to medium-size business owners is less consistent than most.

Social class position defined by occupation is a factor in understanding inequality because people's work sets effective limits on financial rewards and social prestige, influences the stability of employment and the chances for advancement, locates people in systems of workplace authority and power that has consequences that extend beyond the workplace, defines some features of social relations on and off the job, contributes to the way people think about themselves and others, and has enduring implications for their children.

American society, as well as other industrial democracies, can be divided into five broad social classes. A small proportion of the population forms an *elite class*, wielding unusual economic, political, and social power. The elite class is actually composed of two analytically separate groups— an *economic elite*, made up of individuals and families whose power derives from ownership of major economic resources in the form of property and stocks and bonds, and an *institutional elite*, whose power resides in the structural positions they occupy: top leadership in business, the media, government, and other dominant organizations and institutions. Specific individuals may simultaneously be members of both groups, and the extent of this overlap is the subject of much controversy.

The next level, the *upper middle class*, combines occupations based on expert knowledge (professional people such as physicians and scientific personnel) and includes organizational managers who are below the executive level but still exercise a significant level of power. The *lower middle class* includes technicians, lower level administrators, clerical personnel, and most sales workers. In the United States *working class* implies manual work, also called blue-collar work, and describes those who do largely physical labor in the factories and mills. Some are engaged in highly skilled work (auto mechanics), and others do more routine work (on assembly lines). Such skill differentials are an important consideration in understanding how manual workers perceive themselves.

[1] The term social class is widely used, but it has many different meanings. It is one of those concepts that sociologists have been unable to specify to the complete satisfaction of one another, in part because definitions vary with ideology and methodology. Consequently, any conceptualization encounters both critics and supporters. There is no recourse except to note that social class is herein defined in a manner that is not necessarily the same encountered in the work of other sociologists.

At the bottom of the hierarchy are *the poor* [2] those who live on the very margins of the productive system. Numbered in this class are both the *working poor*, who fill the least skilled and most unstable jobs, and those who are unemployed, underemployed, or discouraged because they believe they cannot find work.

Developing an accurate picture of the class structure of American society is a complex task, but the basic outlines are as suggested by Exhibit 1.1.[3] There is a small elite, making up no more than 1 or 2 percent of the population. About one quarter of society can be defined as upper middle class on the basis of administrative, managerial, and professional occupations. Approximately one third of the population holds lower-middle-class jobs in clerical, sales, and administrative support positions. One quarter fills the manual occupations of the working class. Perhaps one in four Americans may be counted among the poor, holding marginal jobs or facing unemployment.

Countless significant rewards are associated with class position, not the least of which is financial. Most economic rewards for the majority of people flow directly from their occupation, with approximately 80 percent of the money people earn coming from their work (Ryscavage, 1986).

Color: Race and Ethnicity

People of color are, to quote a widely used phrase, groups of people who, "because of physical or cultural characteristics, are singled out from

[2]This group was typically called *lower class* in earlier sociological analysis, but that term has been abandoned because it carries pejorative connotations. More recently, it has become commonplace to use "the poor" to identify those occupying the lowest levels of the stratification system, and that convention is employed here.

However, the use of the term the poor is not without problems. One is that it tends to concentrate attention on monetary consequences rather than structural position. It must be emphasized that there are other noneconomic consequences of occupying the lowest levels of the system. A related issue is that it can lead to confusion with official poverty levels. "Poverty" is a measure of economic resources developed by the government in the 1960s and, although a useful tool, is not based on structural position.

[3]There are several unresolved technical and conceptual issues in the definition of classes. One methodological problem is that the most comprehensive and up-to-date national occupational data are collected by government agencies, but the data are not organized and reported in a manner consistent with the class analysis used here. A related difficulty is that not all people are part of the paid work force, requiring an estimation of their class position.

There is also the conceptual problem of defining the unit of class analysis—individuals or family units. Although there is a tendency to dichotomize the issue, both perspectives have merit. It is evident that families are the locus of residence, socialization, lifestyle, and consumption patterns, and that household units frequently include partners at the same class level. However, class differences within families are also common and relevant to the way people experience their position in the stratification system. In addition, increased marital instability and the increase in the number of unmarried adults points up the necessity of focusing on the individual.

Exhibit 1.1
A Model of Social Class in the United States

Social Class	Percentage of the Population	Number Employed (ooos)
Elite	1-2	
Upper middle class	20-25	
Professionals		10,900
Middle managers		7,500
Sales, except retail		7,800
Lower middle class	30-35	
White collar		6,700
Technicians		3,600
Sales, retail		2,600
Administrative support		18,400
Working class	25-30	
Precision production		13,800
Machine operators and fabricators		8,200
Transportation workers		4,800
Protective services		1,900
The poor	15-20	
Private household workers		320
Service workers		6,500
Handlers, cleaners, helpers, laborers		4,800
Unemployed		6,500

Note: Class designations are based on U.S. Bureau of Labor Statistics occupational categories reorganized as follows. Middle managers: executive, administrative, and managerial minus management-related occupations; professional: professional specialty minus teachers, counselors, social workers, recreation workers, and health assessment occupations; white collar: teachers, counselors, social workers, recreation workers, and health assessment occupations.

Source: "Employed Civilians by Detailed Occupation," *Employment and Earnings*, 55 (January, 1991), Table 22.

others in the society in which they live for differential and unequal treatment" (Wirth, 1945: 347). The term people of color currently coexists with the term minority group and encompasses two traditional sociological concepts—race and ethnicity. Race is a social definition of a social category of people, typically based on visible physical characteristics, such as skin color, stature, and facial features. Ethnic groups are identified by cultural (or national) origins, which may be manifest in language, religion, customs, and practices.

Patterns of Intergroup Relations

Societies of any size and complexity typically include subgroups based on race or ethnicity, and the United States is no exception. The bringing together of peoples from diverse cultural and racial origins does not necessarily produce social, economic, or political subordination. A case in point are the Cossacks and Tungas of Manchuria, who coexisted for centuries within a context of political independence and mutual respect (Lindgren, 1938). Unfortunately, though, some form of economic or social subordination is the all-too-common outcome.

Minority groups become members of a society by different paths and this has important implications for subsequent intergroup relations. *Immigration* is the flow of peoples in search of jobs or political freedom, beginning in the United States on a large scale in the 1840s and continuing today as waves of newcomers pour into America. Immigration tends to be voluntary, but there are also several forms of involuntary contact. Groups are sometimes incorporated into a society as the result of *territorial expansion*. A more powerful group, prompted by military, economic, or political goals, encroaches on previously independent populations, as was the experience with Europeans encountering native Americans or Mexicans in the Southwest. Other groups become members of the society through a process of *importation*, typically to provide a work force, as was the case in nineteenth-century Hawaii where Chinese laborers were brought in to harvest sugarcane. Finally, there is *involuntary servitude*, the enslavement of groups for the purpose of providing labor, as in the case of African slaves, or some other purpose for the dominant members of society.

During the 1980s more than 5 million immigrants entered the United States (with the largest numbers originating in Korea, China, Vietnam, and Mexico), joining the literally hundreds of diverse racial and ethnic groups that coexist in America. Minority status has important implications for location in the class system and, in turn, inequalities in wealth, prestige, power, and life chances. Recent decades have witnessed breakthroughs by individuals, but progress has frequently been slow and halting for groups that lag behind in many areas. As shown in Exhibit 1.2, African Americans and Hispanics—the only two groups for which there are reliable data—are underrepresented among upper-middle-class occupations and overrepresented in clerical work, among operatives and in service work.

A brief overview of several of the large minority groups is useful, and serves to emphasize the fact that broad statistical groupings often mask marked differences in culture, religion, and language.

Exhibit 1.2
Class Distribution of Persons of Color in the United States 1990

	All Workers	White	Black	Hispanic
Upper middle class				
Managerial	12.6%	13.3%	7.2%	6.0%
Professional	13.0	13.4	8.7	5.8
Lower middle class				
Technicians	3.2	3.2	2.7	1.9
Sales	11.9	12.4	8.0	8.1
Clerical	15.5	15.4	16.7	13.1
Working class				
Craft	11.6	12.1	8.6	13.2
Operatives	11.1	10.5	16.6	17.8
The poor				
Service	13.3	12.1	23.1	18.9
Laborers	4.2	4.0	6.5	6.7
Nonurban occupations	3.0	3.2	1.9	5.4

Note: Hispanics may be of any race.
Source: "Employed Civilians by Detailed Occupation," *Employment and Earnings* 37 (October, 1990), Tables A-60-61.

MAJOR MINORITY GROUPS IN THE UNITED STATES

Blacks, or *African-Americans*, are the largest single minority group in the United States, numbering over 30 million and making up about 12% of the total population.[4] Scholars continue to debate the original social and political status of the first blacks in colonial America during the seventeenth century, for there is evidence that some came as indentured servants to be freed after serving fixed terms, but it is clear that by the end of the century

[4]The shifting language of identification among disadvantaged groups reflects the social and political realities of their histories. Some American slaves apparentlly favored "African" over the more insulting terms used by their owners, at least until white supremacist groups mounted campaigns to deport freed slaves. "Negro" dominated the social discourse until the 1960s when the former racial slur "black" was adopted as a proud statement of group solidarity and identity. Late in the 1980s, some leaders began to champion "African-American" to encourage people to identify themselves by their history and culture rather than skin color. Recent surveys suggest that "black" continues to be favored by a sizable majority of American blacks although "African-American" is favored by the young and better educated (New York Times, 1991).

slavery was a social and legal reality for Africans. Slavery was supported by an ideology of racism that continues to have contemporary ramifications. Although open expressions of racism have declined, white supremacist groups continue to march, campuses across the nation are frequently marred by racial incidents, and thinly disguised expressions of racism infiltrate social and political life.

The erosion of social and legal barriers to voting, housing, jobs, and education combined with changing attitudes have made it possible for black Americans to achieve upper-middle-class status and even occupy positions among the institutional elite. However, the collective economic, educational, and occupational attainments of blacks continue to lag behind those of white Americans and other minority groups. Black children are more likely to die in infancy than white children and are three times more likely to be growing up in poverty or in a single-parent family. Fewer African Americans than whites attend college; those who do graduate earn one third less than whites with the same level of education. And, the net wealth of black households is one tenth that of whites (O'Hare, et al., 1991: 2).

Hispanic is commonly used to describe all persons of Spanish-language origin, although many prefer to identify themselves as "Latinos." Hispanic is a very loose category, encompassing people from quite different national and cultural traditions. There are approximately 20 million Hispanics in the United States (U.S. Bureau of the Census, 1989). The largest single subgroup (63 percent) is of Mexican descent and is concentrated in the Southwest. Many Mexican Americans describe themselves as "Chicano." Puerto Ricans (13 percent) have tended to settle in the Northeast, and Cubans (5 percent) in Florida. Most of the rest of the Hispanic population is from Central and South America (11 percent) or trace their origins to Spain or other nations (8 percent).

The Hispanic population in the United States grew by about 30 percent during the 1980s, making it one of America's fastest-growing minority groups and leading to predictions that it will become the largest single minority category by the twenty-first century. Sheer numbers have granted Hispanics a growing voice in political affairs, and they hold over 4,000 elected offices at the local, state, and national levels. However, Hispanic high school dropout rates and unemployment rates are well above national averages, and income stands below that of white Americans.

Another large minority group is *Asian*, including peoples from such disparate cultural and religious traditions as India, the Philippines, Korea, China, and Japan. Asian immigration on a large scale began with the Chinese in the nineteenth century, followed by the Japanese at the turn of the century. An ongoing series of political and economic upheavals beginning in the post–World War II period has more recently caused the influx of significant numbers of Filipinos, Koreans, Vietnamese, Cambodians, and Laotians.

The success of Asian students on Scholastic Aptitude Tests has contributed to their being labeled a "super minority," as they are able to compete successfully with white Americans in science and math. But the dark side of race relations cannot be ignored. The death of Vincent Chin, a Chinese American, is a part of it. He was beaten to death in Detroit in 1982 by two unemployed autoworkers who are alleged to have made racist remarks such as "Nip" (thus confusing him with someone of Japanese ancestry) and saying, "Because of you we're out of work" (U.S. Commission on Civil Rights, 1986: 43).

Native American is still another loose statistical category, bringing together peoples as diverse as the Eskimos of Alaska, the Navaho of Arizona, and the Iroquois of New York. It is believed that there were 200 different tribes residing in North America when Europeans first arrived, and although there are no reliable figures on the size of the native population at that point, estimates range from a low of 1 million to a high of 10 million (Feagin, 1984: 177). By 1850, disease and warfare had reduced the native American population to about 200,000. Recent census figures show a population of approximately 1.5 million persons, and nearly one fourth of all native American households must be numbered among the poor. By all accounts, native Americans are the most severely disadvantaged minority group in contemporary society, suffering extraordinarily high rates of illness and alcoholism (Sandefur & Sakamoto, 1988).

Sex and Gender

Male-female differentiation is common to all human societies. *Sex* is used when discussing differences in physiological and biological characteristics, whereas *gender* refers to socially defined roles and behavioral and attitudinal expectations. Gender roles are a part of the social and cultural heritage of a group, and individuals are introduced to them at birth as they begin to encounter different expectations and are exposed to different treatment.

In a broad, historical perspective it appears that gender-based inequalities are associated with the evolution of societies as social systems (Chafetz, 1984). More modest levels of social, economic, and political inequality are found in simple hunting and gathering societies (past and present), and social and economic discrepancies reach their peak in horticultural and agricultural societies and seem to decline with the onset of industrialization.

American women have made significant strides during the last two decades. Legal and customary barriers to education have been eroded, sexist stereotypes are challenged on every front, and occupational success in fields closed to women only a few years ago has been attained. But many forms of inequality persist, and none is more persistent than the wage gap

Exhibit 1.3
Class Distribution of Women in the United States, 1989

	All Workers	White Women	Black Women
Upper middle class			
Managerial	12.7%	11.6%	7.4%
Professional	13.3	15.3	10.8
Lower middle class			
Sales	12.0	13.6	9.4
Clerical	15.7	28.2	25.9
Technicians	3.1	3.2	3.6
Working class			
Craft	11.8	2.2	2.4
Operatives	11.2	6.6	10.7
Protective	1.7	0.5	0.9
Agriculture	2.9	1.2	0.4
The poor			
Services	11.5	15.8	26.3
Laborers	4.2	1.6	2.3

Source: "Employed Civilians by Detailed Occupation,"*Employment and Earnings* 37 (1990), Table 21.

that separates male and female workers' incomes. Women also continue to be concentrated in lower level occupations with fewer opportunities for advancement (Exhibit 1.3).

PATTERNS OF INEQUALITY

All major forms of inequality have a distinct relationship to the intersection of social class, color, and gender. Class position is a major factor in understanding the distribution of financial rewards, assignment of social prestige, and access to power and authority. In addition, the salience of the concept of social class also extends to considerations of life chances and lifestyles.

Economic Inequality

The range of economic inequality in societies may be great or small. Anthropologists have noted that a number of non-industrial societies reveal an almost complete absence of economic inequality (Marshall, 1965;

Holmberg, 1950). At the other extreme are societies where economic resources may be concentrated in the hands of a relatively small number of individuals or families. Historically, it appears that the most rampant inequalities were found in agrarian societies during the twelfth and thir-teenth centuries. At one point in medieval England, the income of the king was estimated at £24,000, 30 times the income of the next wealthiest noble and equivalent to the income of 24,000 field hands, who earned a penny a day (Lenski, 1966: 212). Estimates suggest that perhaps 70 percent of all the wealth in the United States—including about half the value of all real estate and over 90 percent of corporate stocks and bonds—is concentrated in the hands of 10 percent of the population, (U.S. Congress, 1986: 35). At the same time, the poorest 10 percent have no material assets or are actually in debt.

Social Ranking, Prestige, and Association

A second important form of inequality is that of social ranking in terms of superiority and inferiority, usually called social prestige or social status. *Social prestige* or *status* may be described as the social standing, esteem, or honor that positions command. Social prestige is relevant because people are sensitive to the evaluations of others, valuing the admiration and approval of their peers, as is readily evident when people attempt to enhance their social standing through the display of clothing and cars or by their choice of career and lifestyle (Goode, 1979).

Individuals may earn prestige on the basis of their own efforts (athletic ability) or personal attributes (physical attractiveness, intelli-gence), but there is also a powerful structural dimension to prestige. Social classes, occupations, racial and ethnic groups, and the sexes can be ar-ranged in hierarchies of social prestige. For example, at various times and in various places, women and men have formed clearly demarcated pres-tige groupings. In the United States, as recently as the 1950s, it was common for males to be openly rated as superior to females by both men and women (McKee & Sherriffs, 1957). Perhaps the most common rankings are based on occupation, with upper-middle-class work such as lawyer or physician being rated well above working-class jobs such as truck driver or garbage collector.

Moreover, the significance of social ranking extends beyond questions of social approval and ego gratification. Prestige considerations can dictate the form of social interaction between people at different levels. People are likely to show deference to those ranked above them and tend to expect deference from those below them. Social ranking can also lead to exclusion-ary practices designed to limit social contacts and social interaction that show up in residential segregation and other forms of restrictions.

Power, Authority, and Influence

A third, more complex, form of inequality is in the distribution of power and authority in society. Much formal authority in democratic societies is centralized in the various branches of government that write, interpret, and enforce the laws, impose taxes, regulate business and industry, and declare war or pursue peace. One direct measure of access to positions of authority is elected representation, and it appears that some groups have much greater access to government than others. For example, the composition of the 101th Congress showed that of the 535 members, only 24 (4.5 percent) were women and 23 were black Americans (4.5 percent). Members of lower social classes are also disadvantaged. For example, 191 (36 percent) are members of a single occupational group within the upper middle class—attorneys—and 77 percent have incomes over $90,000 a year. Therefore, it would seem that access to Congress is not necessarily evenly distributed across all groups in the society.

Most organizations—corporations, military organizations, educational and government agencies—distribute authority hierarchically. Incumbents of positions at each higher level earn more money, but perhaps equally important, they have some authority to set rules, reward, promote and sanction, and direct the work behavior of subordinates. Moreover, each higher level has more influence on the goals and activities of the organization, with the most authority concentrated in the hands of a few executives at the apex. Access to hierarchial organizational authority also appears to favor some groups over others. This is illustrated by an examination of the major news organizations, which typically have five bureaucratic levels (J. Wilson, 1989). Women fill a large percentage of the jobs at the bottom of these organizations, 53 percent of the news reporters and 61

CASE STUDY:
Hierarchy in Sports

Opportunities for blacks in professional sports reveal an interesting anomaly. Although many are players, and some earn huge competitive salaries, the fact is that few African Americans have been able to move into decision-making or supervisory positions in professional sports organizations. A recent survey shows the following situation that prevailed in the National Football League in 1987. More than half (58 percent) of the players in the NFL were black, but blacks held only 3 percent of the managerial/administrative positions (Shuster, 1987). The specifics were:

Black head coaches	1 out of 28
Assistant coaches	41 out of 284
Game officials	41 out of 107
Referees	0 out of 15

percent of the sales staff. However, their proportions are notably smaller at each higher level. For example, at the fourth level, 26 percent of managing editors are female. At the third level, positions such as advertising director or sales manager, 17 percent are women. General managers form the second level and here 8 percent are women. At the pinnacle of publishers, chief executive officers, and vice presidents, 6 percent are female.

Lifestyles and Life Chances

Max Weber is responsible for popularizing the concept of life chances, and his phrasing remains descriptive: "the typical chances for a supply of goods, external living conditions, and personal life experiences" (Weber, 1946: 180). Thus, *life chances* refers to the role of class in increasing or decreasing the probability of experiencing events, circumstances, or opportunities that enhance or diminish the quality of life. Infant mortality, the chances of going to college, the risk of suffering mental illness, positive self-concepts, becoming unemployed, and countless other incidents are encompassed by this phrase. Life chances are highlighted by considering the probability of being a victim of violent crime (robbery, assault, rape). The poorest in American society are more than twice as likely to be victimized as are the most wealthy (U.S. Department of Justice, 1988: 26):

Family income:

$7,500 or less	49 victims per 1,000 persons
$7,500 to $14,999	34 victims per 1,000 persons
$15,000 to $29,999	26 victims per 1,000 persons
$30,000 or more	20 victims per 1,000 persons

Such examples can only hint at the broad implications of social class.

Members of a society all participate to some extent in the larger culture, but there are also certain differences in behavior that serve to distinguish members of different social classes. The concept of *lifestyles* points out that people who occupy a common location in the social organization of production and distribution sometimes develop distinctive behavioral and attitudinal patterns. In some instances lifestyles represent the outcome of deliberate collective action. For example, many long-standing members of the economic elite conform to a unique style of life that emphasizes genteel manners in social discourse, a singular language copied from British aristocracy, and a passion for breeding certain quadrupeds—dogs and horses (Birmingham, 1987). Many elements of this lifestyle emerged in the nineteenth century as a self-conscious attempt to separate and isolate members of their class from less advantaged classes.

However, the concept of lifestyles also encompasses less explicit and coordinated activities that can be viewed as aggregate responses to common conditions. For example, one theme running through the lives of members of the working class is a sense of detachment from their work that contrasts with the sense of commitment so often found among members of the upper middle class. This orientation would seem to be a way of coping with the routine, unchanging nature of manual work that provides little stimulation, challenge, interest, or chance of promotion. It is not so much an organized response as it is a collection of typical individual responses to the same situation.

THE INSTITUTIONALIZATION OF INEQUALITY

Structural inequality cannot and does not survive isolated from other parts of a society. Patterns of inequality always interact with social values, beliefs, and institutions, are endorsed by laws and informal norms, and are supported by prevailing patterns of power. Therefore, *institutionalization of inequality* is used to describe the configuration of sociocultural arrangements that support and perpetuate social inequalities.

Values

The *values* of society define standards of desirability for members of the group. Values place a premium on such things as material objects, ideals (democracy and opportunity), behaviors (courage or bravery), or symbols (grades) and serve as a guide or justification for the conduct of individual affairs. Widely shared values can support the distribution of rewards. The dignity and worth of human life are a powerful dimension in the social and religious heritage of Western civilization. Thus occupations that contribute to the preservation of life tend to enjoy more social prestige than does "dirty work" which makes no direct or observable contribution to the quality of life. A conspicuous example of the cultural value–prestige link is the Hindu concept of an "untouchable" caste. Hindus considered it wrong to harm any form of life, and thus any occupation such as butcher, hunter, or fisher or even the raising of animals for such purposes were joined in a caste felt to "defile" or "pollute" its members.

At a more basic level it is important to realize that the very salience of wealth, prestige, and power as valuable rewards in the United States is supported by a value system that emphasizes consumption, invidious distinctions of social status, and personal autonomy. Still, property can have much less meaning in other social systems in America. The Amish reject overt displays of wealth in clothing, jewelry, homes, and possessions. Their lifestyle deliberately rejects the materialism of modern industrial systems in favor of a stable, homogeneous, and devout religious value system.

Beliefs

Beliefs are definitions of reality shared by members of a society. Beliefs are not "true" or "false" in any absolute sense, but rather are commonly accepted knowledge. Stereotypes, legends, religious revelations, scientific propositions, and superstitions all qualify as beliefs in that they serve to explain the social and physical world's and interpret the causes of events. By structuring reality, beliefs determine the way in which people perceive the world and react to it.

Beliefs about the individuals and groups in a society can affect the distribution of rewards. It is, for example, common to discover beliefs that suggest racial or ethnic minorities are somehow inherently inferior—socially, culturally, or biologically. Racial and ethnic stereotypes reflect beliefs about the characteristics of members of minority groups. Such beliefs thus serve as the basis and justification for discriminatory treatment, such as channeling minorities into dead-end jobs.

Laws and Norms

Inequality is frequently built into the legal fabric of a society. The exclusion of women from occupations such as law was once upheld by the U.S. Supreme Court. In the absence of formal laws, informal social norms may produce the same results. Women attending law schools were, as recently as the 1960s, subjected to the degradation of a "ladies day" at which they were singled out and humiliated in the presence of their male counterparts.

Social Institutions

Social institutions such as religion, education, and the family also play a role in the perpetuation of stratification. For example, the church has sometimes provided overt sacred support for secular inequality. Medieval feudal estates were imbued with a religious-moral purpose by Christian philosophers who maintained that the feudal system was the only possible way of defending the church against its pagan enemies (Nottingham, 1954). A less direct link between religion and stratification was proposed by Karl Marx in his criticism of organized religion. He claimed the attraction of otherworldly salvation distracted the attention of the poor from their suffering and contributed to their acceptance of the existing system.

Formal educational systems may perpetuate existing patterns of inequality and guarantee that each generation will inherit the same social position as that of their parents. A network of elite preparatory schools and colleges trains upper-class children to assume the reigns of power held by their parents, whereas the rest of the population must depend on the public school system. Tracking systems in the high schools of America tend to benefit the children of upper-middle-class parents, and the children of the poor and the working class are more likely to be channeled into unrewarding, dead-end careers in blue-collar or service work.

Social Stratification

The terms *social stratification* and *systems of stratification* are used interchangeably to describe the hierarchy of groups, the patterns of structural inequality associated with membership in these groups, and the complex of supporting values, beliefs, and institutions. Attention to the idea of a system is an important component of the concept of stratification for the various dimensions are interrelated and mutually supportive. Social and cultural ideas explain and legitimize the arrangement of groups and the distribution of rewards. Social theorists are divided on the temporal priority of these elements. Some argue that patterns of inequality originate in the basic configuration of ideas and ideals in society. Others suggest that social structure emerges to justify or rationalize prevailing patterns of inequality.

Social stratification has taken many different forms at different points in history but it is most instructive to concentrate on four common and recurring types—slave, caste, estate, and industrial class systems. Each arises under different social and economic conditions, identifies different social categories of people, generates alternative kinds of hierarchies, and differs in the scope and magnitude of inequalities.

CONCLUSION: The Interaction of Class, Color, and Gender

When social class is defined by location within the economic system, it is then manifest that gender and color cannot be ignored in understanding the allocation of people among positions. Moreover, considerations of color and gender have the potential to influence people's accomplishments and those of their children. In addition, class, color, and gender may interact to produce different experiences and responses at different class levels. Thus, a comprehensive understanding of the stratification system of industrial societies must include a consideration of the interrelationship among class, color, and gender.

The basic point is that three social factors—social class, minority status, and gender—are decisive in understanding patterns of inequality. It must be noted that not all inequities that exist in a society are included within the concept of structural inequality. Individual variations in beauty, athletic prowess, and intelligence are excluded, for although salient, they are essentially personal traits. However, it will become apparent that societal position can and does influence whether on not individual potential is realized. Also, it should not be suggested that other social characteristics such as age and sexual preference are irrelevant, merely that these three are the most salient.

The broad implications of social stratification in the United States are illustrated by focusing on the relationship among class, color, gender, and income as shown in Exhibit 1.4. A hierarchy of social classes based on occupation is associated with pronounced differences in earnings as exemplified by a gap of at least $10,000 between the upper-middle and lower-middle classes. The income of the clerical sector of the lower middle class, dominated by women (80 percent), is much closer to the working class on the economic dimension. The bottom of the income hierarchy is anchored by unskilled and service work.

However, this broad pattern is modified by considerations of color and gender. Minorities and women consistently command lower than average earnings, but this pattern also varies by class level. Several examples highlight the situation; the earnings of African American men in lower-middle-class clerical occupations are 87 percent those of white males but only about 58 percent in sales work. Hispanic men in the upper middle class earn more than comparable black men. Women's income is always low relative to men's, but the discrepancy widens at higher class levels. Finally, it can

Exhibit 1.4
Class, Color, Gender, and Income

Social Class	White	Black	Hispanic	White	Black	Hispanic
		Men			Women	
Upper middle class						
Professions	$36,975	$28,775	$32,846	$19,324	$21,122	$21,302
Managers	39,273	29,712	32,264	20,800	20,281	19,819
Lower middle class						
Technicians	27,238	19,404	20,402	17,250	16,227	n/a
Sales	28,242	16,358	20,494	10,752	7,937	9,336
Clerical	20,018	17,590	16,417	12,712	14,068	12,498
Working class						
Craftspersons	22,068	18,066	17,246	14,040	13,378	12,994
Semiskilled	19,249	15,501	15,214	10,684	11,167	8,560
The poor						
Service work	10,510	8,595	10,282	6,756	7,855	7,022
Unskilled	12,110	11,041	11,930	8,615	8,113	7,865

Source: U.S. Bureau of the Census, *Money Income of Households, Families and Persons in the United States*, 1989, Washington, DC: Government Printing Office, 1990, Table 40, p. 166.

be noted that minority women in the professions and service work actually have higher average earnings than do comparable white women.

ADDITIONAL READINGS

On Inequality and Stratification

CELIA HELLER, ed. *Structured Social Inequality*, 2nd ed. New York: Macmillan, 1987.

JOHN DALPHIN. *The Persistence of Social Inequality in America*. Cambridge, MA: Schenkman, 1981.

SCOTT G. MCNALL, RHONDA F. LEVINE, and RICK FANTASIA, eds.. *Bringing Class Back In: Contemporary and Historical Perspectives*. Boulder, CO: Westview, 1991.

KEVIN PHILLIPS. *The Politics of Rich and Poor: Wealth and the American Electorate in the Reagan Aftermath*. New York: Random House, 1990.

DANIEL W. ROSSIDES. *Social Stratification: The American Class System in Comparative Perspective*. Englewood Cliffs, NJ: Prentice Hall, 1990.

BRYAN S. TURNER. *Equality*. New York: Tavistock, 1986.

On Social Class

ARTHUR MARWICK. *Class: Image and Reality in Britain, France and the USA Since 1930*. New York: Oxford University Press, 1980.

RICHARD SENNETT and JONATHAN COBB. *The Hidden Injuries of Class*. New York: Vintage, 1973.

ALBERT SYMANSKI. *Class Structure: A Critical Perspective*. New York: Praeger, 1983.

ERIC OLIN WRIGHT. *Classes*. London: New Left Books, 1985.

On Minorities

MARIO BARRERA. *Race and Class in the Southwest*. Notre Dame, IN: University of Notre Dame Press, 1979.

JACQUELINE JONES. *Labor of Love, Labor of Sorrow: Black Women, Work and the Family from Slavery to the Present*. New York: Basic Books, 1985.

STANLEY LIEBERSON and MARY C. WATERS, eds. *From Many Strands: Ethnic-Racial Groups in Contemporary America*. New York: Russell Sage Foundation, 1988.

MICHAEL OMI and HOWARD WINANT. *Racial Formation in the United States*. New York: Routledge & Kegan Paul, 1986.

JOHN STONE. *Racial Conflict in Contemporary Society*. Cambridge, MA: Harvard University Press, 1985.

On Sex and Gender

PAMELA ABBOTT and ROGER SAPSFORD. *Women and Social Class*. New York: Tavistock, 1987.

JANET SALTZMAN CHAFETZ. *Sex and Advantage*. Totowa, NJ: Rowman & Allanheld, 1984.

JOYCE MCCALL NIELSEN. *Sex and Gender in Society: Perspectives on Stratification*, 2nd ed. Prospect Heights, IL: Waveland Press, 1990.

PATRICIA ROOS. *Gender and Work: A Comparative Analysis of Industrial Societies*. Albany: State University of New York Press, 1985.

Chapter 2
Theoretical Approaches to Social Stratification

THEORETICAL TRADITIONS

Inequality and stratification have captured the attention of social philosophers, moralists, intellectuals, and social theorists since the origins of recorded history. Plato may have been the first Western theorist to attempt a systematic examination of the nature and consequences of inequality. One of the central goals of his utopian *Republic* was to construct a society in which inequalities corresponded to the inherent differences among people. But, because of his belief that extremes of wealth and poverty generated undesirable behavior, he also proposed placing limits on the economic resources people could accumulate. The theorists with most relevance to contemporary analysis date from the mid-nineteenth century when industrialization began to reshape the structure of Western societies. Three major theoretic traditions tend to dominate in American sociology.

The works of Karl Marx and Friedrich Engels are the starting point in any consideration of stratification theory, for they were among the first to perceive the internal dynamics of the emerging industrial order. They asserted primacy to be control of the physical means of industrial production and emphasized the social relations inherent in different forms of production and the role of this factor in shaping society and in the dynamics of social change. After the death of Marx, Engels developed a systematic analysis of gender stratification.

Max Weber was one of a number of people who carried on a dialogue with the "ghost of Marx." On several occasions he is quoted as defining part of his work as "positive criticism of materialistic conceptions of history" (Bendix, 1962: 591). This should not imply a single-minded attempt to discredit Marx and Engels; rather Weber challenged some interpretations, admitted some insights, and attempted to elaborate on still others. It is more accurate to recognize that Weber objected to the idea that any single factor such the relations of production could provide a universal explanation of social phenomena; hence he developed a multidimensional model of stratification based on economics, prestige and lifestyles, and power.

American interest in social stratification intensified during the 1930s and 1940s and tended to emphasize social status and patterns of social interaction. W. Lloyd Warner and his associates studied small communities with quaint names such as "Yankee City" and "Jonesville" to disguise their location. Their original formulation emphasized economic considerations, but eventually they came to argue that subjective measures of "status" and reputation superseded economic considerations, but eventually they came to argue that subjective measures of "status"and reputation superseded economic considerations (Warner, et al., 1949). It was Warner who popularized stratification terms such as "upper upper class" and "lower middle class" that have become a permanent part of the American vocabulary. Talcott Parsons's theoretical formulations, and those of some of his students, were particularly influential during this period. Probably the most controversial single contribution was a brief paper by Kingsley Davis and Wilbert Moore (1945) that purported to explain why stratification was universal and necessary. These developments contributed to the emergence of "functional" theories focusing on prestige and an accompanying decline in interest in conflict and political and economic inequalities. Functionalism eventually dominated American sociology for several decades.

The 1990s are a period of multiple models and multiple perspectives on inequality and stratification. Attempts to continue in the classic traditions initiated by Marx and Weber seek to reconcile twentieth-century developments with models formulated in earlier stages of industrialization. Concern with social prestige is evident in the continuing flow of studies attempting to unravel the subtleties of status in societies around the world. The issue of power remains the most difficult to deal with, largely because the exercise of power is so often shrouded in secrecy. With rare exceptions, theories of stratification have failed to devote systematic attention to the interaction of class, color, and gender.

THE MARXIAN TRADITION

Karl Marx (1818-1883) and Friedrich Engels (1820-1895) lived and wrote during a period of rapid and disruptive upheaval stimulated by industrialization and democratization. It has always been difficult to dispassionately discuss the works of Marx and Engels because they were simultaneously social analysts and political reformers. As social critics they were dismayed by the abuses, misery, and oppression found in urban factories although they could not help but recognize the positive aspects of the emerging economic system. In the *Communist Manifesto* there is praise for the capitalist class he called the bourgeoisie, which "during its rule of scarce one hundred years, has created more massive and colossal productive forces than have all preceding generations together" (Marx and Engels, 1959: 8). The development of science, the command over nature, the rise of cities, and the breakdown of rule by the feudal nobility could all be attributed to this group.

But they were also partisan reformers and as Feuer (1959: xviii) has noted, political "prophets have always been dualists," seeing history as a conflict between the forces of good and evil, lightness and darkness and hence they anticipated the revolutionary overthrow of capitalism. Subsequently "Marxism" became the rallying point for a number of political movements around the world. However, numerous Marxian theorists argue that oppressive Leninist-Stalinist regimes bore little resemblance to the socialist ideals of Marx and were merely ways of centralizing and legitimizing political power (Lane, 1976). The more recent political and economic changes reverberating through the Soviet Union and Eastern Europe have been used by some to attempt to finally discredit Marxist thought. Despite controversy and criticism, the writings of Marx and Engels survive as a broad analytic scheme for analyzing and understanding developments in industrial democracies.

Social Stratification

Marx's collaborator, Engels, has provided a frequently quoted passage that is a succinct summary of their conception of history and social stratification:

> The materialist conception of history starts with the proposition that the production of the means to support human life—and next to production, the exchange of things produced—is the basis of all social structure; that in every society that has appeared in history, the manner in which wealth is distributed and the society is divided into classes or orders is dependent on what is produced, and how it is exchanged. From this point of view the final causes of all social changes and political revolutions are to be sought...in changes in the modes of production and exchange. (Marx & Engels, 1959: 90)

Thus, the key to understanding the flow of human history, as well as the distribution of inequality and stratification, has its basis in the organization of the productive forces of the society.

Marx and Engles viewed the whole of human history as divided into a number of major phases—primitive communism, slavery, feudalism, and capitalism—that were destined to be supplanted by socialism and eventually communism. Each period is dominated by a pair of social classes defined by their relationship to the means of production and to each other—masters and slaves or landowners and serfs. Central to the Marxian analysis of capitalism was the belief that the idea of private property created a basic cleavage between those who owned economic resources and those who did not, or to use their terms, *bourgeoisie* (who owned capital) and the *proletariat* (nonowners who had only their own labor to sell).

Inequality of wealth in capitalist societies was directly based on owner-ship of land, buildings, machinery, factories—the means of production. Own-ership is translated into profits at the expense of workers. This wealth is, in turn, translated into power in the political sector by control of the apparatus of government. Systematic consideration of social prestige, which later be-came so vital to the work of Weber and others, was largely ignored by Marx and Engels. They argued that the potential for domination of society is not simply economic and political, but is also social and cultural in that a "ruling class" will be able to shape the laws, values, art, beliefs, and institutions of society—the *ideological superstructure*—to their advantage.

> The ideas of the ruling class are in every epoch the ruling ideas; i.e., the class which is ruling the material force of society is at the same time the ruling intellectual force. The class which has the means of material production at its disposal has control at the same time over the means of mental production. (Marx & Engels, 1959: 78)

These ideas are disseminated through the press, the church, the schools, and the various political institutions and serve to legitimize their advan-taged position.

Class Consciousness and Class Conflict

The concepts of class and social change intersect with the idea of class conflict for the disadvantaged classes spawned by the economic system will be the instruments of social change. Therefore,

> The history of all hitherto existing society is the history of class struggles. Free man and slave, patrician and plebeian, lord and serf, guild-master and journeyman, in a word, oppressor and oppressed, stood in constant opposition to one another, carried on an uninterrupted, now hidden, now open fight, a fight that each time ended, either in a revolutionary reconstitution of society at large, or in the common ruin of the contending classes. (Marx & Engels, 1964: 78)

Because ruling classes never voluntarily relinquish their position, conflict was inevitable. In this context, Marx introduced and explored the critical link between economic position and subjective class awareness. Both bourgeoisie and proletariat form nominal groups as a result of their relative location in the economic system. He called such groups *klasse an sich* (class of itself), with class position defined by structural position. Members of the opposing classes have shared interests by virtue of their position. These common interests are most clearly perceived by the bour-geoisie for it is more readily evident that their advantaged position is based on private property. Yet members of disadvantaged classes need not be aware of their common interests. Their interests may be fragmented by differing religious beliefs, ethnic loyalties, and prestige distinctions or obscured by rhetoric. Therefore, Marx raised the question of conditions that could transform a heterogeneous aggregate into a cohesive, organized group (a *klasse fur sich*, a class for itself) aware of its interests and acting to realize its own interests.

Marx anticipated that a combination of several social and economic forces would combine to produce self-conscious action on the part of workers. A major factor would be economic deprivation. He expected that the discrepancy between the wealth of the bourgeoisie and the proletariat would widen for two reasons. Increases in productivity would produce ever greater profits, and ever more wealth would be concentrated in the hands of an ever smaller number of capitalists as they competed among themselves for a larger share of the wealth. Another factor in awakening class consciousness would be the homogenization of the proletariat. Divergent interests would be rendered less meaningful as they became more similar. For example, technological advances would reduce all workers to unskilled laborers, thus reducing interoccupational rivalries. Finally, continued confrontations with owners (e.g., strikes) would expose their common interests.

Interestingly enough, Marx neither defined class nor developed his ideas about social classes in any systematic way. However, it is clear that he saw class in two separate ways (Wright, 1985: 26-38)—first, structurally defined by ownership (or lack of it) of productive capacity, capital and land; and, second, relationally. That is, classes exist only in relation to one another. Moreover, they are antagonistic in the sense of having opposing interests, and exploitative in that the advantages of one class are gained at the expense of another.

The Middle Class

Critics are quick to claim that Marx was unable to anticipate fully the future of industrialization in the United States and some parts of Western Europe. Politically, the state intervened with social and economic reforms (e.g., minimum wages, unemployment compensation, and social welfare programs) to buffer the vulnerability of workers, and in some instances took basic industries out of the private sector (utilities, health services in some countries). Economically, industrialization raised the standard of living of large segments of the population. Structurally, the vast white-collar "middle class" of office workers, professionals, and managers occupies an intermediate position between workers and capitalists. Marx clearly recognized a growing middle class "who stand between the workman on the one hand and the capitalist and landlord on the other," but he did not work out the long-term implications of this development (Burris, 1986). For example, at one point he merely suggested that intermediate groups such as small business persons, farmers, shopkeepers, and crafts workers would "sink down into the proletariat," although he was not clear about precisely how that might happen.

The proliferation of a broad middle class creates a dilemma for that part of the Marxian system that emphasizes the polarization of society into two opposing groups. Contemporary theorists working in the Marxian tradition have wrestled with the problem of reconciling the reality of a middle class within the theoretical idea of dichotomous classes. Some feel that the evolution of capitalism has produced a new class of technical, professional, and managerial workers that falls outside the traditional bourgeoisie-proletariat dichotomy. It is argued that they have in common the control of a special kind of capital—knowledge, skills, expertise. As a consequence, there is the potential for the development of a distinctive class consciousness among members of this group. Others insist that the basic owner- nonowner dichotomy continues as an accurate description of the most fundamental cleavage in society, for it focuses on the fact that a small minority are in a position to control the labor of the vast majority (e.g., Wright, 1985). What has changed is the development of new kinds of resources in the productive process.

Wright's model highlights the structural predicament of the middle class of managers, supervisors and experts pointing out they are simultaneously proletariat in the sense that they are employees working for others and bourgeoisie because they have resources that allows them to exploit the labor of workers. Hence, they occupy a contradictory class position. His

---

CASE STUDY:
A Contemporary Marxian Approach to Social Class

Erik Olin Wright is one of many contemporary sociologists working in the Marxian tradition. He has long been preoccupied with understanding the broad middle class in advanced capitalist societies (Wright, 1976; 1985). He argues that the industrial transformation has vested new "assets" or resources in the hands of different segments of the middle class that allow them to exploit the working class. Ownership of capital remains a major asset, but as shown in Exhibit 2.1, it must be recognized that there are quantitative divisions within the owners of capital assets. This category also includes those who employ one or two people (small employers) and independent self-employed persons (petty bourgeoisie) who do not exploit workers. The middle class is divided into those who have "organizational assets,"—the hierarchial authority to make policy decisions (managers) or direct the work of others (supervisors), or "skill assets" in the form of educational credentials (experts). By far the largest category is non-owners (workers) who possess neither productive assets nor control over other workers, and consequently do not even control their own efforts. The working class in the United States defined by this criteria would include approximately one-half of all people in the labor force (Wright & Martin, 1987).

Exhibit 2.1
An Interpretation of Class Categories in Capitalist Societies

Class	Employs Others	Makes Workplace Decisions	Supervises Others	Credentials	Sells Own Labor
Owners of Capital Assets					
Capitalists	+	+	+	−	−
Small employers	+	+	+	−	−
Petty bourgeois	−	+	−	−	−
Owners of Organizational Assets					
Managers	−	+	+	−	+
Supervisors	−	−	+	−	+
Owners of Skill Assets					
Experts	−	−	−	+	+
Nonowners					
Workers	−	−	−	−	+

Note: This exhibit reflects the author's interpretation of the work of Erik Olin Wright developed in Erik Olin Wright, *Classes* (London: New Left Books, 1985); Erik OlinWright, et al., *The Debate on Classes* (London: Verso, 1989).

work, still in process, promises to explore many fruitful avenues of research, including the impact of contradictory locations on class consciousness and class action and the possibility of coalitions between members of the working class and different segments of the middle class (Wright, et al., 1989).

Engels and Gender Stratification

Engels is often credited with the first sociological theory of gender stratification (Collins & Makowsky, 1984: 49–54). His approach is a continuation and extension of the basic Marxian perspective. In fact, he links the origins of gender stratification to the first decisive step in the process that eventually produced capitalism—the transition from communal to private property. "The first class opposition that appears in history coincides with the development of antagonism between man and woman in monogamous marriage, and the first class oppression coincides with that of the female sex by the male" (Engels, 1972: 129).

Based on the anthropological research of his time, he concluded that both hunting and agricultural societies were characterized by matrilineal descent and gender equality. (More recent anthropological research does not support the thesis that all hunting societies are egalitarian.) Because they fully participated in the production of food, women enjoyed equal social status. However, as advanced agricultural methods created the potential for an agricultural surplus, males wanted to be able to pass their accumulated property on to their children. Patrilineal descent and monogamous marriages were created to foster this, and women became excluded from economic production and relegated to household tasks. As a consequence of not producing for the market, women become economically subordinate to their spouses.

Thus, Engels effectively linked gender subordination to the dynamics of industrial production systems. More recent thinking in the Marxian tradition has elaborated on that perspective, suggesting that women have been forced into playing a vital but largely invisible role in perpetuating the economic system. They reproduce the working class by bearing and socializing children to become the next generation of workers.

The Legacy of Marxism

In retrospect it is easy to emphasize the flaws in the works of Marx and Engels. They were so wedded to the idea of dichotomous classes that they failed to fully explore the implications of the emerging middle class or fully anticipate the future of capitalism in the West. Perhaps the most salient observation about their work is that they were too much products of their time, and overgeneralized from what was occurring in nineteenth-century England (Bottomore, 1966: 18). It is understandable that they would imagine industrialization leading to the domination of society by a small class of industrial capitalists ranged against an expanding mass of propertyless and impoverished urban laborers. It was the period of some the worst industrial abuses—crowded tenements, hazardous factories, subsistence wages, child labor, and minimal standards of public health. It was also the era of unrest and ferment in the fledgling labor movement. Trade unions and socialist political parties were active and industrial conflict common.

Despite its flaws, their work exerts a strong influence on contemporary thinking about social stratification. The concept of classes based on position in a specific productive system remains a powerful tool for understanding the distribution of wealth, power and privilege in industrial societies. Modern theorists, working in this tradition, continue to wrestle with the issue of precisely defining relations between members of different social classes. The interaction of class and gender in stratification systems is one of the dominant topics in the discipline today. The question of understanding the conditions which hinder or facilitate the emergence of class consciousness and collective action is the subject of continuing interest and research. So too is the question of the Marxian assertion that a industrial elite may form a ruling class in industrial society.

THE WEBERIAN TRADITION

Max Weber's (1864–1920) approach to an analysis of social stratification is more multidimensional in contrast to the Marxian tradition. Weber recognized the central importance of position in the social organization of industrial production, but he emphasized the existence of three forms of inequality in society—economic, prestige, and power. His words are direct:

> Whereas the genuine place of "classes" is within the economic order, the place of "status groups" is within the social order, that is, within the distribution of "honor," ...(and) "parties" live in the house of "power." Their action is oriented toward the acquisition of social "power," that is to say, toward influencing communal action no matter what the content may be. (Weber, 1946: 194)

Class

Weber's economic form of inequality is based on "market situation," which does not differ in principle from the Marxian division of propertied and propertyless (Anderson, 1974: 112). However, Weber specified three different types of market situation: the labor market, which divides society into employers and employees; the money market, which separates creditors from debtors; and the commodity market, which differentiates between buyers and sellers (and landlords and tenants). Accordingly, those who participate in all three markets could be members of three distinct economic classes (Wiley, 1967: 531). In addition, Weber noted that the propertyless have different levels of skill (ranging from the unskilled to the professional worker). Weber's observations about skill differences among those who are without significant capital resources marks his attempt to deal with the question of the emerging middle class.

Weber noted that classes are groups of people who share a common market situation, and, in turn, class position strongly influences their opportunities. (This is where he introduced the concept of "life chances.") Common economic position does not imply or even guarantee a sense of common identity. An awareness of common interests and collective action might emerge, under the right conditions. For example, class action of workers is fostered by a presence of a clear and unambiguous opponent, the physical concentration of workers in a single place, which facilitates interaction and communication, and clear goals articulated by political leaders (Weber, 1946: 180–184).

On the matter of gender stratification, he displayed a strong interest in Engels' analysis of the family and in the feminist theory of his day (Collins, 1986a: 269–271). He challenged Engels' notion of the evolution of sexual domination, but accepted his perspective as making a valuable step toward understanding the situation. His own ideas on the family define it as a set of sexual and economic relationships regulated by political power (Collins, 1986: 277).

Status

Weber termed his second form of inequality *status honor* (or what is today referred to as *prestige)*, grounded in the prevailing values, beliefs, and ideals of the society. Taking this a step farther led him to visualize society as a hierarchy of "status groups" having unequal prestige. Status groups are, in Weber's thinking, communities of people having some degree of awareness of commonality. These communities may be based on property, income, ethnicity, ancestry, education, or occupation, but consumption patterns and styles of life are primary.

The way in which status groups develop is one of Weber's most influential and enduring contributions. Because members of status groups have a shared identity they may develop social rules for maintaining and protecting their position and that of their children. A set of formal and informal exclusionary rules will be established, and members of status groups will selectively interact with others who they consider to be their social equals—socialize with them, invite them to their homes, send their children to the same schools, and join the same organizations. Outsiders will simultaneously be deliberately excluded from such contacts. It follows that marriage partners should also be among social equals, and restricted patterns of interaction will limit the pool of potential partners to members of the same status group.

Weber believed that in the most extreme cases, status groups evolve into "castes" where distinctions of social status are maintained by rigid social conventions or even laws that prohibit marriage outside the caste. Moreover, physical contacts with lower caste members will be considered degrading, as though the lower caste might contaminate them. He felt that caste systems would usually emerge when there were ethnic differences to distinguish members and cites the Jews as the most persistent historical example, along with other cases that can be assumed to include "the untouchables" of Hindu India.

Parties

Finally, Weber focused on the question of *power* and identifies *parties*, groups actually organized for the pursuit of power. His term parties would encompass the contemporary idea of political parties, but is broader, more inclusive, including any group whose "action is oriented toward a goal which is striven for in a planned manner" (Weber, 1946: 180–184). Although vague on the nature of parties and how they coalesce, he does point out that economic or status interests may be important. However, other motives beside class and prestige may be operative. The ways in which parties may gain power can range from naked violence to persuasion, subterfuge, or hoax.

The Legacy of Weber

Weber's contribution to the thinking on stratification is more generalized than specific. Actually, he devoted but one relatively short essay directly to the topic, yet he is widely quoted. His attraction may derive from the multidimensionality of his model, which is more consistent with contemporary thinking that emphasizes the complexity of social phenomena. Thus, while not disputing the Marxian concept of economic classes, Weber did postulate a more complex picture of inequality and stratification. His scheme encompasses a broader view of economic classes and also includes status groups and parties, thus allowing individuals and families to be located on at least three hierarchies of inequality. He asserts that inequalities of lifestyles, prestige, and power can be independent of one another, but concedes the primacy of the economic factor in most situations. "Property as such," he notes, "is not always recognized as a (prestige) qualification, but in the long run it is, with extraordinary regularity" (Weber, 1946: 185).

Although not directly linked to his work on stratification Weber did extensively explore the implications of the role of emerging bureaucratic structures, and correctly predicted that they were destined to be dominant form of social organization in industrial society. Most individuals are subject to some form of bureaucratic control, whether industrial, political, educational, or religious. Obviously, leadership in these bureaucracies is the source of unusual power and influence over individuals and society, a point developed later by other theorists.

One of Weber's most well-known works, *The Protestant Ethic and the Spirit of Capitalism*, develops the thesis that Protestant beliefs set the stage for the emergence of capitalism in the West. His theory earned him quick fame, for he challenged the Marxian premise that gives primacy to economic relations in shaping social institutions, and offered a new connection between religion and economic development (Collins, 1968b: 51). As Weber saw it, the unique combination of religious ideas developed by Luther and Calvin fostered certain kinds of secular behavior—disciplined effort, self-denial, devotion to work, material success, and individual responsibility—values that fostered the emergence of capitalist economic organization. His theory has generated considerable controversy, but it does call attention to an alternative interpretation of interrelationship between social institutions and the stratification system.

THE FUNCTIONALIST TRADITION

The functionalist tradition has diverse theoretical and empirical roots, traceable to the work of Emile Durkheim, a group of British social anthropologists, and the early community studies of W. Lloyd Warner in "Yankee City" (Grabb, 1984). The most influential work in this tradition in the United States was produced in the 1940s and 1950s by Talcott Parsons (1940; 1949; 1953) and two of his students, Kingsley Davis and Wilbert Moore (1945).

Status

Parsons focused on the status (prestige) dimension of inequality, not ignoring differences in wealth and power, but assigning them secondary importance. His emphasis on prestige followed logically from his broader perspective on society, which is directed to a most fundamental question: What makes social order possible? His perspective emphasizes two features of society, a common value and belief system that serves to weld members of society together, and the integrative role of major social institutions in a society. Such an approach differs from those who choose to emphasize divergent interests and disharmony.

In his first article on the subject of stratification, the focus is clear, "the differential evaluation (of members of society) in the moral sense." Within any society, Parsons argues, its members are evaluated and ranked (by other members of the society) on the basis of conformity to a shared value system. The link between societal values and social prestige was made earlier by Weber. Parsons further suggests that some institutions are more important than others and consequently that higher value will be attributed to those who make the most important contribution to society. In industrial societies that will be the economic system; in other societies, at other times, religious or cultural institutions might have higher priority. This led him in the direction of assuming that prestige will be allocated primarily on the basis of the type of work a person does.

Is Stratification Universal and Necessary?

Parsons suggests that a hierarchy of prestige will emerge in every society, and Davis and Moore address the question of why it is apparently universal. They take the position that if it is universal it must serve some vital social function, for functionalists emphasize that the social institutions and social patterns that prevail in a society must play some fundamental role in the survival of that society. Their view is that every society is confronted with the need to motivate people to fill essential positions and perform them effectively and diligently. Phrased differently, it is the question of how society can ensure that people will want to become physicians (or judges or scientists). This is a crucial issue, for such jobs require lengthy and costly training, involve scarce talents, and are more crucial to the survival of society than others.

Their answer is direct: Those positions must be handsomely rewarded. "Social inequality is thus an unconsciously evolved device by which societies ensure that the most important positions are conscientiously filled by the most qualified persons" (1945: 249). Medicine is an apt example. Training is costly, arduous, and long and people would not be inclined to become physicians without the lure of societal rewards. The Davis-Moore functional theory of stratification can thus be reduced to a series of propositions as given in the accompanying case study.

Inequality thus has its origins in consensus and ensures that the most competent and well-trained persons will conscientiously fill the most important positions in a society. Because it is a general framework, functional theory it does not claim to explain either the relative degree of inequality or the form of stratification in a particular society, for that will depend on social values, external conditions, level of development, and historical circumstances.

CASE STUDY:
A Functional Theory of Social Stratification

Some positions in society are more important than others for the survival of the society.

Some positions require more training and/or talent than others.

The continued functioning of society requires that such positions be filled by qualified people.

Rewards are an incentive to motivate qualified people to fill the positions.

Therefore, society allocates proportionately greater rewards to those positions which are more important and /or require unusual scarce talents.

Inequality and stratification are thus socially evolved mechanisms for enhancing the potential survival of society.

Inequality and stratification are both indispensable and positively functional for society.

Source: Davis & Moore, 1945; Davis, 1953.

The Legacy of Functionalism

Despite its more narrow focus, it must be noted that functional theory did have a powerful influence on theory and research in sociology during its ascendance. Probably the most important single consequence was to direct attention on the distribution of social prestige. Sociologists have accumulated a large body of research on prestige rankings in societies across the world (e.g., Treiman, 1977). This research tends to reveal a high degree of consensus on the ranking of occupations lending some credence to the contention that members of society are united by a common value system.

Functional theory has also generated much critical comment, which can be organized into three categories. The first group of critics imputes an ideological bias, claiming that it is merely a rationalization for an existing system of inequality when it suggests that the most rewards go to the most important positions. Some have gone so far as to draw an analogy between Parsons approach to society and totalitarian government propaganda (Lane, 1976). It should be noted that proponents of the theory claim ethical neutrality, arguing that they are seeking to explain social patterns, not judge them.

There is a second category of criticism which, while relevant, does not invalidate the basic theory. One weakness of the theory, recognized by the authors themselves, is that there is no guarantee that the most qualified persons will actually be able to gain access to the highly rewarded positions (Tumin, 1953). At a minimum, wealthy and advantaged parents will be able to provide their children with access to the education and other advantages which are prerequisites to more desirable rungs on the ladder of prestige. Moreover, as Weber pointed out, members of groups that enjoy privileged positions can actively close off access to others. Consequently, there is the need to analyze the ways in which social classes and occupations act self-consciously to protect their position.

The third form of criticism focuses on specific methodological problems. Functional importance is, at best, a vague idea, meaning that there are no objective criteria for establishing the relative functional importance of social institutions or positions. Although there have been a number of attempts to test this theory, none have been able to provide consistent empirical support for the theory (e.g., Cullen and Novick, 1979).

CONCLUSION: Structural Realism versus Evolutionary Liberalism

These disparate theoretical traditions provide vital insights into the dynamics of inequality and social stratification, and contemporary sociologists continue to pursue answers to the issues raised by earlier theorists. It has been suggested that the study of stratification tends to be divided into two very broad intellectual and ideological traditions sometimes called structural realism and evolutionary liberalism (Pease, Form & Rytina, 1970; Rossides, 1990).

The structural realism model suggested by the Marxian and Weberian traditions accentuates societies divided into distinct social classes. This approach is grounded in the belief that social classes are embedded in the economic structure of society. Classes are groups of people or families who share a common location within a system of production and distribution. The Marxian tradition emphasizes social class divisions based on ownership or control of the means of production, and the Weberian tradition encompasses other economic indicators. Moreover, there is agreement that inequalities of income, power, and prestige are the direct outcome of structural position. It is recognized that people are not necessarily sensitive to the implications of their location or that they have shared interests with others, and the conditions that foster or inhibit class consciousness are to be found in the social and political conditions of the time. However, the more advantaged are sensitive to their position, and are likely to attempt to solidify their position and ensure those privileges are passed on to subsequent generations.

Evolutionary liberalism tends to deemphasize structural position and stresses that inequalities are the result of individual accomplishment within increasingly open industrial systems. This approach emphasizes the progress industrial societies have made toward rewarding individual effort and overcoming constraints imposed by class, color, and gender, especially through education. Moreover, inequalities that do exist in society form more or less continuous hierarchies, lacking clear boundaries and shared interests between classes. In this model, "classes" as such are not structural entities but rather aggregates of people who enjoy similar economic or social rewards or educational attainments.

ADDITIONAL READINGS

On Stratification Theory

ANDRE BETEILLE. *Inequality and Inequality: Theory and Practice.* New York: Oxford University Press, 1983.

RANDALL COLLINS and MICHAEL MAKOWSKY. *The Discovery of Society*, 3rd ed. New York: Random House, 1984.

EDWARD G. GRABB. *Social Inequality: Classical and Contemporary Theorists.* New York: Holt, Rinehart and Winston, 1984.

JONATHAN H. TURNER. *Societal Stratification: A Theoretical Analysis.* New York: Columbia University Press, 1984.

JONATHAN H. TURNER and LEONARD BEEGHLEY. *The Emergence of Sociological Theory.* Homewood, IL: Dorsey Press, 1981.

On the Marxist Tradition

RALF DAHRENDORF. *Class and Class Conflict in Industrial Society*. Stanford, CA: Stanford University Press, 1959.

PETER KNAPP and ALAN SPECTOR. *Crisis and Change: Basic Questions of Marxist Sociology*. Chicago: Nelson-Hall, 1989.

DAVID MCLELLAN. *Karl Marx: His Life and His Thought*. New York: Harper & Row, 1974.

ERIK OLIN WRIGHT. *Classes*. London: New Left Books, 1985.

On the Weberian Tradition

RINEHARD BENDIX. *Max Weber: An Intellectual Portrait*. Garden City, NY: Doubleday, 1962.

RANDALL COLLINS. *Weberian Sociological Theory*. New York: Cambridge University Press, 1986.

RANDALL COLLINS. *Max Weber: A Skeleton Key*. Beverly Hills, CA: Sage, 1986.

H. H. GERTH and C. WRIGHT MILLS, eds. *From Max Weber: Essays in Sociology*. New York: Oxford University Press, 1946.

On the Functionalist Tradition

MARK ABRAHAMSON. *Functionalism*. Englewood Cliffs, NJ: Prentice Hall, 1978.

DONALD J. TREIMAN. *Occupational Prestige in Comparative Perspective*. New York: Academic Press, 1977.

Chapter 3
Types of Stratification Systems

SYSTEMS OF STRATIFICATION

Stratification systems vary from society to society and at different points in the history of any given society. Despite such diversity, it is still possible to identify four fundamental forms of stratification that have existed at more than one time and in more than one place—slave, caste, estate, and industrial class systems. Each is intricately linked to the social, economic, and political system in the society. Slave systems create an unfree group, often for the purpose of ensuring a pool of labor. Caste systems tie people to hereditary occupations. Estate systems are based on control of land and expropriation of the products produced by agricultural workers. Each system is the basis of major forms of structural inequality—legal, social, economic, and political.

There are variations within each of these types, for each system is shaped by its own history, demographics, culture, and specific circumstances. Thus, slavery in Russia differed in several important aspects from that which prevailed in the United States. Moreover, no system is static, meaning that it will have different features as it evolves and changes. However, the value of this topology is that it identifies the basic features of each system, defines the sources of inequality, and reveals the ways in which systems are established and legitimized. Familiarity with different forms of stratification also has relevance because some aspects of these systems still prevail in the contemporary world. For example, the vast landholdings that characterized feudal societies have continued into the present in England and Latin America. Another instance surfaced in India in 1990, when scores of people were killed in riots set off by government attempts to reserve some jobs for members of the lowest castes. Moreover, structures and perspectives shaped during one point in history frequently survive into the present. For example, social arrangements surrounding the middle-class division of labor along color and gender lines are a late nineteenth-century development, but continue to influence and shape the class position of these groups in contemporary American society.

SLAVE SYSTEMS: Unfree Labor

The U.S. Department of Justice regularly investigates scores of allegations of people being held against their will. Cases have surfaced in places as diverse as Los Angeles, California, Tyler, Texas, and Ann Arbor, Michigan, and frequently involve illegal immigrants forced to perform agricultural work. Although such incidents are commonly referred to as "slavery," they do not meet the criteria for *slave systems*, for they are situations that violate the legal and social codes of the nation. For a slave system as a form of social stratification to exist, persons must by law and/or custom be defined as the property of other persons or the state (Derrick, 1975: 13).

Slave systems in antiquity were found in Mesopotamia, Egypt, Greece, and Rome and have persisted into the twentieth century in parts of Africa, South America, and the Middle East. The final, formal, international abolition of slavery was adopted at a United Nations Convention in 1956 and subsequently ratified by virtually all nations. Yet it is believed that slavery still exists in several places scattered around the globe. A celebrated case occurred in Mauritania in western Africa in 1980. Worldwide attention focused on the nation because of the public sale of a 15-year-old woman (Sawyer, 1986: 16). The government officially reaffirmed its non-slavery position, but it is alleged that slavery flourishes in most of the nonurbanized areas of the nation. Although the French officially abolished slavery there in 1905, the government acknowledges that the practice survives, and estimates range as high as 200,000 men, women, and children are subject to being bought and sold (Gordon, 1987: x). Slave owners are likely to be Moors and slaves the descendants of the original black inhabitants, the Bafours.

Many different motives explain the origins of slave systems. Slavery has been imposed to provide victims for ritual sacrifices, as a penalty imposed on debtors or criminals, as a means of pacifying conquered peoples, or to provide rulers with concubines, but the most common basis of slavery is to provide compulsory labor—the lure of an efficient and profitable pool of low-cost laborers.

The key feature present in all slave systems is the division of society into two basic categories, free and unfree. Slaves are typically denied political and civil rights granted other segments of the society. Some of the key features of slavery in both ancient Rome and nineteenth-century United States were stipulations that slaves could not own property, enter into contracts of any kind (including marriage), or make a will (or inherit anything) and they were excluded from participation in most legal proceedings (Sio, 1965). Thus, those relegated to slavery can be denied their freedom, endure personal indignities, be deprived of the rights and privileges of others, and suffer severe economic and social deprivation. Scholars sometimes debate how well owners treated their slaves, but they miss a fundamental point: Perhaps the most important consequence is that slavery strips people of their basic humanity, relegating them to the status of property.

Although involuntary servitude is a common feature of all slave systems, it is important to note that colonial American slavery early on included a racial dimension.[1] Slaves and masters came from different racial and cultural backgrounds—African and European. In addition, Europeans who had immigrated voluntarily tended to think of America as their home and see displaced Africans as outsiders, meaning that even second- and third-generation slaves, although born in the United States, were still considered aliens. Consequently, slavery was intermingled with claims of racial inferiority. The result was that involuntary servitude, race, and social definitions of inferiority became inextricably linked; race meant inferiority and race was the basis for slave status (Sio, 1965; Davis, 1966; Kolchin, 1988). This is not always the case in compulsory labor systems. Greece, Rome, and Russian serfdom made no such link; slaves were not inferior persons, merely legally *unfree* persons. Once an ideology of innate differences among the races becomes institutionalized there are enduring consequences. Among the most important is that although the formal abolition of slavery can grant legal rights to former slaves, it cannot guarantee them social rights. Emancipation does not necessarily bring about the demise of the ideological underpinnings that exist to legitimize and justify enslavement.

CASTE SYSTEMS: Heredity And Endogamy

Caste systems are based on a hierarchy of hereditary groups. Children inherit the caste of their parents, and this distinction is not subject to alteration by individual effort. Hence, there is virtually no opportunity for social mobility. Often the members of castes are subject to rules that define the occupations they may enter, the neighborhoods where they may live, whom they may marry—caste systems are endogamous (marriage is limited to other members of the same caste). A caste system thus locks people in positions of relative advantage or disadvantage, and guarantees the perpetuation of such inequities. Caste systems of stratification have existed at various times in Rwanda (East Africa), Swat (Pakistan), Japan, Tibet, Korea, and India (Berriman, 1973).

The Indian Caste System

Perhaps the most well-known, but generally misunderstood, caste system has prevailed for centuries in India. Although it began to be

---

[1]Historians continue to debate whether the link between color and slavery existed from the beginnings of enforced labor or developed over a period of time. There may be no definitive answer, but it is clear that the connection was institutionalized by the eighteenth century.

formally dismantled in the 1850s vestiges remain in many rural areas. Four basic groups called "varnas" were documented as early as 1500 B.C. At that point they may have reflected functional divisions of society— Brahmins (priests and scholars), Kshatriyas (rulers and warriors), Vaisyas (artisans and merchants), and Sudras (unskilled workers). Although historical records are often unclear, there are several theories on the origins and development of varnas. One theory suggests that Aryans imposed the system on native Indians as a means of controlling them. In contrast, others have suggested that the emergence of the system coincided with transition from a hunting and gathering economy to a settled agricultural economy, when some clans were able to dominate others and appropriate the agricultural surplus. There is also some debate over the historical point at which the varnas were transformed into true castes, but the caste system was certainly in place by the ninth century A.D. (Kolenda, 1985: 34). By then, a fifth caste had also solidified. These were the "outcasts," later commonly called "the untouchables" and more recently "scheduled castes." The origins of this caste are obscure, but perhaps they were criminals, or the children of illicit marriages.

It is important to understand that the caste system as it developed in India operated at different levels in society. At a societal level, castes (varnas) were social, religious, and legal categories, linked by a common name, occupational specialty, and subcultural lifestyle. Sociologist Max Weber identified about 25 such castes early in this century. Among them were the Baniya (shopkeepers), Lohars (blacksmiths), and Untouchable Chamars (leather workers). However, there were thousands of local castes and subcasts. Thus, Brahmans in one province were divided into 200 major castes, none of whom could intermarry. Moreover, they enjoyed different levels of social prestige. Traditional Hindu law spelled out relations between members of castes and the privileges reserved for castes. Among the more stringent codes were those directed against the scheduled castes. They were, for example, denied the right to give evidence against members of other castes and were excluded from studying or even hearing the sacred religious texts. In rural areas they were denied access to communal village wells. More recent data show that most of India's 100 million untouchables are illiterate and landless agricultural laborers, overwhelmingly in debt to local moneylenders or shopkeepers (Josi, 1986: 2–3). Moreover, they are often the victims of acts of degradation and brutality. Official records for 1989 registered 14,000 acts of violence, including more than 1,000 murders and rapes (Desmond, 1990).

At the village level, castes combined political, economic, and social inequality. Each village, or network of villages, was composed of a set of endogamous and hereditary castes. A dominant caste exercised economic control, either by control of the farm land or by coercion. Lower castes were locked into a network of interdependent occupations and forced to cooperate in order to function. Communities were usually spatially divided, with "untouchables" always isolated at the outskirts of town or in a physically separate area somewhat distant from the main village.

Familiarity with the Hindu concept of purity and the related concept of pollution is vital to an understanding of the institutionalization and perpetuation of the caste system. A central tenent of Hindu rituals is offerings to the gods to ensure societal tranquillity (Kolenda, 1985: 62–70). A Brahmin priest must be "pure" in order to communicate with the gods. All things—gods, individuals, groups, animals, and objects—can be ranked on a scale of purity, and contacts with the impure have the potential to "pollute." It appears that purity is directly related to distance from biological excretions, human waste products, and death. For example, as priests prepare for religious services, they purify themselves of the pollution of their own bodies and contacts with polluted places and people. They fast, purge themselves, bathe, and don fresh garments. The hereditary occupations and dietary habits of castes and their members are ranked on the purity-impurity scale. Occupations are more or less polluting. Barbers work with bodily wastes (hair), washers clean clothing soiled by human excretions such as sweat, butchers deal with dead animals, and sweepers remove human discards. Dietary habits are more or less polluting. Purer castes such as the Brahmins are likely to be vegetarians, middle castes may eat chicken, and untouchable castes may partake of the most polluting of all meats—pork and beef. Thus, each caste occupies a position on a scale of permanent purity, with Brahmins at the top and sweepers at the bottom.

In addition, temporary impurity occurs by contacts with impure places and things and impure caste members. Consequently, in some places, elaborate rules specified the physical distance at which caste members could safely approach each other. In one village, lower caste members could not come closer than 32 feet to a Brahmin (Beteille, 1965: 126–128). Where intercaste contacts are unavoidable, as at work, in public places, or during transactions in the marketplace, clearly defined rules are followed to avoid pollution. For example, taking cooked food from the hand of a person is more polluting than accepting dry food; brass utensils are less polluting than porous pottery vessels (Mahar, 1959).

Thus, once established, the caste system was internally justified and self-perpetuating. Higher castes were purer, due to their lifestyles and work; simultaneously, each has a monopoly over the very attributes that grant higher status. Subsequent generations inherit the same traits and the same location in the stratification system. The system was further reinforced by the belief in successive incarnations of the soul. A person's place was in large part determined by actions in a previous incarnation, thus placing responsibility for a person's present caste location on his or her own behavior.

Industrialization has served to undermine traditional caste relations, at least in urban areas (Kolenda, 1985). Modern industry generates countless new occupations that have no traditional association with a particular caste and are thus "ritually neutral" and may be filled by members of any caste. Moreover, there have been a long series of attempts to improve the social, legal, and economic status of women. Women occupied a degraded position in the caste system well into the nineteenth century (Srinivas, 1966). The lower status of females was also embedded in the concept of purity. The normal but exclusively female biological processes of menstruation and childbirth were defiling events. Two of the more onerous customs that symbolized the degraded position of women in the caste system were the practice of *sati* or *suttee*, which called for the burning of a widow on the funeral pyre of her husband, and female infanticide. Although officially prohibited in the nineteenth century, these practices are alleged to have survived into the present in some more remote areas. Men and women also had differential legal rights. As a general rule women could not inherit property; sons, grandsons, and great-grandsons inherited property before anything would go to a widow or a daughter. Males could legally have several wives, but monogamy was the rule for females. Such discrepancies were formally eliminated in the mid-1950s.

Caste in South Africa

In the aftermath of World War II South Africa established a racially based caste society. Internal discontent supported by international disapproval is producing ongoing changes in the system, but the consequences of those earlier policies are likely to survive well into the future. South African castes take the form of "population groups" based largely on social definitions of race. There are four, and the official names have been altered several times. *Africans* or *blacks* (currently numbering about 25 million people) are the original, indigenous people of the area. *Whites* (about 5 million people) are largely Afrikaaners descended from the original Dutch, German, and French Huguenot settlers who brought slaves from Southeast Asia with them and descendants of British settlers. *Indians* or *Asians* (0.8 million) are descendants of laborers imported from India in the nineteenth century to work the sugar plantations. *Colored* (2.8 million) are descendants of marriages and sexual unions between early settlers and slaves or the native population.

The task of assigning people to "population groups" was until 1991 the responsibility of white "race inspectors," who visited hospitals and inspected babies under the Population Registration Act. Appearance (fingernails, hair, shape of the face) was the major criterion, but if there some suspicion that a "white" infant may have had an "African" ancestor an investigation was mandated and relatives summoned to be scrutinized and interrogated. An abandoned child whose parents were unknown could cause a major dilemma, and in cases where physical features were ambiguous and scientific analysis inconclusive there was a tendency to apply the "colored" label (*Time*, 1983).

A policy of "separate development" (officially called "apartheid" between 1948 and the mid-1960s) established a number of rules to enforce endogamy. Sexual relations and intermarriage across color lines were prohibited by such acts as the Immorality Act of 1950, since repealed. Separate residential areas were established. Other rules shaped the present and future distribution of inequality among the castes. Nonwhites were effectively denied access to many high-skill occupations by the Job Reservation Act, which generally limited them to menial jobs, except during periods of labor shortage. Moreover, pay for similar jobs was graded by caste and gender. For example, a male teacher's salary is 10 percent higher than a female's, and a white teacher earns 30 percent more than a colored teacher and 50 percent above an African (Finnegan, 1986: 23). It is estimated that white per capita income is $7,276 whereas blacks in segregated areas average $1,467 (Jolidon & Keen, 1990).

Separate and unequal educational systems were established for members of each group, which helps to limit the occupational attainments of future generations. The teacher-pupil ratio in white schools is 16 to 1, compared to 41 to 1 in black schools. Some indication of the relative quality of the schools is suggested by per capita expenditures for education during 1980: whites, 1,169 rands; Indians, 389 rands; colored, 234 rands; and Africans, 91 rands (Finnegan, 1986: 45).[2] Thus, while white literacy approaches 100 percent the rate for blacks hovers around 50 percent (Jolidon & Keen, 1990).

The system was also arranged to deny many political rights to all but the highest caste. All nonwhite groups were denied representation in parliament until 1983, when Indians and colored were granted seats in separate chambers. Finally, censorship of certain ideas was enforced. For example, non-white castes were forbidden from seeing certain American films, especially those that showed blacks in positions of authority over whites.

ESTATE SYSTEMS: Land and Power

Estate systems existed in ancient Egypt, the pre-Columbian civilizations of Central and South America, Imperial Russia, feudal England, and prerevolutionary France. *Estate systems* are usually found in advanced agricultural societies where land is the most important economic resource, and are characterized by the concentration of economic and political power

---

[2] In 1991, the exchange rate for the rand was approximately 2.5 per U.S. dollar.

in the hands of a small minority. There are always at least two estates, a powerful political-military group able to accumulate vast holdings of land and a peasantry tied to the land. It is estimated that a minority of 2 or 3 percent of the population typically own from one third to two thirds of the land and claim not less than half the total income (Lenski & Lenski, 1987: 185). Peasants might own the land they farmed, or rent it. In either case, economic obligations imposed by more powerful estates usually took much of what the peasants could produce. The church imposed tithes, the state taxed, and landlords expected obligatory gifts (Hanawalt, 1986: 5). The extremes of economic inequality could be dramatic. The aristocracy of medieval England practiced a lavish lifestyle as the very poorest peasantry often languished in poverty (Hanawalt, 1986). A peasant family might normally survive on a diet of bread, cheese, and vegetables, occasionally supplemented with meat. Some slept on straw, lacking beds or other furniture.

Another usual feature of estate systems was a dual legal system. The English nobility exercised special rights, such as the right of private revenge. They were not subject to arrest, except for treason, felony, or breach of the peace, were free of the obligation to testify in court, and were tried by different juries than were common felons (Stone, 1965: 17). Further, estate membership tended to be hereditary, with marriage into different estates usually prohibited by law or custom.

In the twelfth century Europe was dominated by a manor system and a threefold arrangement of estates—aristocracy, clergy, and peasantry. Religion played a vital role in the institutionalization of European estate systems. It supported a model of society that emphasized the functional interdependence of estates. The responsibility of the aristocracy was to rule (sometimes by "divine right"), protect society, and maintain social order by providing services such as the resolution of disputes. Peasant families owed tribute (taxes) to noble families, who in turn were obligated to provide protection and some civil services. The clergy ministered to the religious needs of all—commoner and landlord. Thus, each estate was portrayed as playing a distinctive and vital role in the total functioning of society.

Contemporary societies often retain traces of earlier estate systems. Land is vital in agricultural nations, and many Latin American nations continue to concentrate much of the land in the hands of a few owners. For example, in the agricultural sector of Brazil 2 percent of the landowners control 60 percent of the usable land while 70 percent of the rural households lack enough land to support themselves, producing high levels of malnutrition and infant mortality (Riding, 1989). Such vast inequities can generate mass discontent and challenges to ruling classes. Indeed, it has been suggested that mass political violence in Latin America is more likely to occur in societies with the greatest inequities in landownership (Midlarsky, 1988).

CASE STUDY:
Modern Landowners in Britain

The legacy of vast landholdings created during the feudal period also prevails in industrial societies such as Great Britain. Recent estimates show that Queen Elizabeth II, as monarch, technically owns 280,000 acres of land in Great Britain, including 350 acres of prime land in central London (Caborn, 1988: 23). Actually, the revenues of about $60 million from these holdings are paid to the Royal Treasury, which in turn, distributes a salary of $8 million to her. The queen does personally own 36,000 acres worth $90 million, which generates about $1 million annually. Her son and future king, Prince Charles, has 127,000 acres of land, which generates about $3 million annually.

Most of the wealthy landowners with ties to the feudal past are unknown and anonymous people, but have great wealth based on property. One of the oldest estates in London belongs to the ninth Viscount Portman, who owns 100 acres of London land along Oxford Street. The land was granted to the first viscount in 1533 by King Henry VIII. Europe's largest private landowner is believed to be the Duke of Buccleuch, with 258,000 acres of land in England and Scotland.

INDUSTRIAL CLASS SYSTEMS:
The Industrial Transformation

Prior to the middle of the eighteenth century most people were engaged in some form of agriculture, and the family was the basic unit of production and consumption. The Industrial Revolution began to reshape the world, often displacing slave, caste, and feudal systems of social stratification with those based on class. Industrialization is sometimes viewed in the restricted sense of technological innovations in the mechanization of the productive process—the cotton gin, assembly lines and laser technology—but is more appropriately understood as a complex and interrelated set of economic, demographic, and organizational changes that transformed whole societies. The list of major developments includes: the shift to paid urban employment, the growth and concentration of corporate power, the segmentation of labor markets, the expansion of government activity, bureaucratization, and the knowledge explosion. The internal politics of industrializing nations took them in different directions, with some embracing different stands of communist socialism, others such as the United States following a capitalist model, and still others creating mixed democratic-socialist economies. Vital differences in politics should not obscure the fact that industrialization also produces some common structural arrangements and major similarities in the class structure.

The Shift to Paid Urban Employment

Industrial production accelerates urbanization and the shift spells the decline of individual autonomous workers and the increase in the proportion of people working for pay. Nearly 75 percent of all Americans lived on farms in 1820, compared to less than 3 percent today, and many contemporary farmers supplement their incomes with paid employment. The number of people running small family farms, self-employed crafts workers, and independent shopkeepers has declined in favor of a paid work force of employees. Less than 10 percent of the American labor force is currently defined as "self-employed," most either in professional or skilled blue-collar work.

The Growth and Concentration of Industry

In the first stages of capitalism relatively large numbers of small companies compete with one another within countries, but over time there is a tendency for larger firms to eclipse smaller ones. For example in 1904 thirty-five separate firms were manufacturing automobiles in the United States, but the Chrysler Corporation's purchase of American Motors in 1988 left only three major American manufacturers. These firms are also in a position to capture firms in other countries, as when Ford Motor Company acquired British Jaguar in 1990 for $2.6 billion. Despite these moves both companies lag behind the General Motors Corporation, the largest U.S. automaker. General Motors employs some 600,000 people worldwide and had sales of $124 billion in 1990 (*Business Week*, 1991). Thus, industrial production has tended toward the evolution of massive business and financial organizations with tremendous economic power and influence.

Segmented Labor Markets

In the 1960s the term dual economy was coined to emphasize broad structural divisions within the economic system. Different analysts have focused on different aspects of the dual economy—industrial sectors, firms, capital investment, or occupations—but the same logic applies to any specific approach: The components of the economy are divided into two broad sectors. For example, those who analyze industrial companies contend that they can be conveniently apportioned between central (or primary) and peripheral (or secondary) firms (Baron & Bielby, 1984). Businesses in the central sector are large, stable, efficient, highly profitable, and oligopolies (where a few companies dominate). Firms in the auto, steel, and oil industries illustrate this idea. One important feature of central firms is secure employment and another is the presence of *internal labor markets*, a hierarchical system of jobs that allows workers to progress into positions of more responsibility and higher rewards within that company. Peripheral firms tend to be small, unstable, marginal, and competitive. The clothing industry is a good example, where many relatively small manufacturers compete among themselves resulting in low profit margins and, in turn, lower wages, poorer working conditions, less reliable employment, and few opportunities for advancement.

Government Expansion

Industrialization, urbanization, population growth, and shifting attitudes about the role of government have stimulated tremendous growth in the size and power of governments. Some indication of the sheer numerical expansion of government is reflected in the number of government employees. Between 1900 and 1990 the number of employees increased from 5,000 to 2.5 million. During this same period the activities and the potential power of governments expanded to include education, the regulation of industry, public works, defense, and social welfare. The United Nations (1981) estimates that Western industrial democracies on average expend at least one third of the national income of these states.

A different way of looking at the role of government is to focus on ownership of basic industries. Communist-socialist governments of Eastern Europe owned virtually all of the productive capacity of the society until the 1990s. The United States is at the other end of the continuum, with government ownership generally limited to railroads and some major utilities. The democratic-socialist nations of Western Europe have taken a different stance, attempting to strike a balance between widespread private ownership and government ownership of fundamental industries/services. Definitions of "fundamental industry" differ among nations and shift with changes in political control, but has included public control of such things as: airlines, banks, telecommunications, health care, and coal mining (*Economist*, 1978). This development takes ownership of economic power out of private hands but adds to the power of the state. Regardless of the political system, all governments centralize some unusual economic and political power in the hands of a small segment of the population.

Organizations, Bureaucratization, and Taylorism

The sheer size of industrial and government entities creates massive organizational problems—the need to plan, manage, and coordinate the activities of literally hundreds of thousands of people. As Max Weber pointed out there is a tendency toward the bureaucratization of organizations. *Bureaucracy* refers to several key structural features of organizations: specialization of organizational roles, formalization of procedures, proliferation of rules, and hierarchial authority.

One of the most important occupational consequences of bureaucracy is the creation of a vast cadre of clerical and administrative support personnel. At the beginning of the twentieth century approximately only 3 percent of the work force was in the clerical classification, but the end of the century that proportion approaches 20 percent. However, it may be that the most far-reaching consequence of bureaucratization is found in the patterns of authority that have developed. All bureaucracies involve some degree of centralized decision making at the upper levels of the organization. This means that a small group of individuals will be in a position to direct the activities of subordinates and establish organizational goals and objectives. One bureaucratic tendency has been for top-down decision-making, for all major judgments, to be concentrated in the hands of those at the apex of the organization. The result has been that most technical, clerical, and blue-collar employees have very little input into activities of the organization and very little control over the structure of their own work. Strong trade union movements have challenged this trend in some West European nations, notably Germany and Sweden. Here a policy of codetermination has limited the unilateral expression of managerial authority. Swedish law, for example, requires negotiations between labor and management on such issues as work assignments, production methods, supervisory appointments, market policies, and even broad corporate strategy (Haas, 1983).

In the United States the social organization of industrial firms was also strongly influenced by the thinking of Frederick W. Taylor and a school of thought called scientific management. In the interests of efficiency and productivity whole categories of work were highly specialized and precisely proscribed.[3] The result was that countless blue-collar and lower level white-collar jobs became narrow, highly specialized tasks. The work involved continuous repetition of one task that could be closely monitored.

Science and Technology: The Knowledge Explosion

The first scientific journal appeared in the middle of the seventeenth century because practitioners felt that new knowledge was accumulating so fast that they needed some mechanism for sharing that information. The rate of growth of new knowledge obviously continues to accelerate at an unprecedented rate and the "knowledge explosion" has several impor-

---

[3]Motives other than productivity were probably operative in this process, specifically control of the work process and weakening the potential for working-class solidarity (e.g., Braverman, 1974). Narrow specialization of work tasks reduced many jobs to unskilled labor and made workers more easily replaceable.

tant implications. One is the creation of new occupations: Countless modern occupations are devoted to the manipulation of knowledge in one way or another, whether to create it (scientists and engineers), apply it (medical personnel, computer programmers), process and record it (clerks, accountants), or disseminate it (teachers). In addition, knowledge has elevated the importance of formal education, especially higher education.

CONCLUSION: Industrial Classes

The industrial transformation altered societies and combined to create the class structures of modern industrial societies. The evolving features of class systems can be seen in the changing occupational structure of the United States during the twentieth century (Exhibit 3.1). The trend away from the land has culminated in an agricultural work force of less than 3 percent. The expansion of organizations is apparent in the growth of the managerial cadre and the clerical and sales occupations. The knowledge-based professions con-

Exhibit 3.1
Occupational Trends in the United States in the Twentieth Century

Occupation	Percentage of Paid Workers					
	1900	1920	1940	1960	1980	2000
Professional	4.3%	5.4%	7.5%	11.4%	16.0%	17.0%
Managerial	5.8	6.6	7.3	10.7	11.2	10.8
Clerical	3.0	8.0	9.6	14.8	18.6	17.3
Sales	4.5	4.9	6.7	6.4	6.3	11.7
Crafts	10.5	13.0	12.0	13.0	12.9	11.4
Operatives	12.8	15.6	18.4	18.2	14.2	9.0
Laborers	12.5	11.6	9.4	5.4	0.6	3.7
Service	3.6	4.5	7.1	8.9	12.6	16.0
Private household	5.4	3.3	4.7	2.7	1.2	0.6
Farm workers	37.5	27.0	17.4	7.9	2.8	2.4
LABOR FORCE (in millions)	29.0	42.2	51.7	65.7	99.3	136.2
Rates of participation:						
Females	20.6	23.7%	25.8%	34.5%	51.5%	62.6%
Males	n/a	n/a	n/a	83.3	77.4	75.9

Note: Labor force data are not strictly comparable over time due to changes in methods of enumeration.
Sources: U.S. Bureau of the Census, *Historical Statistics of the United States*, 1975, Washington, DC: U.S. Government Printing Office, 1975; U.S. Department of Labor, *Handbook of Labor Statistics*, Washington, DC: U.S. Government Printing Office, 1985; U.S. Department of Labor, *Employment and Earnings*, 47 (January 1981); George Silvestri and John Lukasiewicz, "Projections of Occupational Employment, 1988-2000." *Monthly Labor Review* 112 (November 1989); 42-65.

tinue to expand. Blue-collar jobs employed over one third of the work force for a long period but have begun to decline, being replaced by service occupations.

Although industrial class systems dominate in many parts of the contemporary world, there are many variations on the single theme of industrial classes. The democratic-socialist systems of Western Europe tend to manifest a class structure similar in many ways to that found in the United States, but with two notable differences. One is that the government intervenes in the economic system to a much greater extent, notably in the ownership of a large slice of the productive capacity of such basic industries as oil, steel, coal, telecommunications, and railroads. The other is that the state expends a higher proportion of the nation's wealth on social welfare programs such as health care. Overall shifts in the occupational structure were accompanied by the institutionalization and legitimation of inequality (discussed in Chapter 4).

Communist-socialist systems moved in many different directions and are currently in the process of restructuring, making generalizations difficult. The Soviet Union moved toward a command economy by virtually eliminating private ownership, and vested economic and social control in a powerful "governing class" or Nomeklatura that controlled the government, economy, military, education, communications, and other major social institutions (Voslensky, 1984). It was a self-perpetuating oligarchy in that access to the Nomeklatura could only be gained through sponsorship by current members. Thus, although there was no economic elite as found in the industrial democracies there was an institutional elite enjoying special privileges (e.g., government cars, homes, exclusive stores) that enabled them to enjoy lifestyles not available to the rest of the society.

Below the governing elite was a group of upper-managerial personnel and scientific workers similar to the upper middle class in the West. Skilled manual workers and salaried professionals occupied the next level, and lower white-collar and manual workers were below them. At the bottom were as many as one quarter of the population living in poverty and homeless because of a shortage of dwelling units (Dentzer and Trimble, 1989). The relative economic position of the classes was generally similar to that found in Western nations, although there was not as wide an earnings discrepancy between the poor and the upper middle class (Akszentievics, 1982). In addition, prices were controlled and housing and health care were subsidized. Occupational segregation based on gender was common, with women often channelled into "female work" such as teaching, medicine and bookkeeping with low pay and prestige (Lapidus, 1978). Political and social revolutions set in motion late in the 1980s make it impossible to assess the current form of stratification systems or to fully anticipate the future directions of these societies.

ADDITIONAL READINGS

On Slave Systems

EUGENE D. GENOVESE. *The Political Economy of Slavery*. New York: Pantheon, 1965.

MURRAY GORDON. *Slavery in the Arab World*. New York: New Amsterdam, 1987.

PETER KOLCHIN. *Unfree Labor: American Slavery and Russian Serfdom*. Cambridge, MA: Harvard University Press, 1987.

BERNARD LEWIS. *Race and Slavery in the Middle East: An Historical Enquiry*. New York: Oxford University Press, 1990.

MARIETTA MORRISSEY. *Slave Women in the New World: Gender Stratification in the Caribbean*. Lawrence: University Press of Kansas, 1989.

ROGER SAWYER. *Slavery in the Twentieth Century*. New York: Routledge & Kegan Paul, 1986.

On Caste Systems

ANDRE BETEILLE. *Equality and Inequality: Theory and Practice*. New York: Oxford University Press, 1983.

LOUIS DUMONT. *Homo Hierchieus: The Caste System and Its Implications*. Chicago: University of Chicago Press, 1970.

WILLIAM FINNEGAN. *Crossing the Line: A Year in the Land of Apartheid*. New York: Harper & Row, 1986.

G. M. FREDERICKSON. *White Supremacy: A Comparative Study in American and South African History*. New York: Oxford, 1981.

LEONARD THOMPSON. *A History of South Africa*. New Haven, CN: Yale University Press, 1990.

On Estate Systems

H. S. BENNETT. *Life on the English Manor: A Study of Peasant Conditions, 1150–1400*. New York: Cambridge University Press, 1960.

MARC BLOCH. *Feudal Society*. London: Routledge & Kegan Paul, 1961.

BARBARA A. HANAWALT. *The Ties That Bound: Peasant Families in Medieval England*. New York: Oxford University Press, 1986.

HENRI PIRENNE. *Economic and Social History of Medieval Europe*. New York: Macmillan, 1933.

On Class Systems

DAVID LANE. *The End of Inequality? Class, Status, and Power Under State Socialism*. London: Allen & Unwin, 1982.

ARTHUR MARWICK, ed. *Class in the Twentieth Century*. London: Harvester Press, 1986.

GORDON MARSHALL and others. *Social Class in Modern Britain*. London: Hutchinson, 1988.

ERIC OLIN WRIGHT. *Classes*. London: New Left Books, 1985.

MICHAEL VOSLENSKY. *Nomenklatura: The Soviet Ruling Class*. Garden City, NY: Doubleday, 1984.

Part Two

Social Class in America

The United States can be divided into five broad social classes, with a small wealthy and influential elite at the top of the stratification system and a broad base of employed and jobless poor at the bottom. The majority of the society is ranged between these two extremes with an upper middle class of managerial and professional people, a lower middle class of technical, clerical and sales workers, and a working class of manual workers.

Chapter 4 traces the evolution of the "dominant ideology" of individual effort and responsibility and a set of perceptions and beliefs about the poor, women, and people of color that supports and legitimizes their position in the class system. Chapter 5 provides a broad overview of the class system in America and establishes a link between class standing and family structure and dynamics. Chapter 6 explores the way in which people think about the class system and their place in it.

Chapter 4
Institutionalizing and Legitimizing Inequality

ON THE ORIGINS AND MAINTENANCE OF STRATIFICATION SYSTEMS

The social, economic, and political changes accompanying industrialization divided American society into a system of five broad social classes. Class position has broad social and economic consequences, including expansion or limitation of opportunities. However, recognition of the nature and effects of class has in the United States been overwhelmed by an emphasis on the individual effort and performance that tends to deemphasize the structural.

Two analytically separate processes are involved in the origin and maintenance of structured inequality. Therefore, it is helpful to differentiate between the "institutionalization" and the "legitimation" of inequality. The institutionalization of stratification refers to the process of establishing various forms of structural inequality—the systematic exclusion of categories of people from education, housing, and well-paying jobs is one dimension of the process. In contrast, the rationale or justification for such discriminatory treatment is a different process, a process that sociologists refer to as legitimation. The two processes interact, and cannot be understood independent of one another.

The Institutionalization of Inequality

The *institutionalization* of inequality refers to the collection of laws, customs, and patterns of interaction that combine to produce inequality based on class, color, and gender. Discriminatory laws and codes have often played a role in this process. For example, African Americans were long formally excluded from labor unions, schools, and neighborhoods, and the exclusion of women from combat roles in the military survived long after other forms of legal discrimination were toppled. In other cases inequality is based on custom or openly accepted informal social understandings.

Early in this century contractors openly advertised to pay "whites" $1.50 per day and $1.15 to "Italians" (Feagin, 1984: 123).

The institutionalization of inequality is supported by a variety of social and political forces. In extreme cases sheer force and intimidation are used to create and maintain inequality. The period between the American Civil War and World War II in the South witnessed the exercise of both private (the Klan) and public violence and intimidation. As late as the 1940s, city police departments were involved in forcibly providing workers for the cotton plantations (James, 1988). However, institutionalized privilege, discrimination, exclusionary practices, and violence seldom cannot exist in social isolation; it is typically legitimized in some manner.

Legitimation and the Ideology of Inequality

Robert Nisbet (1970: 183–184) explains legitimation in this way, using the term status in lieu of class:

> No (position) will long survive widespread belief in its loss or lack of legitimacy. Ages that are truly revolutionary...are ages in which the sense of legitimacy regarding the status system of a social order terminate rather sharply. The traditional prerogatives of high status in the society are challenged, and the traditional limits put upon low status are seen as so many illegitimate fetters, to be cast off. The high status of the patriarch, the man of knowledge, the businessperson, or of the titled aristocrat will survive only so long as a determining part of the population...regards each as legitimate, as properly entitling their possessors to the privileges which go with their status.

Thus, in the context of stratification, the term legitimation refers to the evolution of social definitions and social beliefs that support, rationalize, and justify patterns of inequality. When these ideas are organized into a more or less consistent collection of definitions and ideas, they may be said to form an *ideology*. An obvious example of an ideology is the caste system idea that lower castes are ritually impure. A different illustration is the belief that slaves are inherently inferior, docile, and born to be enslaved. Current terms such as "racism" and "sexism" must be used in this way if they are to have any meaning—as organized beliefs and ideas that support discrimination against socially defined groups. It is important to emphasize that ideologies need not be logically consistent, nor based on an accurate picture of the situation.

Several points about ideology must be understood at the outset. First, the elements of an ideology may be consciously recognized and accepted by dominant members of society or they may operate below the conscious level. Long-standing ideologies often enjoy the force of tradition. Patterns are learned and passed on to subsequent generations through the social-

ization process, and seem to have no other justification than their antiquity. This kind of ideology is often evident in *social stereotypes*, tacit, often
unrecognized, beliefs and assumptions about categories of people.

Second, ideologies may be elaborate and coherent systems of ideas,
deliberately promulgated by a dominant group, or they may be loose
collections of ideas that emerge in the process of every-day social relations
among groups. In the former category are formal or explicit ideologies
developed and advanced by specific groups, and that justify inequality
(Barrera, 1979: 198). For example, medieval European aristocrats es-
poused the position that they were the descendants of the Teutons (later
called Aryans) who had defeated the Romans, and commoners were descendants of the Romans and other inferior cultures. Members of the
aristocratic class were thus members of the line responsible for the flow-
ering of Western civilization and hence destined to rule. Later versions of
this civilization ideology showed up in the United States in this century
among those who sought to erect barriers to the influx of immigrants from
eastern and southern Europe. Not all ideologies are deliberately created
(Shibutani & Kwan, 1965: 248). Rather, they may be understood as
emerging in a more unsystematic way when certain ideas are selected out
and embraced simply because they can be interpreted to justify inequality.

Understanding the analytic distinction between institutionalization
and legitimation is vital to understanding the dynamics of inequality. The
two processes interact to create and support a stratification system; one
has little meaning independent of the other. This distinction is also
important in understanding the persistence of inequality through time.
Discriminatory practices may be outlawed or discredited, but underlying
ideologies (attitudes, beliefs, and stereotypes) may persist long after formal
barriers to opportunity have crumbled. Any number of contemporary
examples can be phrased in this way. Blue-collar workers when compared
to white-collar workers enjoy less social prestige; how this pattern emerged
is one question, but why it continues may be a different question. Black
workers began to be systemically excluded from some craft unions late in
the nineteenth century is one issue, but why this pattern has continued
into the 1990s in some instances, is another matter. The question of the
origins of pay differentials between women and men is different than the
issue of contemporary manifestation of monetary inequities.

CLASS AND THE IDEOLOGY OF STRATIFICATION

Contemporary American attitudes and perceptions of the class structure
and distribution of inequality continue to be influenced by a complex
system of ideas, the origins of which can be traced to the Protestant
Reformation of the sixteenth century. A key element in this religious
philosophy was the emphasis individual responsibility for one's own fate

(both religious and secular). Puritans brought this individualistic spirit with them, and it came to form the centerpiece of the American cultural value system. The importance of independence and self-reliance was solidified and elaborated by the unique circumstances of a frontier society and later by the celebration of emerging capitalism.

This is often called the *dominant stratification ideology*, and when reduced to its most basic form may be phrased as follows (Huber & Form, 1973; Feagin, 1975; Klugel & Smith, 1986):

a. There are abundant economic opportunities.
b. Individuals should be industrious and competitive.
c. Rewards in the form of jobs, education, and income are, and should be, the result of individual talent and effort.
d. Therefore, the distribution of inequality is generally fair and equitable.

Although there may be a weakening in the power of this ideology, especially since World War II, it continues to have relevance for significant segments of the population. The origins of this ideology may be traced to the Protestant Reformation, but it also had some unique American features.

The Puritan Ethic

Protestantism of the sixteenth century must be understood as a rejection of the elaborate bureaucracy of the Catholic church and the doctrine that a Christian was unable to achieve salvation without the active help of the church. Reformers such as Martin Luther and John Calvin emphasized the individual's responsibility for his or her own actions and fate. Work was a key part of individual responsibility. Prior to the Reformation, all work except religious endeavors was perceived as a burden to be endured as a means of survival. Martin Luther elevated all occupations to the level of "a calling," arguing that every form of work played an integral part in God's worldly plans. Influential ministers demanded relentless industriousness in pursuit of a person's occupation, no matter how menial. Hard work offered countless rewards; it was intrinsically worthwhile, but also was a way of serving God and a protection against the temptations of the secular world. More than one Calvinist theologian defined lack of employment as a crime or a sin. The unemployed were, in several colonies, subject to imprisonment or whipping (Feagin, 1975: 25).

There can be little question that Benjamin Franklin was the chief spokesperson for this Puritan ethic. Writing in 1726 he resolved, "To apply myself industriously to whatever business I take in hand, and not divert my mind from my business by any foolish project of growing suddenly rich;

for industry and patience are the surest means to plenty" (Franklin, 1961: 183). It was these traits that attracted the attention of Max Weber, who argued they fostered the spirit of capitalism.

There was also religious sanction for social inequality, for economic success, or the lack of it, became associated with personal character and virtue. For a brief historical period, Calvinists proclaimed wealth as a worldly sign of God's grace, for God would certainly not allow the damned to prosper. Hence, if persons are responsible for their own economic fate, failure must be an indication of some personal defect. Some groups, such as the Quakers, spoke out against this view, but without much impact, and the powerful emphasis on individual responsibility for success or failure was established.

The Frontier and the Land of Opportunity

The American version of Puritan individualism was supported and reinforced by the abundant opportunities that existed here, and none was more important than the lure of the western frontier. The frontier was much more than a distant geographic boundary, it was a symbol of unlimited opportunity (Turner, 1920). The image of plentiful land on the western frontier created a convenient mythology for the nation. There was no reason for anyone to fail, for there was always the vast untapped land to the west, with prosperity awaiting the strong and talented who were willing to seize the opportunity. This image was fostered in the mid-nineteenth century with discovery of gold in California, and in 1862 the passage of the Homestead Act guaranteed cheap land to everyone. The inherent risks—the desire to displace the native population, unchartered land, social isolation, and lack of law and order merely emphasized the rewards for the self-reliant. This led to the celebration of the rugged individualist, perhaps symbolized by the cowboy.

This ideology could flourish in a largely agrarian economy with an abundance of inexpensive land, and lacking traditional class barriers to success (with the notable exception of slaves). Industrialization offered a different kind of opportunity, urban jobs, and because the nation was a leader in industrial development it soon became the "land of opportunity." The image of a nation of apparently limitless economic opportunity was to attract waves of immigrants fleeing from poverty and famine in their native lands. Most non-English immigrants met with discrimination and open hostility, and were typically relegated to the least rewarding work in the factories. Yet their economic status was often better than it would have been in the lands they abandoned, and there were enough opportunities for economic success for those from humble origins to support the belief system. Those who did not themselves prosper were sustained by the notion that their children would enjoy the benefits of a better life.

Social Darwinism

An ideology of individualism and self-reliance has more salience and appeal in an agricultural society of independent craftspersons and small household farms. With the emergence of laissez-faire capitalism, increasing numbers of persons become employees of others, subject to their authority. Toward the end of the nineteenth century a different variation of the dominant ideology, more suited to an industrial economy, emerged. Charles Darwin published *On the Origin of the Species* in 1859, and soon it became the basis for a full-blown social ideology. Themes such as the "struggle for survival" and "survival of the fittest" were appropriated from a biological theory of evolution and grafted onto an economic system. John D. Rockefeller, speaking at a church school, explained: "The growth of a large business is merely a survival of the fittest....This is not an evil tendency in business. It is merely the working out of a law of nature and a law of God" (Feagin, 1975: 35).

Soon thereafter the sociologist William Graham Sumner lent academic legitimacy to Social Darwinism in his discussion of the rich: "(M)illionaires are a product of natural selection, acting on the whole body of men to pick out those who can meet the requirement of certain work to be done....They may fairly be regarded as the naturally selected agents of society....There is the intensest competition for their place and occupation (and) this assures us that all who are competent for this function will be employed in it" (Sumner, 1914: 90).

Therefore, he concluded, there should be no attempt to redistribute wealth or interfere with the evolutionary process. He believed that hard work could triumph over the most humble circumstances. Hence he had these words of advice for the impoverished urban worker: "Let every man be sober, industrious, prudent and wise, and bring up his children to be so likewise, and poverty will be abolished in a few generations" (p. 57).

Challenges to the Ideology of Individualism

Americans still generally identify their country as a land of opportunity, although increasing numbers are expressing some skepticism. A clear trend is evident in adherence to the belief that there is "plenty of opportunity" in the United States: 88 percent endorsed this statement in 1952, 78 percent in 1966, and 70 percent in 1980 (Kluegel & Smith, 1986: 46). It must be assumed that general perceptions reflect a degree of sensitivity to the well-publicized declining economic position of the United States in the global economy, and the perceived threat to jobs caused by worldwide economic competition. In addition, it reveals an awakening (or perhaps a public acknowledgment) of the fact that structural barriers to access prevail, especially for minorities, women, and the poor.

The themes of individualism, self-reliance, and boundless opportunity were difficult to sustain when the Great Depression struck. More than 6 million workers were thrown out of work between 1929 and 1930, and that figure doubled by the mid-1930s. No amount of individual effort could protect them from joblessness. The economic chaos of the period stimulated government intervention in the economic system, and social welfare legislation such as unemployment insurance and the social security system for older workers were instituted.

Further challenges to the situational and structural limits on individual achievement surfaced during the turmoil of the 1960s. The civil rights and women's movements and the rediscovery of persistent structural poverty left little doubt that discrimination and structural barriers placed artificial limits on the chances of economic success for many segments of American society. Social scientists marshalled evidence that allocated responsibility for lack of success in the economic system to failures of institutions such as the schools. These developments challenged exclusive reliance on individual success or failure and focused on social, political, and economic factors beyond the direct control of individuals, however highly motivated they might be.

Class Ideology in the 1990s

The ideology of opportunity and individualism that dominated American society and culture for much of its history survives, but flourishes more powerfully among some segments of the population than in others. Although ideologies are complex social phenomena, they can sometimes be highlighted by a single issue, a single topic, or a single question. Many social scientists believe that asking people to define the causes of wealth or poverty accomplishes this. "The poor" represent those at the bottom of the class structure, and beliefs about the reasons for their situation demand that people distill their feelings and attitudes into a single response.

When confronted with this question, Americans divide into three almost equal categories (see Exhibit 4.1). One segment of the population is willing to blame the poor themselves due to lack of effort, and another third locate the causes of poverty in circumstances beyond their control. The remaining third endorse the idea that both reasons must be considered. It should also be noted that this is not a neutral issue, for very few people have no opinion on this matter.

Subgroups within the general population diverge from the overall pattern. Men are somewhat more likely to subscribe to the importance of individual responsibility than women. As would be expected, racial minorities are more sensitive to structural rather than individual sources of poverty. Finally, lower-middle-class workers (clerical and sales) place

Exhibit 4.1
Perceptions of the Causes of Poverty

Group	Lack of Effort	Circumstances	Both	No Opinion
Overall	33%	34%	31%	2%
Sex				
Male	36	31	30	3
Female	29	37	31	3
Racial/ethnic group				
White	35	30	33	2
Nonwhite	15	67	16	2
Hispanic	11	44	38	7
Social class				
Upper middle	36	32	31	1
Lower middle	41	36	23	<1
Working	29	36	31	4
Not in labor force	31	37	31	4

Note: Data based on a national sample of 1,505 adults conducted during 1984. The question was worded as follows: "In your opinion, which is more often to blame if a person is poor—lack of effort on his own part, or circumstances beyond his control?"
Source: "Blame for Poverty." *The Gallup Report* no. 234 (March 1985), p. 24. Copyright © 1985 by The Gallup Report.

greater emphasis on personal effort than blue-collar workers, who are more inclined to stress structural factors. In addition, explanations based on individual effort are more likely to be found among older people and those with higher incomes.

More detailed analysis of individualist responses reveal the survival of the traditional values of Ben Franklin. The major causes of poverty are identified as the absence of some positive personal trait such as lack of thrift or proper money management, lack of effort, lack of ability and talent, or loose morals and drunkenness (Kluegel & Smith, 1986: 79). In contrast, when asked to explain the sources of great wealth, a majority favor factors such as personal drive, willingness to take risks, hard work, and initiative, although it is conceded that inherited wealth is some advantage. Those who emphasize social structure see the sources of wealth or poverty, success or failure originating with social barriers or in the circumstances that individuals confront in their own backgrounds. They assign the greatest weight to factors such as discrimination, exploitative wages, or failures of the school system.

A large group occupies the middle ground, endorsing elements of both extremes. On issue after issue we find large numbers of people taking the position that structural barriers exist but that individual effort also plays a role. These people refuse to accept a dichotomous explanation and *volunteer* the answer that poverty is the outcome of the interaction of these two explanations. The same pattern emerges in other surveys; for example, when asked if the government should improve the living standards of the poor or should they care for themselves, most people choose a middle ground that encompasses both points of view (E.C.L., 1987: 23).

The convergence of these various elements form the dominant ideology that stresses individual responsibility over structural position in understanding the rewards that people enjoy. This evident in the aversion to the term "social classes" in American society (DeMott, 1990). Acceptance of social classes admits that society is divided into levels whose opportunities and rewards are enhanced or limited by the workings of the economic system.

GENDER AND CLASS STRATIFICATION

Anthropologists and historians have compiled extensive analyses of gender roles in non-industrial societies, and documented that a sexual division of labor is a common feature of human societies (Chafetz, 1984; D'Andrade, 1966). Biological or physiological differences do not contribute a great deal to the explanation of gender differences because the tasks assigned to men in one society may be the province of women in another, and because they change over time. There are many instances of such diversity. Clerical work in the nineteenth century in the United States and Britain was a male domain, only becoming feminized as the twentieth century proceeded. Sales work in contemporary Philippines is dominated by women (69 percent female), but an almost exclusively male occupation (1 percent female) in the United Arab Emirates (Jacobs, 1989: 19). The conclusion that derives from this research is that gender is a social construct, reflecting the convergence of social, political, economic, and demographic forces.

Women have always formed part of the paid labor force, but the most dramatic increases have occurred in the last 4 or 5 decades. The rate of female participation has increased steadily and is expected to continue to expand. Overall rates of participation mask differences among women, with poor and blue-collar women and women of color apparently always more likely to be working for wages than their more advantaged counterparts. A dominant feature of employment is gender segregation with numerous jobs dominated by members of one sex or the other. Thus, origins of these enduring patterns can be traced to the industrial transformation that reshaped a largely agricultural society (see Kessler-Harris, 1982; Bose, 1987; Anderson, 1988).

From colonial times to the beginning of the nineteenth century, the individual household in the United States was the basic unit of production and consumption for the majority of the free white population. There were, of course, wealthy landowners and urban merchants at one extreme, and slaves and sharecroppers at the other extreme. It appears that labor in family farms was generally divided along gender lines, with men having primary responsibility for agricultural production and women largely responsible for the inner economy—food, clothing, and child care (Anderson, 1988). However, both sexes easily crossed these lines, with husbands involved in the socialization of children for adult community and religious roles, and being especially active in preparing sons to follow agricultural pursuits. Wives participated in production through keeping inventories, caring for livestock, supervising farm hands as well as helping with planting, cultivating, and harvesting during peak periods. Households were largely self-sufficient, but cash was needed for the purchase of equipment and services (such the milling of grain) and wives often produced the products and services that generated extra cash income, either by weaving, growing food on small plots, or even working as midwives (Jensen, 1980). This pre-industrial division of labor still survives on contemporary small independent farms (Boulding, 1980).

Gender and Work in the Nineteenth Century

The first stirring of industrialization began about the turn of the eighteenth century with the introduction of factories and textile mills. Displaced rural men and young women and children provided the labor force for those early factories. At first the women were the daughters of rural families who contributed to household income through paid work, but they were soon supplemented by foreign-born immigrants (Kessler-Harris, 1982). A major pool of low-paid labor was provided by the waves of Irish-Catholic immigrants that began to reach the United States in large numbers in the 1840s. The men worked the docks and the textile mills, built the railroads, dug the canals, and supplied farm labor. Wives, daughters, and single women were most likely to end up as domestic servants for the wealthier classes. In 1855, 75 percent of all domestic workers in New York City were Irish (Feagin, 1984: 93).

Historical convention locates the era of rapid industrialization to the period between the Civil War and World War I. One measure of the industrial transformation is the fact that within two decades after the Civil War industrial workers outnumbered farm workers for the first time in American history. The family farm did not disappear, but there was a shift toward commercial production for the market. Consequently, the urban household and industrial work became the center of attention. This was a decisive period in the evolution of gender roles, for it was during this period

that a number of forces combined to crystalize a more dichotomous separation of men's and women's occupational and social roles. It is also an
extraordinarily complex period, as a number of different forces were at
work.

A most obvious difference between agrarian and urban industrial
economies is that the workplace became physically separated from the
residence. That made it more difficult for women with child rearing
obligations to combine domestic responsibilities with full-time paid work.
Some continued in various forms of income-producing work at home. The
wives of lower-middle and working class men were doing laundry at home
or taking in boarders as a means of supplementing family income well into
the 1920s and 1930s (Kessler-Harris, 1982; Jensen, 1980). Countless
others did industrial "home work," jobs such as sewing clothing, making
lace or buttons, or even rolling cigars that were decentralized in private
homes on a piece-work basis.

Many women joined the labor force on a more or less full-time basis.
Although census data of the time are notoriously unreliable, in 1900 at
least one in four paid workers was female. Black women, their options
severely limited by overt discrimination, were relegated to agricultural or
domestic work while factory work was largely the province of young single
white women, usually immigrants or the daughters of immigrants, who
toiled under some of the worst working conditions in the disgraceful
sweatshops. As a result women were active in fighting for improved
working conditions, both in the larger trade union effort and in organizing
along gender lines with groups such as National Women's Trade Union
League (Bose, 1987: 275).

Some enduring forms of gender segregation of occupations emerged
during this period. Women were often exploited as pawns in the struggle
between employers and workers. For example, early working class solidarity between men and women in the printing industry was eroded over the
course of the nineteenth century when unskilled women were used to
displace skilled male printers or were employed as strikebreakers (Baron,
1980). Printers worried that the "petticoat invasion" threatened to depress
their wages and undermine the skilled traditions of their craft. Consequently, gender cooperation faded in this and other areas, and women came
to be perceived as competitors for scarce jobs. This pattern was repeated
in many other craft unions leading to exclusionary practices that made the
crafts the province of white males.

The segregation of occupations along gender lines was legitimized
and fostered by a configuration of gender stereotypes and attitudes toward
the appropriate social and occupational roles of men and women (Deaux &
Kite, 1987: 97). These ideas did not emerge during this period, but were
thrown into strong relief by the process of industrialization. In some cases
gender-based beliefs were invoked as justification for occupational segregation as is evident in mass production industries where auto assembly

came to be dominated by men while 80 percent of electric light-bulb assembly was done by young women (Milkman, 1983: 166). One justification for this division of labor was that women had more skillful and delicate hands, and more patience for tedious work.

Gender stereotypes were specifically articulated to explain the rejection of women who sought to surmount occupational barriers. When, for example, Myra Bradwell sought a license to practice law in Illinois in the 1870s, she was refused by state courts and an appeal to the U.S. Supreme Court also brought rejection. Her suit was denied on Constitutional grounds, but Justice Bradley located the decision in broader historical and social context:

> Law, as well as nature herself, has always recognized a wide difference in the respective spheres and destinies of man and woman. Man is, or should be, woman's protector and defender. The natural and proper timidity and delicacy which belongs to the female sex evidently unfits it for many of the occupations of civil life....The paramount destiny and mission of women are to fulfil the noble and benign offices of wife and mother. This is the law of the Creator. And the rules of civil society must be adapted to the general constitution of things. (*Bradwell v. Illinois*, 1873: 141-142).

The male protector and defender ideology also had an economic dimension. For example, it was used to support the fight for a "family wage." The family wage issue was used by labors unions as a strategy for seeking improved wages for their male constituents on the grounds that it was the husband's responsibility to act as protector and provider for his family. Samuel Gompers, speaking in 1905, proclaimed, "In our time, ...there is no necessity for the wife contributing to the support of the family by working" (Foner, 1964: 224). There is a powerful residue of this concept in contemporary society for some husbands at all class levels tend to be resistant to accepting working wives as co-providers (see Chapter 5).

Another manifestation of this ideology surfaced in the early part of the century when a wide variety of protective legislation was introduced to protect women from workplace hazards. In retrospect, it is noted that considerations other than health were at stake, for most of the protected jobs were traditional male jobs and often the best paid. The U.S. Supreme Court in 1908 in *Muller v. Oregon*, ruled that special legislation for women was appropriate because women were not as strong as men, were dependent on men, and were the mothers of future generations. Perhaps the key feature of the decision was that it placed all women in a separate legal classification because all women were potential mothers. Legislation beginning in the 1960s largely eliminated this situation, although the exclusion of women of childbearing age from some jobs on the grounds of "fetal protection" was not eliminated until 1991. It is apparent from the perspective of the twentieth century, that the family wage, protective legislation, and occupational segregation benefited some men by excluding women from competition from the more lucrative jobs in the paid labor force.

The assumption that women and men have inherently inferior intellectual and psychological characteristics was reinforced by "scientific" research on sex differences. Craniometrists proceeded from the observation that there were average differences in stature, to conclude that this produced intelligence, leading social psychologist Gustave LeBon to conclude in 1879 that, "All psychologists who have studied the intelligence of women recognize today that they represent the most inferior forms of human evolution and that they are closer to children and savages than to adult, civilized men" (Deaux & Kite, 1987: 93). Thus, the research was prompted by a belief that there were sex differences, and the findings (however unfounded they might have been), in turn, buttressed the belief.

Gender and Work in the Early Twentieth Century

While segregation along gender lines was occurring in the occupational sphere, households was also changing. Among the most important developments was the shift away from internal production for the family. This was largely an upper middle class phenomena, but the impact extended to other levels in the society because the lifestyles of this class were a model for others. Their new affluence combined with the introduction of mass produced clothing and prepared foods rendered home work less necessary, creating a "domestic void" by stripping women of meaningful work in form of goods and services for the family. They were caught up in the emergence of a home economics movement that transformed housework into an unpaid occupation (Ehrenreich & English, 1979). The home economics movement itself represented the convergence of several broader trends—wider availability of single-family homes, concern with the breakdown of the traditional, tightly knit family, the rise of scientific child-rearing, and medical science's discovery of the germ theory of disease (making wives responsible for cleanliness).

Advocates of Frederick Taylor who were seeking to rationalize the workplace also turned their attention to the home, encouraging housewives to study and analyze the best way to perform tasks such as peeling potatoes, maintaining household records, and holding to rigorous schedules. Out of this emerged a new social ideal for upper-middle class women, often called the "cult of domesticity." This ideal demanded dedication to home decoration, cleanliness, nutrition and meal planning, and child rearing. The cult of domesticity served to legitimize certain patterns. One was that it located the male role in the paid labor force (the public sphere), and female role in the home (the private sphere). It is not at all clear how many women were actually able to realize this ideal, for many working class wives, immigrants and women of color continued in the paid labor force but the ideal was spread through the media and advertising.

The flourishing upper-middle class ideal for homemaker flourished as the century progressed. Aided by technological innovations directed toward work in the home (vacuum cleaners and washing machines) and prompted by mass advertising and the proliferation of women's magazines, upper-middle class wives were expected to attain new heights in neatness and cleanliness in the home and in creative cooking. The more affluent could afford domestic servants, relegating unpleasant physical tasks to a corps of black women (Palmer, 1989). Continuing into the 1960s, housewives devoted increasing hours to housework. More importantly, wives' income and social status came to be defined by their husband's occupational attainments, and the expectation that personal success and satisfactions were subordinate to those of spouses and children.

Trends in occupational segregation that had been set in motion earlier intensified between the two world wars, as did the gender stereotyping of work. A whole range of occupations proliferated during this period, and they tended to split along gender lines. The professions—law, medicine, science, engineering—proliferated, but along sex lines. The feminization of clerical work began at the end of nineteenth century; women outnumbered men by the 1920s and by the 1990s held over 90 percent of clerical jobs such as bank teller, secretary, and typist. It has been suggested that men abandoned clerical work at least in part because it did not enable them to demonstrate masculine traits (Lockwood, 1958), but it may also have been influenced by the lack of mobility opportunities.

Work and Ideology Since the 1940s

World War II was to have a major impact on women's roles. The influx of women into the labor force to replace men in the armed services set the stage for the eventual blurring of the distinction between the public and private sectors. Women filled jobs of all kinds (in both civilian industry and the military), including those that they presumably lacked the psychological traits to master. As the war wound down, an overwhelming majority expressed a desire to remain in the work force, although many were eventually displaced to make room for returning servicemen. However, the rate of participation of women in the paid labor force was to begin an increase that has become permanent (Exhibit 4.2). An expanding economy created hundreds of thousands of new jobs. Older (over 45) married women with diminished child-rearing responsibilities were the first group to seek work in larger numbers, and since the 1970s it is younger married women.

Social and legal change diminished occupational barriers in some areas. Law schools, once an almost exclusively male domain now enroll approximately 40 percent women. However, the segregation of jobs along gender lines that emerged during earlier phases of industrialization often

Exhibit 4.2
Labor Force Participation Rates for Women, 1946–1987

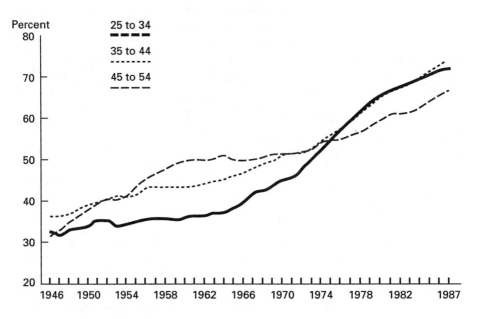

Source: Susan E. Shank, "Women in the Labor Market: The Link Grows Stronger," *Monthly Labor Review*, 111 (March 1988), Chart 2, 5.

Exhibit 4.3
Gender Segregation in Selected Occupations, 1989

Occupation	Percentage Female
Auto mechanics	0.7
Carpenters	1.6
Aerospace engineers	3.7
Clergy	7.8
Dentist	8.6
Textile sewing machine operators	90.5
Registered nurses	94.2
Teacher, K and pre-K	97.8
Dental assistant	98.9
Secretary	99.1

Source: "Employed Civilians by Detailed Occupation, Sex, Race, and Hispanic Origin." *Employment and Earnings* 37 (January, 1990).

continues. This is underscored by examining the proportion of women in some specific occupations (Exhibit 4.3). The distorted occupational distribution is nicely summarized by one observation; three out of five employed women would have to shift jobs to match the distribution of employed men (Bella, 1984).

Contemporary Gender Beliefs

Large numbers of people hold a configuration of perceptions and beliefs about masculine and feminine traits. They may be defined as *gender beliefs* or *sex-trait stereotypes*, convictions and assumptions about the characteristics of women and men. All stereotypes are generalizations about groups of people. Members of a society may disagree over the origins of such traits, with some emphasizing inherent sex differences and others feeling they have their origins in socialization practices, but there is consistent evidence that gender beliefs do prevail. These generalizations are complex and varied and people certainly recognize diversity within each sex and seldom attribute the extremes of these traits to individuals, but there does appear to be a high level of consensus in American society and other industrial nations (Williams & Best, 1990).

Beliefs about the characteristics of women and men are a major factor in understanding their position in the class structure. Prompted by the cross-cultural work of anthropologists, the social scientific analysis of gender beliefs emerged during the 1940s and produced a wealth of information about the way members of society perceive gender. One consistent pattern that emerges is the perception that gender involves two broad clusters of traits. Men tend to be viewed as stronger and more active, with potent needs for achievement, dominance, autonomy, and aggression. Women are seen as less strong and less active, with powerful needs for affiliation, nurturance, and deference. Moreover, there is a general consensus (among both men and women) on these configurations of characteristics, and some indication that a number of these traits show up in other cultures (Williams & Best, 1990).[1]

Stereotypes are more than perceptions; they also have a normative dimension, setting broad standards for appropriate gender behavior. Such popular beliefs can work to the advantage or disadvantage of men and women in the occupational sphere in more than one way. If persons are persuaded of the salience of stereotypes, they can disqualify themselves

[1]Such findings articulate the debate over the relative contribution of differences grounded in sex differences as opposed to the impact of socialization practices. This debate is beyond the scope of this book, but there are a number of useful summaries of the issues and the research. See, for example, Maccoby and Jacklin (1974), Fausto-Sterling (1986), and Williams and Best (1990).

from the pursuit of specific occupations. It is more likely that they are held back or disqualified as they encounter barriers based on the assumption that they lack the traits necessary to function in certain fields or at certain levels. For example, women lawyers who choose criminal defense confront perceptions that they lack the requisite "coolness" and "aggressiveness" required for success in the crucible of the courtroom. Ironically, displaying that competitive behavior can also be interpreted to their disadvantage. This dilemma is described by a lawyer, "If a woman lawyer begins to argue with another lawyer, it may seem...that (she) is becoming too emotional or agitated.... If a woman tries to be unemotional she may be accused by being hard or unfeminine" (Blodgett, 1986).

There is an important quality about the way in which people view these traits in the United States. They tend to be dichotomous and polar opposites. This means that there is a tendency to place a person in one category or another, masculine or feminine, with little tolerance for neutrality. In addition, if people are described as lacking one set of traits, it will be assumed that they possess the opposite. Thus, a male who is not dominant is assumed to be submissive; the female who is not warm is

---

CASE STUDY:
Sex-Trait Stereotypes and Management Careers

Research on sex-trait stereotypes is typically approached through the use of lists of adjectives. Male traits in the United States tend to cluster around terms such as independence, self-direction, and control, whereas female traits cluster around caring, expressiveness, and sensitivity to interpersonal relations. The following listing of adjectives in Exhibit 4.4, summarized from a broad body of research, provides an outline of the perceived attributes of women and men (Schein, 1973; Williams & Bennett, 1975; Deaux & Lewis, 1984; Brenner, et al. 1989; Williams & Best, 1990. Attempts to capture the essence of these clusters in a single word or phrase has popularized expressions such as "instrumental," "competency," "task-orientation" or "agency" for men and "expressive," "social orientation," or "communion" for women.

The link between occupational attainments and stereotypes is highlighted by considering the characteristics, attitudes, and temperaments necessary for success in certain kinds of jobs. Management careers present a direct illustration. It is more common to associate male characteristics (aggressive, self-reliant, stable) than female characteristics (helpful) with success in management, at least among men (Schein, 1973; Brenner et al., 1989). This discontinuity between female sex traits and managerial success means that women are perceived as less likely to have abilities to compete in the high-powered world of administration. The characteristics of successful management may also be stereotypes, but their existence has the potential to place women at a disadvantage.

Exhibit 4.4
Perception of Male and Female Traits

Men	Women
active	affectionate
aggressive	changable
confident	emotional
courageous	gentle
daring	helpful
forceful	poised
inventive	sensitive
rational	sophisticated
stable	submissive
unemotional	sympathetic
unexcitable	warm

pictured as cold. This visualization of people falling into dichotomous/polar opposite categories is a general characteristic of the society, also showing up with respect to sexual preference: Homosexuals are assumed to possess the social traits of the other biological sex.

Dramatic social changes propelled into the public consciousness in the 1960s stimulated a reexamination of contemporary gender roles. It is conventional to date this development from 1963, when Betty Friedan labeled the middle-class ideal a "comfortable concentration camp" for women, but she merely touched a responsive chord in the society. Prompted by the second women's movement and other social changes, members of society became more sensitive to patterns of institutionalized inequality called into question the validity of the ideological legitimation of such inequities. Many formal, legal barriers to women's achievement fell during the 1970s, but inequalities remain, perpetuated by disadvantageous structural arrangements, deeply ingrained attitudes and beliefs inherited from earlier periods, and patterns of socialization that help to perpetuate them.

PEOPLE OF COLOR AND STRATIFICATION

Race or ethnicity is often the basis of relegating minorities to the lowest levels of society. There have been many different attempts to explain the origins and legitimation of minority stratification. All focus on the question of how the jobs reserved for minorities tend to the most unstable, hazardous, dead-end, undesirable, and lowest-paying forms of employment. These theories can be grouped in many different ways, but seem to fall into three categories.[2] One approach focuses on competition for scarce resources; a

[2] It is impossible here to do full justice to the many attempts to explain racial/ethnic stratification. There are several useful summaries and comparisons; see, for example, Barrera (1979, Chap. 7) or Feagin (1984 Chap. 2).

second, labeled colonialism, emphasizes deliberate coercive exploitation of minorities; and assimilation theorists emphasize the sociocultural disadvantages that minority group members suffer by placing them at a disadvantage in a system dominated by members of a different culture.

Competition Theories

Donald Noel (1968) maintains that the emergence of racial or ethnic stratification is the outcome of the interaction of three factors—ethnocentrism, competition for scarce resources, and the ability to exercise control. When groups of different racial, cultural, or religious backgrounds come in contact, they are often separated by feelings of *ethnocentrism*, the tendency of one group to view its own standards and perspectives as superior. The religious dimension is a prime example for most religious belief systems define their creed as "the one true faith," thus establishing an unequivocal basis for judgments of inferiority. Cultural values, by virtue of defining what is "right," operate in the same manner. Ethnocentrism thus emphasizes social differences among groups, but is not necessarily or inevitably a source of stratification, for there been instances of peaceful pluralism.

Stratification emerges, Noel argues, only when there is *competition for scarce resources*. Certainly the history of relations between native Americans and Europeans can be seen as a struggle for land that was eventually decided by the superiority of weaponry and military personnel. A different form of competition centers on jobs. Organized occupational groups frequently limit minority access. For example, the legal profession during the 1920s and 1930s erected barriers to limit the number of African American and East European immigrants (Auerbach, 1976). During the post–Civil War period the dramatic and relatively sudden competition for working-class jobs between blacks and whites was set in motion by emancipation. One estimate suggests that 100,000 of the artisans in the South in 1865 were black (Brooks, 1971: 243), and it is not surprising that some white artisans worried about the threat to their jobs posed by the newfound freedom of skilled black carpenters, blacksmiths, and tailors. The situation was, of course, more complex than just a struggle between working-class whites and African Americans for skilled jobs. Other groups had vested interests. Large landowners also stood to benefit from the presence of a large pool of black workers excluded from skilled blue-collar work, and thus available as a cheap labor force.

The subordination of a racial ethnic group ultimately depends on the ability to *control access* to such valued resources. Frequently, racial competition was settled by violence, either actual or threatened. However, exclusion of blacks from jobs also took less extreme forms. For example, white-controlled unions systematically excluded blacks from membership and from apprenticeship programs, and unions prohibited their members from working with nonunion members, thus pressuring employers to exclude blacks (Foner, 1964). Such practices were part of some union constitutions into the 1940s.

Although the focus is on jobs, discriminatory behavior is not limited to the occupational sphere alone. It takes place within the larger context of exclusionary practices designed to keep minorities poor, uneducated, and powerless, thus discouraging competition and ensuring another generation of workers.

Internal Colonialism

Colonialism refers to a pattern of global political and economic expansion and exploitation by powerful nations over weaker nations. A number of people have expanded this approach to include processes that occur within the borders of a nation, and hence use the term internal colonialism (Blauner, 1972). The thesis is embedded in economic imperatives and it argues that non-native groups are explicitly exploited as a pool of low wage workers, thus generating profits for agricultural landowners or industrial employers. For example, Indians were encouraged or forced to enter South Africa in the nineteenth century to work the plantations. This approach can be used to illuminate the American experience of a number of nonwhite groups, starting with the forced importation of blacks as slaves, and continuing in the mid-nineteenth century with the importation of Chinese workers to work the mines and build the railroads, and on to the influx of Mexicans in this century to do fieldwork in the Southwest.

Assimilation Perspectives

The assimilation perspective grew out of an attempt to understand the experience of waves of immigrants to America during the nineteenth and twentieth centuries (Gordon, 1964). The pattern occurred with newcomers from Ireland and Italy and is projected to be repeated for succeeding groups. Most members of each immigrant group tends to be concentrated at the lowest levels of society due to a combination of hostility and discrimination by members of the dominant group and their own characteristics (lack of marketable job skills, absence of educational credentials, language barriers) that handicaps them in the competition for work and homes.

The assimilation perspective predicts the decline in the salience of racial, ethnic, and religious differences over time as assimilation occurs along several different dimensions. Succeeding generations should be able to improve their position by adopting the social and cultural attributes of the host society, a process called cultural assimilation. As this takes place the salience of their differences should decline allowing second and third generations to achieve structural assimilation, acceptance into neighbor-hoods, clubs and institutions of the host society, and ultimately marital assimilation as prejudice and discrimination decline. Research with this model has been unable to confirm the process for all groups, especially Hispanics and African Americans (e.g., Williams & Ortega, 1990). This issue is explored in more detail in Chapter 8 in the context of social evaluations and social relations.

Legitimation of Racial/Ethnic Inequality

Discriminatory and exclusionary practices interact with ideologies that define minorities as different and deserving of unequal treatment and rewards. There are important differences among the experiences of differ-ent groups such as blacks and Hispanics in the United States, but there are also some recurring themes.

Black Americans and the Ideology of Racism

The word racism refers to an ideology that defines physically different groups as having inferior intellectual and psychological characteristics (cf. Feagin, 1984: 5). Slavery was established in the colonies by the middle of the seventeenth century, and some historians suggest that Africans were enslaved because they were members of societies that were politically and militarily weaker. Others feel that a form of ethnocentrism—religious—was a major factor, initially more salient than race in legitimizing slavery. It is argued that the fact that Africans were non-Christian was the rationale for enslaving them (Franklin, 1974). There is little doubt that early accounts by traders and missionaries were often dominated by religious and cultural, rather than racial, considerations. As one put it, "cultivating none of the practices of civilized life as these are found among the rest of mankind" (quoted in Gordon, 1964: 25). Although the origins of negative attitudes are unclear, racist stereotypes were established and articulated by the eighteenth century. With the breakdown of legal sanc-tion for slavery, elaborate pseudo-scientific theories of biological racism flourished. One was a theory of polygenesis, which held that the various races evolved at different times, and blacks, who theoretically evolved first, were consequently the most primitive. Moreover, this theory proclaimed that culture is the product of biological capacity, and hence less advanced races could neither create nor carry the culture of higher races.

Consequently, over the course of the nineteenth and twentieth cen-turies many different themes were elaborated, all of which were said to demonstrate that all African blacks exhibited biological and personality traits that handicapped them and justified discrimination. For example, it was long fashionable to stereotype blacks as "lazy" and "childlike," which makes it logical to exclude them from positions of authority and responsibility. Scholarly journals produced "scientific" evidence to prove the mental inferiority of blacks, thus justifying limiting their educational opportunities to inferior schools. Sexual images infiltrated also, with black women seen as lacking in conventional morals, thus providing some justification for the sexual exploitation of black women by white men.

There are, in addition, subcategories for women of color. One is the myth of the aggressive and domineering "strong black woman," having more masculine than feminine traits. Bell Hooks (1984) points out the usefulness of this stereotype in legitimizing broad patterns of racial inequality. The reasoning follows this logic: The strengths of black women violate broader social expectations of women and consequently emasculate black men and cause the breakup of the family, which in turn causes poverty. The function of the stereotype is thus to locate the causes of problems within the personality of the victims rather than focusing on structural problems that produce poverty.

The Case of Mexican and Chinese Women

Broad racist stereotypes directed at Mexicans can be traced to the middle of the eighteenth century through the selective perception and interpretation of events. The defeat of the Mexican army in the struggle for territory in the 1840s generated stereotypes of cowardice rather than a recognition of superior military force. A period of internal turmoil produced by the Mexican struggle for independence was transposed into "political incompetence," a people not capable of self-government.

Mexican women in the United States often faced special problems created by the work patterns imposed on their husbands by employers. Male Mexican workers working the mines, farms, and railroads in the Southwest were frequently required to leave their families behind and live in all-male labor camps (Glenn, 1987). In those cases families were disrupted and circumstances demanded that women single-handedly bear the burden of maintaining the family, albeit with the help of the extended family. This was not a unique case, but rather one that was frequently repeated. In the case of Chinese women in the middle of the nineteenth century wives were left behind in their native land, prohibited from immigrating with their spouses. There they often lived with their husband's kin, who received money from him and acted on his behalf. A few never saw their husbands again, and others only occasionally during rare visits back to China.

These are specific instances, but women of color tend always to face a common problem. Men of color are channeled into the worst-paying jobs and because husbands earn minimum-level wages, wives are forced into the paid labor force to supplement family income, in addition to having responsibility for regular household chores. They, too, face the discriminatory environment of the larger society, and most end up concentrated in service work, as servants or domestics.

The Perpetuation of Stereotypes

Racial stereotypes and ideologies are transmitted through the socialization process and reinforced by countless social patterns, including such apparently trivial mechanisms as ethnic jokes. Given the pervasiveness of racism, it is not surprising that well into the 1960s at least one third of Americans admitted to a belief that blacks were intellectually inferior to whites, and favored the continuation of racially segregated neighborhoods (Brink & Harris, 1967). In the same period, a full one third of Californians endorsed the notion that Mexicans were "shiftless and dirty."

Overt manifestations of this ideology held sway well into the 1950s and 1960s, when it finally began to dissipate under the pressures of the civil rights movement. One indication of the decline in the legitimacy of racial ideology is measured by the weakening of negative stereotypes of blacks (Gordon, 1986). Moreover, survey research indicates that open manifestations of prejudice toward blacks declined steadily during the 1970s and mid-1980s (Schuman et al., 1988; Firebaugh & Davis, 1988). This pattern holds for all regions of the country, including the South, and is explained in part by the fact that more younger and less prejudiced people are surveyed. All such data must be interpreted with some caution, for it has become socially unacceptable in some areas to express prejudice openly, and in fact, such expressions in some cases leave people liable to legal action.

In many cases, overt behavior belies the expression of more tolerant attitudes. A recent study by the Center for Democratic Renewal counted over 1,000 violent incidents directed against people of color during the 1980s, including assaults, shootings, and murders (Millican, 1988). There were, in addition, another 1,800 cases of vandalism and nonviolent harassment. Some acts are attributed to groups that openly hold to racial supremacist ideologies, a mix of relatively small activist groups, including self-proclaimed skinheads and a dozen different Ku Klux Klan groups. These groups tend to adhere to an extreme position that focuses on any race, religion, or sexual preference that deviates from white, heterosexual Protestantism. But many others are the acts of members of the general population, including a large number occurring on upper-middle-class college campuses.

CASE STUDY:
Ethnic Jokes

"Did you hear that their national library burned down? Not only were both books destroyed, but they hadn't finished coloring them."

Ethnic jokes and one-liners such as this are found in many societies, but those focusing on the alleged stupidity of ethnic minorities seems to be found only in western industrial democracies according to Christie Davies (1982). The following pattern of victimization of ethnic groups prevails:

Country	Ethnic Victims
Australia	Tasmanians
Canada	Icelanders
Denmark	Norwegians
England	Irish
France	Belgians
Sweden	Finns
United States	Poles

The enduring popularity of ethnic jokes and their place in the popular culture of these societies suggests they serve important social functions. The most obvious is that they perpetuate negative stereotypes about ethnic groups in a society, attributing a lack of intelligence to all members of the group. However, this does not explain why those groups are singled out as victims of these jokes, nor the importance of these traits. Davies suggests ethnic jokes emphasize the social and moral boundaries between a dominant group and ethnic minorities. By projecting negative traits to ethnics they reinforce their separation from them and elevate their own status. In addition, the jokes reaffirm the legitimacy of the stratification system for they are directed at groups in the class hierarchy and imply that the lower level of attainment is deserved and just.

CONCLUSION: American Dilemmas

The development of systems of inequality and social stratification is a complex process. On the one hand, mechanisms for the subordination of groups develop—exclusion from economically rewarding positions and opportunities for attaining them. The institutionalization of inequality is buttressed by ideologies such as sexism or racism that maintain that members of groups are inferior in some way—biologically, socially, behaviorally—that causes their position in the class system.

Gender and racial ideologies lend legitimacy to specific exclusionary practices, but it is important to note that they also function at a more general level. A phrase introduced by the Swedish sociologist Gunnar Myrdal (1944) in exploring the situation of black Americans is useful. He called attention to an "American dilemma": A society founded on democratic and individualist principles simultaneously discriminates against a proportion of its citizens, creating a moral contradiction. Ideologies function to resolve this apparent contradiction (Nash, 1962). Sexism or racism provides a moral justification for systematic deprivation by confirming that some members of the society are culturally or biologically inferior. In that way it allows members of the dominant group to reconcile obvious discrepancies between societal values (e.g., democracy) and discriminatory behavior.

Recent research illustrates the dynamics of this process with respect to African Americans. The 1980s was a period in which fewer Americans came to attribute the concentration of blacks at lower levels of the class system to innate differences between the races (Kluegel, 1990). However, individualist interpretations focusing on the dominant ideology of personal motivation still tend to eclipse explanations that emphasize structural barriers. A survey that asked white Americans how they felt about blacks compared to whites reveals that 62 percent see blacks as less hardworking (6 percent define them as more hardworking) and 53 percent as less intelligent (14 percent more intelligent) (Kanamine, 1991). It is important to note that this position is widely held, even among people who do not favor traditional discriminatory practices such as residential segregation. The coexistence of these beliefs contributes to an understanding of the common paradox, a belief in racial equality coexisting with a lack of support for policies to reduce racial inequalities (Kluegel, 1990).

ADDITIONAL READINGS

On Class Stratification

BENJAMIN DeMOTT. *The Imperial Middle: Why Americans Can't Think Straight About Class.* New York: Morrow, 1990.

RICHARD HOFSTADER. *Social Darwinism in American Thought.* Boston: Beacon, 1955.

JOAN HUBER and WILLIAM H. FORM. *Income and Ideology.* New York: Free Press, 1973.

JAMES R. KLUEGEL and ELIOT R. SMITH. *Beliefs About Inequality.* New York: Aldine De Gruyter, 1986.

On Gender Stratification

ALICE KESSLER-HARRIS. *Out to Work: A History of Wage-Earning Women in the United States.* New York: Oxford University Press, 1982.

CHARLOTTE G. O'KELLY and LARRY S. CARNEY. *Women and Men in Society: Cross-Cultural Perspectives on Gender Stratification.* Belmont, CA: Wadsworth, 1986.

BARBARA F. RESKIN and PATRICIA A. ROOS. *Job Queues, Gender Queues.* Chicago: Nelson Hall, 1990.

SHEILA M. ROTHMAN. *Woman's Proper Place: A History of Changing Ideals and Practices, 1870 to the Present.* New York: Basic Books, 1978.

JOHN E. WILLIAMS and DEBORAH L. BEST. *Measuring Sex Stereotypes: A Multination Study.* Newbury Park, CA: Sage, 1990.

On Minority Stratification

RODOLFO ACUNA. *Occupied America: A History of Chicanos.* New York: Harper & Row, 1981.

BART LANDRY. *The New Black Middle Class.* Berkeley: University of California Press, 1987.

WILLIAM P. O'HARE, KEVLIN M. POLLARD, TAYNIA L. MANN, and MARY M. KENT. *African Americans in the 1990s.* Washington, DC: Population Reference Bureau, 1991.

ALPHONSO PINKNEY. *The Myth of Black Progress.* New York: Cambridge University Press, 1984.

WILLIAM J. WILSON. *The Declining Significance of Race: Blacks and Changing American Institutions.* Chicago: University of Chicago Press, 1977.

Chapter 5
Class
and Lifestyles

SOCIAL CLASS: An Overview

Social classes are here defined as groups of individuals and families occupying a common position in the economic system of production and distribution in industrial societies. Position in the economic system is largely determined by occupation, except for members of that group referred to as the "economic elite" who derive their advantaged position from inherited wealth. Social class has broad and significant implications. The ramifications of social class are both direct and straightforward and subtle and indirect. The configuration of economic, social and political rewards deriving from social class are covered in subsequent chapters. This chapter, and the one that follows, concentrate on analyzing how experiences encountered at work influence the way people respond to their specific jobs and to show that these experiences have the potential to extend beyond daily routines to shape their lifestyles and perceptions of the larger society and their place in it.

This approach emphasizes that work must be visualized as much more than simply the collection of physical and mental tasks that individuals perform. Four other relevant aspects of work must be considered (Kohn & Schooler, 1983; Bensman & Lilienfeld, 1991). First, occupations differ in the stability of work, offering relatively secure futures to some while confronting others with the unending threat of financial devastation. Second, occupations are unequal in promotion opportunities with some, such as those in corporate management, having career paths that provide chances to improve one's position and rewards. In contrast, others, especially unskilled and service work, offer few (if any) chances for upward movement. Third, work locates individuals in a system of authority, either organizationally or interpersonally, rendering them more or less under the control of others. Fourth, jobs offer differing degrees of personal autonomy and discretion. Some enjoy high levels of responsibility and initiative and control over the pace and performance of work tasks while others perform routine and repetitive acts. The work environment of upper-middle-class professionals typically offers much more freedom than that available to machine operators or people trying to keep pace with an assembly line. Confronting the combination of these factors on a regular basis at work has the potential to extend to more general attitudes and perspectives toward conformity and self-direction, and feelings of efficacy and control (see Case Study).

CASE STUDY:
Class, Values, and Personality

Melvin Kohn and Carmi Schooler (1983) are among the sociologists who have undertaken the most direct analysis of the implications of social class position on lifestyles. Their thesis, referred to as the learning-generalization hypothesis, argues that lessons learned in one sphere of life are carried over into other areas of life. Consequently, experiences on the job may come to dominate not just perspectives toward work but also broader social values, social orientations, self-concept, and intellectual functioning. More specifically, people at each higher level in an occupationally based stratification system experience more challenge and are able to exercise more self-direction. The general lack of control over job structures and processes that characterize the low-skill jobs of the poor stands in stark contrast to the situation of upper-middle-class professional and managerial workers who enjoy more complex and intellectually challenging work and have greater autonomy in determining the pace and scope of their own work. The fundamental lesson is this: Self-direction at each higher level is allowed, encouraged, and rewarded, but it is discouraged at each lower level, where conformity is demanded and rewarded.

This led Kohn and Schooler to explore the ways in which such lessons shape more general perspectives or values. They found a direct relationship between social class and positive self-evaluations such as having "good sense and good judgment," "self-reliance," and "responsibility," all of which may be interpreted as consequences of having greater opportunities to wield responsibility on the job. There are also class differences in the characteristics people hope to instill in their children. Considerations of success, honesty, and happiness are widely defined as important, but others are apparently organized differently. There is an inverse relationship between class and an emphasis on conformity to external standards of behavior—obedience, personal neatness and cleanliness, having good manners. Thus, people at lower levels value in their children the kinds of traits that are demanded by their class position. This pattern is replicated in other nations, such as Australia, Italy, and Poland, suggesting that such value orientations may have their origins in industrial class systems (Kohn and Slomczynski,1990). It would seem that people's values are shaped by their work experiences, coming to value those traits which are attainable, and subsequently attempting to inculcate them in the children.

The implications of the conditions of work also contribute to some variations in lifestyles among different classes. This is illustrated by focusing on patterns of family structure and dynamics, one of the areas where work structure has consistently been shown to have an impact (Voydanoff, 1988). Any discussion of families must be read and interpreted carefully. Any single characterization invariably blurs internal variations within classes.[1] Moreover, family units may be made up of spouses occupying different class levels, rendering any analysis much more complex.

THE ELITE

The apex of the American stratification system is occupied by a small group of individuals and families who enjoy unusual wealth and power. Position in the *elite* is based on occupational position and/or accumulated wealth. They are the group that is defined by ownership and/or control of major productive resources.

The Institutional Elite

The expansion of large organizations concentrates unusual authority and influence in the hands of the executives who direct those establishments. In some cases a handful of organizations dominates a significant segment of the society. Thomas Dye (1986: 12) refers to them as a national *institutional elite* and identifies some 7,314 specific leadership positions. In the corporate sector it is the top executives of the 215 largest industrial corporations, banks, insurance companies, and investment firms. Combined, these organizations control over half of the nation's total corporate assets. In the government sector are the president, vice president, cabinet officers, chairs of major congressional committees such as finance and armed services, Supreme Court justices, and staff rank members of the military. In the public interest sector are executives of the major media (the ten major newspaper chains that reach one third of total circulation, the newsmagazines, and television networks), the 25 largest private colleges and universities, the 50 largest foundations (which control about half of all endowments), the senior partners in the 25 largest law firms, and

---

[1]One of the unresolved issues in the context of family structure is the interaction between class and color, and the variation among minority groups. In some cases there are significant gaps in the literature. For example, there are no studies that compare Hispanic and non-Hispanic middle-class families (Vega, 1990). In other cases studies of minority families fail to systematically control for social class standing. One consistent finding that does seem to prevail at all levels in the class system is that minority families are more likely to be involved in extended family relationships than whites (Taylor et al., 1990).

various civic and cultural organizations (Red Cross, Kennedy Center for Performing Arts). It is clear that this relatively tiny group has tremendous potential to shape society.

The Economic Elite

Another segment is the *economic elite*, individuals and families who possess vast economic resources in the form of money, property, and stocks and bonds. There are some families where wealth has passed through several generations. They often have familiar names—Ford, Mars (the candy people), Rockefeller (oil), Heinz (foods), and duPont (chemicals), and are called "old money" to underscore their tradition of wealth. Others, typically referred to as the "new rich," have amassed their fortunes more recently, people such as Sam Moore Walton, who founded the Wal-Mart retail store chain and amassed a personal fortune of over $6 billion.

There are, of course, more than a few cases of a convergence of economic and institutional elites in specific individuals or families. The Ford family is a prime example within the corporate world, both owning and controlling the auto company that bears its name. And in some cases there is movement between the two spheres, as is the case of several members of the Bush family straddling both institutional and economic elites. The broader issue of the overlap between institutional and economic elites is the subject of some debate. Some sociologists such as William Domhoff argue that members the economic elite also dominate the institutional elite, leading him to see the existence of a "ruling class" that effectively controls the destiny of the nation (1983). In contrast, Dye (1986: 194) estimates that only 30 percent of the positions in the institutional elite are held by people of inherited wealth. Most of the remainder come from upper-middle-class backgrounds. Thus, although over-represented, they are not able to control the institutional sector.

Members of the two segments of the elite often do travel in the same social circles, and the parties of the late Malcolm Forbes provided a showcase for them. His parties were always media events, but one of the most famous took place in 1989 on his seventieth birthday. Forbes spent an estimated $2 million to host 600 guests for his birthday party at his villa in Morocco. Guests were flown to Tangiers on chartered jets, met by an honor guard of 274 mounted cavalry, entertained by 600 belly dancers, and waited upon by 271 servers. They toasted each other with 216 magnums of champagne.

Forbes's publicity machine always afforded the public the chance to glimpse the elite at play. His guest list included entertainers (Elizabeth Taylor, Beverly Sills, Mike Jagger), entrepreneurs (Donald Trump), journalists (Barbara Walters, Ann Landers), old money (David Rockefeller), state governors (California, New Jersey, Rhode Island), CEOs (General Motors, Chrysler, American Express, Pepsico, Citibank), media giants (*Washington Post*, *US News & World Report*, *Playboy*), and various current (White House chief of staff, and attorney general) and former (Henry Kissinger) government officials (Alter, 1989).

Some members of this group apparently deliberately live an extravagant life, encouraging television and the tabloids to peek into their homes and personal lives (Taylor, 1989). A few have even gone so far as to purchase British titles—a Texas businessman became Lord of Beedon Manor for $30,000 (Jones, 1990). Thorstein Veblen's (1899) insights into the lifestyles of the rich at the end of the nineteenth century continue to have relevance. He explained their ostentatious and extravagant expenditures as nothing more than "conspicuous consumption," open and public displays of wealth for the express purpose of flaunting their vast wealth. Wealth is further validated by "conspicuous leisure," dedication to nonproductive endeavors that vividly demonstrate that they are so rich they need not work. As Stephen Birmingham (1987) has pointed out, raising and racing thoroughbred horses became a favorite form of conspicuous leisure in the nineteenth century, and members of this group still meet each August in Saratoga Springs, New York.

CASE STUDY:
ZIP Code 90210

The contemporary geographic capital of conspicuous consumption may be Beverly Hills, California, where many of the newly rich reside (Weiss, 1988). It boasts the wealthiest ZIP code in the nation with an average household income of $154,776 (compared to the national average of about $35,000). The least expensive homes start at $500,000 and go as high as $30 million (Ferrell, 1990). Originally the home of stars of the movie industry, it has since become the locale for those whose wealth originated in popular music, the television industry, professional athletics, real estate, or finance.

Beverly Hills is a relatively small city of 33,000 permanent residents (and 45,000 cars), yet each year $2 million is spent to decorate the streets for Christmas (Stewart & Dunn, 1989). The influx of tourists, city workers, shopkeepers, bankers, gardeners, real estate brokers, and tourists inflates its population to 150,000 during the day. The community houses 170 beauty salons, 122 jewelry stores, 65 banks (with deposits of $9 billion), 24 furriers, 14 limo services, 22 auto dealers, and at least one department store requiring an appointment for the privilege of spending money. Stores on the famed Rodeo Drive feature such items as $25,000 leather jackets.

The Family and the Transmission of Privilege

The most enduring segment of the elite is that group born to wealth and power. Consequently, the group's members are dedicated to the maintenance of their advantaged social position through the preservation of the family and the class. Families play a central role in this process because the family line is both the source of position and the mechanism for transmitting social position to future generations. Consequently, as Ruth Caven observes, they think of themselves not so much as individuals, but as "a stage in the development of a historical family" (1969: 85). Moreover, because the fortunes of specific families are linked to the survival of the elite class, there are powerful allegiances with other members of the same class.

The socialization of each new generation is organized around the perpetuation of family and class. Primary responsibility for teaching appropriate behavior and instilling proper attitudes falls to mothers (Domhoff, 1970: 34). From the start children are taught that they are different from the children of other classes, and a clear element of moral superiority is instilled (Ostrander, 1984: 70). Socialization means immersion in the elegant lifestyle that wealth offers and a strong emphasis on correct behavior. This includes the need for sons to follow parents in careers as business and government leaders. For daughters there is emphasis on participation in community activities (Daniels, 1987). For both there is stress on "good marriages," which, of course, means a union with another member of the elite. Good marriages are facilitated by limiting the children's circle of acquaintances to other members of the elite. This is accomplished through a complicated system of informal social activities, private schools, exclusive clubs, and debutante activities.

Children are expected to assume positions of influence and work to maintain family fortunes, but they also face some unique problems. One of the most troublesome is that their privilege denies them the opportunity to prove their own self-worth through individual accomplishment. Most people in today's society prove themselves in the occupational world, often measuring success with income. The children of wealth lack this challenge, for not only are they born to wealth, but their route to future positions of influence is virtually guaranteed. Consequently, some are destined forever to wonder how well they might have fared on their own merit. Another challenge to their self-worth is evident in relations with others where there is the constant suspicion that people around them are attracted to their wealth and position and not to them as people. Thus, in every generation a few who renounce their wealth or change their names to disassociate themselves from their wealth, and a few are driven to seek psychiatric help in order to cope with the need to create a meaningful life.

It has long been noted that upper-class families tend to be conservative and emphasize tradition values (Warner & Lunt, 1941; Blood & Wolf, 1960). Families tend toward patriarchy, with husbands having control of major decisions within the context of the family—decisions about jobs, housing, and major expenditures. This pattern seems to prevail despite the fact that most wives have substantial wealth inherited from their families, which in other classes is translated into higher levels of power within families. Although the pattern is an apparent source of marital dissatisfaction among elite wives, it seldom produces open challenges to husbands' authority.

It has been suggested that the tradition of patriarchy which has been somewhat eroded in other classes, survives here for several reasons. One of the most important is that upper-class women do not perform the burdensome housework tasks that fall to wives in other classes. Another reason is that they derive their social identities from their class position and community work, not through their family roles. But perhaps the most salient reason is the economic and political position of upper-class men outside the family, where they dominate their communities and the society. The men are accustomed to control and would be unlikely to relinquish power voluntarily in any area.

Noblesse Oblige

A recurrent theme running through both the socialization of children and the activities of economic elite class families is the emphasis on the responsibility for the less advantaged members of society, the concept of *noblesse oblige*. A member of the Rockefeller family recalls, "My mother and father's greatest fear was that their children might take their wealth for granted and grow up spoiled and arrogant. They wanted us to learn that with wealth comes responsibility" (*New York Times*, 1989 :4F). Consequently, members of the elite are active in countless local activities, from fundraising for charitable causes to acting as caretakers for vast international philanthropic organizations. The Rockefeller Foundation alone has assets of $2 billion, and is used to support higher education, the arts, and environmental causes.

Noblesse oblige activities serve different motives. Some members of the elite sincerely accept this as a moral obligation accompanying inherited wealth. At a different level it is a means of moving into positions of authority and influence where the activities of these organizations may be directed in the ways they see as most appropriate. There is also the matter of justifying and legitimizing privileged position. The devotion of time, money, and effort to public service may help to deflect potential criticism, and as such is a way of perpetuating the position of their family and class.

THE UPPER MIDDLE CLASS

Virtually all members of the *upper middle class*, largely managers and professionals, are college graduates, and increasing numbers hold advanced degrees. At the upper reaches of this class are managers, administrators, and the professionals who occupy the middle and higher levels of large public and private organizations. This includes plant managers, directors of human resources, deans, research scientists, chiefs of surgery, and undersecretaries of cabinet departments in the federal government, along with an ambiguous plethora of assistant and associate managers. Their authority is circumscribed, limited to specific areas and usually subject to limitations by higher levels of authority. Yet, most are likely to be free from routine and direct supervision, granted latitude in the conduct of their work, and allowed to establish their own schedules within broad limits. Most occupy career paths that offer opportunities for upward mobility, and a small number may realistically look forward to movement into the elite.

Members of established professions such as law, dentistry, university education, science, engineering, and medicine form the remainder of the upper middle class. They typically manifest the same combination of expertise and autonomy. Moreover, their income and social prestige allow them to maintain lifestyles similar to those of managerial personnel and to socialize with them.

Perspectives on the "New Class"

The upper middle class is sometimes called the "new class" for two reasons—first, to emphasize that it proliferated on a large scale relatively later in the process of industrialization, and second, that it currently forms a stratum between a powerful elite class and those who do the more conventional office and factory work. Thus, although it is relatively easy to identify the upper middle class on the basis of a combination of income, authority, expertise, and autonomy, it is more difficult to locate this class within the overall class system of production and distribution.[2]

[2]The situation of the upper middle class has been the subject of analysis for nearly a century (Burris, 1986), first by Marxian theorists, then by a series of other scholars who claimed to have discovered the "managerial revolution," the "white collar," the "new petty bourgeoisie" (Poulantzas, 1975), the "new working class" or the "new middle class" (Mills, 1951), a "professional-managerial class" (Ehrenreich & Ehrenreich, 1979), "self-regulating professions" or "middle layers" (Herring, 1989). The one point of agreement is that this group, the product of emerging industrialization, occupies an intermediate position between the controlling elite and the working class. Current debate often centers on the question of the future of this group, and more specifically whether it is becoming proletarianized.

   The location of salaried professionals and managers is at best ambiguous. The sources of ambiguity are partly structural. Most managers and
increasing numbers of professionals are organizational employees, lacking
ownership of significant productive resources beyond their own expertise
and carrying out decisions enacted at higher organizational levels. On
these criteria alone they have something in common with all employees in
the lower middle and working classes, although they are granted much
greater discretion. Moreover, they also have responsibility for organizing
and directing the activities of subordinates. In fact, some occupations (e.g.,
paralegal, hygienists) have evolved as structurally subordinate to established professions, and the parameters of their work are set by these
professions. It has also been argued that the upper middle class organizes
and directs the lives of those below them in the class structure (the lower
middle class, the working class, and the poor). Barbara Ehrenreich (1989:
139) interprets relations between the upper middle class and the bulk of
society as a one-way dialogue, with managers, judges, teachers, physicians,
and lawyers issuing commands, instructions, and judgments.
   There is some indication that perceptions of the class system by
members of the new class are differentiated by employment in the private
or public sector (Ehrenreich & Ehrenreich, 1979; Herring, 1989). Those
working in the private sector—here limited to employment in profit-mak-
ing industrial, commercial and financial organizations and industries—do
not see themselves serving the interests of either the elite or workers, but
rather occupying a position between the two classes. In contrast, those in
the public sector—education, government, religious, health care—are
more likely to be sensitive to the inconsistency introduced by the need to
control subordinates.
   The structural contradictions of class thus produce some ambiguity,
but there are other sources of ambiguity, even insecurity (Bensman &
Vidich, 1987; Ehrenreich, 1989). Lifestyles are part of it. Upper-middle-
class positions are often well paid, especially when compared to the bulk
of white- and blue-collar workers, and allow most to enjoy a comfortable
lifestyle, measured by such things as homeownership, second cars, and
college educations for their children. At the higher end of the upper middle
class it means vacation homes and trips abroad, but still not approaching
the costly lifestyle of the elite. At the lower end it is a lifestyle not much
different from that available to some members of the lower middle and
working classes.
   The insecurity of members of the upper middle class is also traced to
their origins in lower-middle or working-class families, having succeeded
on the basis of educational credentials. However, their claim to upper-middle-class position—skill and knowledge—unlike real capital, cannot be
hoarded, preserved, or bequeathed to their children (Ehrenreich, 1989: 15).
Consequently, the education of their children looms large in their thinking.

One poll found that many included *private* secondary schools and colleges for their children on their list of the "necessities" of life (Sperling, 1989).

Dual-Career Families in the Upper Middle Class

Much attention focuses on the structure and dynamics of families where both husband and wife hold upper-middle-class positions, in careers that offer significant economic rewards and opportunities for advancement (Zussman, 1985; Hertz, 1986; Hochschild, 1989). Consequently, Rosanna Hertz (1986) suggests that the central issue facing such couples is the need to negotiate three careers—hers, his, and theirs (the marriage). It is often assumed that members of this group should have the most egalitarian attitudes toward careers and the division of household tasks because they are well-educated and both careers offer substantial rewards that would allow them to overcome the traditional emphasis on the primacy of the husband's career and weaken adherence to the male role as provider and the accompanying gender division of work within the home. In some cases this is true, but there are also potential sources of conflict in this kind of family.

One such source of stress shows up in the need to accommodate two earners in the family. It appears that there is some resistance to accepting wives as co-providers, and this is often the source of conflict and dissatisfaction within the family for some couples (Thompson & Walker, 1989). Evidence of this shows up in the tendency for upper-middle-class husbands with employed wives to be less satisfied with their marriages and their personal lives and to have lower self-esteem than those who are the sole financial supporters. Further, such dissatisfactions are greater as wives' incomes are closer to their husbands' (Fendrich, 1984; Stanley et al., 1986; Haas, 1986). Ironically, this may well be due to the husband's level of financial success. Men feel that it is their responsibility to provide for the family, and some, because they earn salaries large enough to support their lifestyle comfortably, depreciate the importance of their wives' jobs and earnings. The absence of the financial incentive means that some husbands view their wives' work unnecessary to sustaining the lifestyle of the family. Rather wives' careers may be seen as a matter of individual fulfillment. Although they may be supportive and proud of their wives' accomplishments, these husbands do not see the income in the context of financial need. In addition, there is the consideration that working wives are less able to devote time to husbands' needs.

In some instances the occupational demands of two careers may come into conflict: overtime, travel, or in extreme cases a promotion that requires a geographic move. Geographic moves to advance husbands' careers are the most costly, disrupting wives' careers and stimulating feelings of social isolation. Both husbands and wives tend to accommodate to each other by restricting their own mobility (Sharda & Nangle, 1981), but working wives do make more accommodations in their own careers than do their husbands (Morrison & Lichter, 1988). In some instances it reflects a conscious decision based on the logic that husbands' careers are more promising. This, in turn, is an accurate generalization of the reality of the workplace considering the concentration of women in lower-level upper-middle-class work, the persistence of barriers to advancement, and the gender gap in wages.

Another potential problem is that in some families the presence of two earners introduces status competition. Occupation and income are clearly one standard by which individuals judge themselves relative to others. Consequently, both husbands and wives in professional or managerial occupations may feel some element of competition with spouses which, in turn, is a source of stress within the family unit.

Any problems that do exist are compounded by the presence of young children in the family. One company found that two thirds of its people had serious concerns about their ability to manage the competing demands of work and family (Trost, 1988). Women are more likely to express this concern, but it is also widely experienced by men. It is clear that working wives continue to do a disproportionate share of household and child-care tasks, which is true at all class levels. Work in the home thus becomes, in the words of Arlie Hochschild (1989), a "second shift" of work. It seems that husbands of working wives do increase their contribution to home and child care, although generally only marginally.[3] Working wives may try a number of strategies to cope with the competing demands of home and family. Some continue to attempt to do both full-time jobs—to be super-moms—and others reduce the commitment to one or both; many are frustrated by the lack of their husband's contributions.

The problems confronting upper-middle-class dual-career families are complex. Certainly many-dual career families accommodate and flourish, but among those that do not the sources of problems may be found in the dynamics of class, status, and traditional gender roles. Both are in jobs that exact a heavy toll in time and effort and define success in terms of promotions. Employers generally have been slow to adopt child-care policies. The socialization experiences of men do not prepare them to assume

---

[3]Studies of the distribution of household and child-care responsibilities raise complex substantive and methodological issues. Although there can be no doubt that women devote more time and effort to such activities, the magnitude of such differences is not always clear. Couples may underestimate the contribution of the other (Hiller & Phillbier, 1986). In some cases women overrate how much their husbands help (Hochschild, 1989). The level of sharing varies with the specific activity being considered, with, for example, money management being a commonly shared task while washing clothes is rarely shared by husbands. Finally, it must be remembered that generalizations can mask great internal variation, meaning that in some families a great deal of work is shared and in other very little is.

easily the responsibilities of housework and child care. Women feel resentment and frustration at the unequal distribution of obligations.

THE LOWER MIDDLE CLASS

Most members of the *lower middle class* occupy the lower levels of white-collar hierarchies either in retail sales work (cashiers, clerks), or in jobs identified as clerical, or in the currently more fashionable parlance as "administrative support personnel" (secretaries, bookkeepers, shipping clerks, insurance policy processors, bank tellers, data entry operators, timekeepers, postal service workers, dispatchers, stock clerks). These people generally are directly supervised by members of the upper middle class. Most work for an hourly wage—called "nonexempt" in corporate parlance (compared to "exempt" and the salaried status of most professionals and managers)—and this is often emphasized by a powerful symbolic distinction for they, unlike the people they work for, must punch a time clock or sign in or in some other way validate the hours they work. Much of the work is routine, lacking responsibility. A certain percentage can look forward to rising to first-line supervisory positions, but careers are largely blocked beyond that level. Levels of income are moderate, in many instances below those of crafts workers and operatives.

Also included in this class are a range of expertise-based professionals (paralegals, nurses, teachers, social workers) and technicians (physical therapists, drafters, dental hygienists). A large proportion of the members of these occupations in the United States are women. They, too, are college graduates. Their expertise grants them some degree of autonomy in the performance of their wok, but significantly less than either managers or professionals. There are notable differences between this group of occupations and upper-middle-class groups in income, authority, and prestige. But perhaps the most significant difference is that there are very limited opportunities for career advancement.

There is a large group of workers—approximately 4 million people—holding supervisory jobs at the lowest levels of organizational authority with job titles such as foreperson or team leader. Their position involves overseeing the performance of relatively small groups of either lower-middle-class white-collar workers or blue-collar workers. By some criteria they could be viewed as members of the upper middle class, especially authority over the activities of subordinates. Moreover, they are nominally defined as the lowest levels of management. However, the scope of their authority is typically narrowly circumscribed, seldom extending to decision making about job structures or rates of production, decisions made at higher levels. Rather, their responsibilities are interpersonal, centering on assigning individuals to jobs, maintaining quality control, or monitoring productivity.

It is frequently noted that this situation produces tensions with the people they supervise, and is made more complex for those supervisors elevated from the ranks of factory or office work because their background can link their allegiance to their former co-workers. Management-initiated demands for productivity impel them to impose output requirements, often the source of rancorous interpersonal conflict. Consequently, because first-line supervisors are structurally distanced from the authority of the upper middle class above them and share patterns of subordination and limited discretion with the lower middle or working classes they supervise, they are most appropriately located with them.

Class and Status in the Lower Middle Class

When C. Wright Mills (1951) undertook the first major analysis of the position of the lower middle class, he focused on their apparent concern with social status and social respectability.[4] He argued that social status considerations were evident in pride in the ability to acquire the visible images of purchasing power—consumer goods, homes, cars—and that respectability took the form of adherence to traditional standards of behavior—hard work, honesty, and religion. It was his contention that these things mattered because their work denied them social prestige in the larger society. In fact, Mills argued, long-term trends had actually eroded the social standing of this group.

As clerical work began to emerge on a large scale accompanying the growth of industrial and government organizations, it had attributes that distinguished it from manual labor (Mills, 1956; Lockwood, 1958; Glenn & Feldberg, 1977). Clerical work required special skills not yet common in the population—-reading, writing, numbers. The pay was superior to that of blue-collar work (good in many cases) and the work offered at least some possibility for mobility into the managerial class. Working conditions were superior to the hazardous and unpleasant conditions found in the factories and mines. Even those who failed to rise in the office derived prestige from their personal contacts with the bankers and merchants and industrialists. Consequently, clerical work in the mid-nineteenth century enjoyed a special measure of social prestige, and clerks were often derided by manual workers for their pretentious attempts to emulate the upper classes in dress and demeanor.

However, over the years offices were affected by a complex of social, economic, and technological changes that were to alter dramatically the nature and position of clerical work. As members of the working class were

---

[4]It should be noted that this research is less current and less abundant than that available for other classes, reflecting the relative neglect of this class in academic research.

able to improve working conditions, wages, and social status, members of the lower middle class found their position degraded. The income advantage narrowed, the work became more routinized, and authority was lost. Consequently, Mills suggested, the most salient overall trend confronting the lower middle class was declining social prestige. Status and respectability are thus ways of emulating the lifestyles of the upper middle class and maintaining social distance from manual workers.

Within the family there is some indication that lower-middle-class marriages are more likely to be egalitarian than those found at other class levels (Kahl, 1957; Vanfossen, 1977). This, too, may have some basis in the position of lower-middle-class jobs in the larger society. *Resource theory* links the distribution of influence in the family to resources such as income and prestige in the occupational sphere. They are jobs not highly rewarded economically or socially, resulting in a high proportion of women in the paid labor force. Relatively modest male occupational attainment combined with wives contributing as co-providers make it less likely that the traditional division of labor could survive.

Lower-middle-class families tend to be strongly family-oriented and child-oriented, especially in the area of education. They encourage strong aspirations in their children, and this reflects the hope that their children will be able to succeed in the occupational sphere where their own accomplishments are modest by societal standards.

THE WORKING CLASS

There are many versions of *blue-collar work*, but the bulk of manual work demands physical labor, often strenuous and under unpleasant and dangerous conditions. Skill differentials are an important consideration, producing an internal division between the more skilled crafts workers (construction trades, automotive technicians) and the less skilled work of machine operators and assembly-line workers. Blue-collar life is likely to be invisible in a popular culture dominated by debonair and clever lawyers, physicians, and executives: and when it does appear, it is too often peopled by stereotyped bigots or crude, overweight construction workers.

Factory Work

Much work is standardized and repetitive, leaving little room for individual initiative. Assembly-line workers, machine operators, and truck drivers typify this. There are powerful social and economic pressures for productivity: assemblers constantly compete to keep pace with the unremitting pace of the line, and others work under piece-rate systems that link wages to output. Consequently, supervisors regularly and continuously

---

CASE STUDY:
Blue-Collar Health

The very nature of manual work places blue-collar workers at great risk to their safety and health. Factories are often very physically dangerous places and also expose workers to a whole range of toxic substances. Moreover, blue-collar work produces unexpected forms of risks to health. Despite the widespread emphasis on the dangers of the fast-paced, high-stress life of the corporate executive or the surgeon, the evidence suggests that lower white-collar and blue-collar workers are the most likely victims of workplace stress and heart disease (Rundel, 1987; Adler, 1989). In fact, when white-collar workers are compared to blue-collar workers, blue-collar workers are 43 percent more likely to fall victim to coronary disease. A combination of work-related stress factors contributes to this situation, including repetitive and boring tasks (garment workers), unremitting pace (assembly lines), and continual deadlines (bus drivers, waiters). All are factors over which the individual has little or no control.

Social class differences in lifestyles that have health implications are another factor. Upper-middle-class persons appear to have been quicker to adopt lifestyle changes that reduce the risk of heart disease. This includes such behaviors such as smoking, exercise, and diet. However, it is important to note that lifestyles are not always simply a matter of individual choice, but are also a matter of opportunities. For example, there are class differences in the way health programs are offered and organized (Rundel, 1987). Corporate-supported wellness and health programs are much more likely to be aimed at members of the executive and managerial levels than the production workers on the factory floor. In some businesses, the health facilities remain an executive prerogative, a status symbol. Moreover, even where programs and facilities are available to all workers, blue-collar workers will find it more difficult to gain access to the facilities. It is difficult for hundreds of them to use the company fitness facilities during the same fixed lunch break, and they do not have the flexibility of scheduling that executives do.

---

monitor their levels of effort. Work is also very dangerous to the health of blue-collar workers for both physical and social reasons.

Another characteristic of their position is economic insecurity. Consequently, very few see themselves free of economic worries, one of the factors that contribute to the large number of two-career families. For some, this economic insecurity is a direct consequence of modest wage levels, but there is also the added dimension of uncertainty of employment. Unemployment rates for blue-collar workers are consistently above those of white-collar workers. Moreover, changing economic conditions in the United States have produced a net loss of large numbers of blue-collar jobs in auto, textiles, and steel; during the 1970s and 1980s 600,000 jobs in textiles and clothing disappeared (Rosen, 1987: 23).

Craft Work: Skill and Pride

Craft work is built on a solid body of expert knowledge. Carpenters, auto mechanics, and construction workers complete extensive formal and on-the-job apprenticeship training. This idea of participation in an exclusive group of skilled workers contributes to a strong sense of pride and identification with other crafts workers. Medieval guilds were their first attempts at collective association and they often called their organizations "mysteries" to emphasize their exclusiveness. Guilds and, later, trade unions were organized around the protection of their autonomy from the encroachment of employers.

Some crafts workers, such as printers, construction workers, and machinists, have developed a powerful sense of pride. When construction workers gather to share a drink—and they do tend to socialize among themselves—their conversation often turns to their work, and their sense of accomplishment is evident in their comments, "I get a hell of a kick when I see a building I helped put up. You know the Edgewater Hotel down by the lake.... I worked on that...and sometimes I drive down there just to see the damn thing" (LeMasters, 1975: 23). They are also known for their tenacious defense of their prerogatives. Construction workers, for example, have been known to openly challenge their supervisors over the quality of their work (Cherry, 1974).

The Segregation of Work and Social Roles

Much blue-collar work is intellectually uninteresting, offers few opportunities to demonstrate creativity, and holds little chance of winning meaningful promotions. Consequently, blue-collar workers tend to segregate their work and social lives and seek fulfillment in other areas such as leisure activities (Shostak, 1969; Halle, 1984). Large blocks of free time are devoted to active participation in softball, bowling, hunting, and fishing and attendance at spectator sports such as football and baseball. Neighborhood bars, taverns, and clubs are the locale for watching games on television as well social drinking.

Blue-collar men do express a preference for male companionship, and there is a tendency for social activities to be segregated along gender lines. (This is not a firm line, and many leisure activities are joint husband-wife activities. Some wives are involved in sports, and visiting with family and friends is done together.) The male friendship system may have its roots in the occupational sphere that developed during the earlier part of this century. Whole categories of higher skill craft jobs became a male province, and within factory jobs there is segregation into men's and women's jobs. Thus, separate male and female work environments prevailed, and male friendships provided a social environment in which men felt more comfortable and could share leisure activities. Countless instances of marital disputes have their origins in a conflict over the division of time between male friendships and marital activities (Halle, 1984: 55).

Working-Class Husbands and Wives

The division of labor and power within blue-collar families has long been divided along gender lines. Husbands filled the role of provider in the paid labor force and wives assumed responsibility for the home. Accompanying this was the location of authority in the family with male superiority legitimized on the ground that he provided the economic support for the family unit. At least some blue-collar husbands, especially poorer ones, became quite authoritarian, imposing severe restrictions on the lives of their wives, attempting to dictate how they could spend their time and money, and even who they could visit (Rubin, 1976).

As more and more blue-collar women become financial contributors to the family income due to economic insecurity and the desire to enhance their purchasing power, there has been some renegotiation of authority within the family (Rosen, 1987). Major decisions become joint endeavors, and husbands assume a larger (albeit not equal) role in domestic chores (meals, laundry, shopping) once delegated almost exclusively to the wife. Their financial contribution to family income also allows wives to resist their husbands' preference for a nonworking spouse.[5]

Many blue-collar wives understand that the traditional role of provider is a central feature of the male role at work and in the larger society. Hence, while negotiating a larger role in decision making and shared domestic tasks, they continue publicly to define their husbands as the major provider, or "breadwinner," and devote their paychecks to "extras" such as consumer goods that enhance their lifestyle and validate their success in the larger society. This social fiction is a way of avoiding marital conflict.

It should be noted that blue-collar wives, like women at all class levels, assume a disproportionate share of domestic tasks. This exacts a heavy toll in time and effort, but blue-collar women place value on both paid employment and unpaid domestic work (Ferree, 1985). Paid work offers economic rewards that allow a degree of financial security and an enhanced standard of living, but is felt to be cold and impersonal and exploitative. The family is hierarchical, but simultaneously offers support, intimacy, and love. Thus, each role offers what the other cannot. Domestic

[5]Some research calls into question the survival of the blue-collar emphasis on traditional gender roles (Smith & Fisher, 1982; Earle & Harris, 1989). Although more suggestive than definitive, this research indicates that although most blue-collar males tend to hold to the idea of husband-centered decision making, there is also support for women's careers and shared household tasks.

life permits a partial escape from the inhumane demands of factory work, whereas paid work allows temporary escape from patriarchal domination (Rosen, 1987: 8).

Gender distinctions between provider and homemaker roles are generally not as rigid in black families as in white families (Taylor et al., 1990). An important factor in understanding this is the fact that African American women historically have had high labor force participation rates because of the lower earnings of black men. Despite a weaker adherence to a household division of labor along gender lines, though, black married women still perform a majority of domestic tasks in the home.

THE POOR

The use of the term the poor to identify this class often produces semantic confusion. One problem is the assumption that *the poor* exactly coincides with those living at or below the government's official poverty level.[6] Although the poor includes those at this level, it also includes people above this arbitrary line. Another erroneous conclusion is that the problems of the poor are only financial deprivation; rather, economic deprivation is merely the most visible consequence. The poor are better understood as those who fill the most marginal jobs in the economic system, those who do routine physical and mental labor, usually in unpleasant conditions with rigid and often harsh supervision, for low pay, and experiencing high levels of periodic unemployment. It then becomes evident that the poor are actually a diverse group. The poor includes some with regular or periodic employment—often called the working poor—as well as those not currently in the labor force. Defined in this way means that the poor can include Census Bureau categories of unskilled labor, domestics, and some forms of service work.[7] Minorities have been concentrated in these forms of work at every stage of the industrialization process in the United States.

Some of the poor have jobs, year-round full-time jobs, and others are separated from work by their circumstances. Therefore, the question of unstable employment deserves special attention. It is important to note at the outset that joblessness is largely a structural problem, defined as the inability of the system to provide stable work for its members. The nature

[6]To avoid confusion, the term poverty is reserved for that group of people living below the government's official poverty level, and "poor" will always refer to structural class position.

[7]There have been a number of attempts to operationalize "marginal jobs," not always consistent with one another (Sullivan, 1978; Kemp & Coverman, 1989). A strict definition of marginal jobs would include the following combination of factors: low skill requirements (e.g., stock handlers), employment in decentralized and competitive industries (e.g., apparel, laundries), working conditions in violation of safety and health standards (e.g., cooks and dishwashers), unstable employment, and lack of advancement opportunities. There are no precise enumerations of marginal jobs, and the data used here are estimates.

of unemployment can be thought of in this way: On any given day, even in the most prosperous of times, 6 to 10 million specific individuals are unemployed. About half find work within six weeks and most will eventually find work, but they are replaced by others (or they themselves reappear). Over the course of a decade approximately one person in four is at risk (Duncan, 1984), with people in unskilled and service jobs the most vulnerable.

Official government unemployment figures stand as the basic measure of the number of people who are jobless. Unemployment rates reached 10 percent early in the 1980s, and the 1990s begin with a rate of 5 percent of the labor force officially unemployed. Official data underestimate the extent of joblessness because they include only those who are "available for work" and have made a specific attempt to locate work within the last four weeks. The job-search requirement excludes many others who are not working and would like paid employment. There are, for example, hundreds of thousands of *discouraged* workers who want jobs but are not actively seeking work because they feel unqualified or believe there are no jobs. There are also another 4 million *underemployed*, people involuntarily working part-time schedules due to material shortages, seasonal slack periods, or the inability to locate a full-time job.

It is also important to understand the sources of unemployment. In any given year less than 10 percent of the unemployed voluntarily leave jobs, the majority (about 60 percent) are displaced due to plant closings, industrial transformations that eliminate jobs, and other kinds of layoffs (steel manufacturing and textiles are prime examples). Some are temporary, seasonal layoffs (agricultural workers, auto workers, construction workers). Thus a large part of unemployment can be traced to the vagaries of the economic system. The remaining 30 percent are young people entering the work force for the first time or older workers attempting to reenter the work force. Adult women are overrepresented, attempting to rejoin the paid labor force because of a change in family status or at the conclusion of child-care responsibilities.

Life at the bottom of the stratification system is often overshadowed by financial deprivation and economic insecurity. It is composed of those in the most insecure and unstable part of the economic system. Many of the poor work, but unemployment is a common and constant reality. A significant proportion are members of minority groups suffering long-term discrimination and more recent immigrants lacking the social and cultural skills that would enable them to compete for better jobs. The problems of economic insecurity are compounded by the social position of the poor in American society. The work they do carries little prestige, and the individualistic themes that have long dominated society mean that a segment of society holds them in disrepute, believing that they are largely responsible for their own plight.

There is also an element of political vulnerability. The poor live in a society that professes dedication to social welfare programs designed to buffer the effects of economic deprivation. Unemployment insurance, minimum wage laws, and Aid to Families with Dependent Children are all manifestations of such public concern. Yet such programs seem to have the lowest political priority, especially in periods of declining revenues. Between 1970 and 1990 the maximum benefit for a three-person family in a typical state grew from $184 to $364, but that increase lagged behind increases in consumer prices, meaning that the purchasing power of welfare income actually declined by 39 percent (Pear, 1991).

Considering the social and economic handicaps encountered by the poor, it might be anticipated that they would have lost faith in the dominant ideology of hard work and open opportunity. In fact, this is generally not the case (Goodwin, 1972). Some do express less optimism about the system and their chances in it than do the more affluent, but a majority still see an open opportunity structure and are optimistic about their own chances for economic success. Despite the apparent limits on advancement for those lacking a high school degree, and earning less than $12,000, only about one fifth feel they have a less than average chance for success (Kluegel & Smith, 1986: 68–72). Women generally see the system as less open, perhaps reflecting a realistic appraisal of the more limited occupational chances for females. African Americans at all levels also have a less favorable assessment of the opportunity structure, and among the poor a large majority of blacks feel they have not had a fair chance to succeed.

Growing Up Poor

One of the largest segments of the poor are children. Official poverty statistics consistently show that children have a greater probability of being poor than working-age adults. One out every five children in America—over 12 million—are growing up in poverty (U.S. Bureau of the Census, 1989a). This includes over 45 percent of all black children and 39 percent of Hispanic children. Despite the often dreary prospects imposed by poverty, most parents tend to sustain positive aspirations for their children. As a result the majority of children of the poor tend to be imbued with aspirations and hopes not dissimilar from those of the more advantaged, albeit at a different level of achievement. Their aspirations often center on stable blue-collar work—manufacturing, construction, the military—certainly not the lofty professional and business careers held by the children of the middle class, but a stable and constructive place in the class system. For example, a poor urban teenager rehearses a future that is not unlike the aspirations of children of the more advantaged, "I'll have a regular house, y'know, with a yard and everything. I'll have a steady job, a good job. I'll be living the good life, the easy life" (MacLeod, 1987: 5).

The challenge of stimulating and sustaining the aspirations of this segment the poor is an even more complex problem than the relatively direct goal of providing a floor under wages through such devices as minimum wage structures or unemployment insurance. Certain government and private innovations have proved to be at least partly successful in accomplishing this goal. Head Start, for example, has a record of stimulating greater educational and occupational attainments (Weikart, 1985). The combination of early education, good nutrition, and parental involvement helps to reduce dropout rates, unemployment, and criminal involvement during the teenage years. However, for most of its history the program reached only about 25 percent of eligible children. In addition, other initiatives focus on the same goal. For example, subsidized day-care programs allow parents to participate in the labor force or rehabilitative education dealing with adult illiteracy.

The Poorest of the Poor: An Enduring Underclass?

There appears to be a segment of the poor that faces persistent and prolonged deprivation, a group commonly called the underclass.[8] Although there is no consensus on the definition or measurement of this segment of the poor, William J. Wilson's definition is widely cited:

> That heterogeneous grouping of families and individuals that are outside the mainstream of the American occupational system. Included in this group are individuals who lack training and skills and either experience long-term unemployment or are not members of the labor force, individuals who are engaged in street crime and other forms of aberrant behavior, and families that experience long-term spells of poverty and/or welfare dependency. (1987: 8)

In short, a group of people at risk of being trapped in a cycle of persistent poverty and lacking the resources to break free—a bleak prospect for both society and the individuals involved.

Actually, there has been little success in identifying this group due to problems with the definition or measurement of the term underclass. Attempts to identify this group have used poverty, geographic location,

[8]The word underclass was apparently first used by the Swedish sociologist Gunnar Myrdal (1944). During the 1980s the term itself has become the subject of debate. Some feel that it has been used indiscriminately, rendering it devoid of any analytic meaning. Others worry that it has taken on racist connotations as a consequence of a media tendency to focus disproportionate attention on the problems of black Americans. Still others believe that the emphasis on the behavioral traits of this segment of the poor has directed attention away from the structural sources of poverty. William J. Wilson, one of those who has systematically examined the topic, has recently suggested that it be abandoned and replaced with a more neutral term such as "ghetto poor" (DeParle, 1990).

education, and behavior. Several points emerge from research that focused on the concentration of deprivation in certain geographic areas (Ricketts & Sawhill, 1988). First, there are some areas with unusual concentrations of people with low educational attainment, high rates of crime, and unemployment and of welfare recipients. Second, it is a small segment of the poverty population identified by the Census Bureau. Underclass neighborhoods by these estimates contain somewhere between 1 and 2.5 million people. Third, although it is a heavily minority population, it includes less that one in five of the blacks living in poverty.

There is a fundamental debate over the origins and future of the underclass (Mead, 1989; Wilson, 1989: Danziger, 1989; Sawhill, 1989; Jencks & Peterson, 1991). One interpretation stresses individual behavioral pathology as the root cause, evident in a lack of commitment to jobs and the future that causes people to fall into a cycle of poverty. In contrast another interpretation traces the creation of an underclass to a combination of economic, political, behavioral, demographic and institutional sources. Among them are a contracting economic system, unresponsive and underfunded schools, the flight of jobs and the middle classes from center cities, the lure of a lucrative underground economy, discrimination, and ineffective public policies. Depressed levels of effort thus grow out of frustration and dejection, but could be revived by redress of the causes of failure.

CONCLUSION: Small Businesses and the American Dream

The overall trend toward the expansion of massive organizations should not obscure the existence of small businesses in the economic system. Included in this category are grocery stores and restaurants, consulting firms, very small factories, fishing boats, service stations, and tailor shops. In many ways the independent small business person epitomizes the American dream. Countless people aspire to having their own business, and many risk it each year although the failure rate is high. The lure of self-employment is a powerful element in American society and has many sources, both individual and structural. Monetary rewards are one enticement, but other factors may well outweigh the potential for making money. There is some indication that major attractions are independence, freedom from supervision, and the opportunity to exercise some initiative (Peterson et al., 1982). Among members of the National Association of Women Business Owners in the United States, it is the challenge of succeeding, the chance to test oneself (Fetterman, 1989). For others, such as auto workers, the lack of realistic opportunities for advancement serves as a push toward opening bars or service stations (Chinoy, 1955). At a broader level, others are propelled by the lack of meaningful employment opportunities.

Minority groups in industrial societies show a penchant for small businesses: Greeks and Koreans in the United States, Indians and Turkish

Cypriots in Britain, the Chinese in Southeast Asia (Cobas, 1986). In some ways this pattern is readily explained in the case of people of color, for they experience the most discrimination and disadvantages in the labor market (Light, 1972). It is, for example, more difficult for professional and managerially trained immigrants to find employment in upper-middle-class jobs. There are, in addition, other factors at work. Racial and ethnic minorities may be able to take advantage of opportunities, some unique to members of the group (Cobas, 1986; Aldrich & Waldinger, 1990). The opportunity for small businesses may present itself because of the demographics of residential segregation. The concentration of minorities in urban enclaves may create "protected markets," markets for goods and services that can be better met by minority businesses that have special insight into minority community tastes and preferences. In addition, these are often in geographic areas abandoned by larger national firms. This is, for example, often true for Asian Americans. In contrast, the African American experience in the United States never offered such protected markets (Boyd, 1990). Founding and operating a small business is in some instances enhanced by the cultural traditions of minority communities. Asian immigrants, for example, bring with them the practice of informal community savings and loan arrangements that allow aspiring businesspersons to borrow money at low rates.

Small businesses do not ordinarily bring great economic rewards, and the failure rate is daunting—less than 50 percent survive for five years. However, small businesses continue to be attractive. For white American women and men, a small business seems to hold out opportunities for independence and autonomy, and for people of color, it is one means of overcoming the social barriers that societies erect. Considering their diversity (in terms of income, size, and ethnic composition) and highly transitory nature, small businesses do not fit neatly into the class system of industrial societies, but they have powerful symbolic meaning.

ADDITIONAL READINGS

On the Elite

PETER W. COOKSON, JR,. and CAROLINE HODGES PERSELL. *Prepping for Power: America's Elite Boarding Schools*. New York: Basic Books, 1985.

G. WILLIAM DOMHOFF. *The Higher Circles*. New York: Random House, 1970.

SUSAN A. OSTRANDER. *Women of the Upper Class*. Philadelphia: Temple University Press, 1984.

On the Upper-Middle Class

BARBARA EHRENREICH. *Fear of Falling: The Inner Life of the Middle Class.* New York: Pantheon Books, 1989.

ROSANNA HERTZ. *More Equal Than Others: Women and Men in Dual-Career Marriages.* Berkeley: University of California Press, 1986.

ARLIE HOCHSCHILD. *The Second Shift.* New York: Viking, 1989.

RICHARD SOBEL. *The White Working Class: From Structure to Politics.* New York: Praeger, 1989.

On the Lower-Middle Class

RICHARD COLEMAN and BERNICE L. NEUGARTEN. *Social Status in the City.* San Francisco: Jossey-Bass, 1971.

HERBERT GANS. *The Levittowners: Ways of Life in a New Suburban Community.* New York: Random House, 1967.

HAROLD HODGES, JR. *Social Stratification: Class in America.* Cambridge, MA: Schenkman, 1964.

C. WRIGHT MILLS. *White Collar.* New York: Oxford University Press, 1951.

On the Working Class

DAVID HALLE. *America's Working Man.* Chicago: University of Chicago Press, 1984.

MIRRA KOMAROVSKY. *Blue-Collar Marriage.* New York: Random House, 1962.

E. E. LEMASTERS. *Blue-Collar Aristocrats: Life-Styles at a Working Class Tavern.* Madison: University of Wisconsin Press, 1975.

LILLIAN RUBIN. *Worlds of Pain: Life in the Working Class Family.* New York: Basic Books, 1976.

On the Poor

GREG DUNCAN. *Years of Poverty, Years of Plenty.* Ann Arbor: Institute for Social Research, University of Michigan, 1984.

CHRISTOPHER JENCKS and PAUL E. PETERSON, eds. *The Urban Underclass.* Washington, DC: Brookings Institution, 1991.

JAY MACLEOD. *Ain't No Making It.* Boulder, CO: Westview, 1987.

U.S. COMMISSION ON CIVIL RIGHTS. *A Growing Crisis: Disadvantaged Women and Their Children.* Washington, DC: U.S. Government Printing Office, 1983.

TERRY WILLIAMS and WILLIAM KORNBLUM. *Growing Up Poor.* Lexington, MA: D. C. Heath, 1985.

WILLIAM J. WILSON. *The Truly Disadvantaged: The Inner City, the Underclass and Public Policy.* Chicago: University of Chicago Press, 1987.

Chapter 6
Class Consciousness

SUBJECTIVE PERCEPTIONS OF INEQUALITY AND STRATIFICATION

It is apparent that people are sensitive to the extremes of social inequality in their society. In fact, when asked if there is anything they are not particularly proud of about the United States a full one third volunteer either "inequality" or "poverty" (Robinson, 1983). Such responses are not unexpected, for it is virtually impossible to miss the social and economic discrepancies manifest in the clothing, homes, consumer goods, and life-styles of the people we all encounter in the everyday routine of our lives. Even the more comfortable middle-income group, socially insulated from direct contact with both the poor and rich, cannot escape the media that bring them details of those living at the extremes of society. Popular magazines glorify the lifestyles of the rich and famous while television documentaries present graphic images of the plight of the poor and homeless.

The broader question of perceptions of a class structure is a much more complex matter than merely being sensitive to gross economic inequalities. *Class consciousness* as a general term focuses on subjective sensitivity to the division of society into relatively distinct groups or classes. There are different forms of class consciousness, ranging from the cognitive—recognition of a hierarchy of classes—to the behavioral—taking direct action to enhance class-based interests.

For analytic purposes it is possible to identify, as shown in Exhibit 6.1, five different levels of class consciousness (Morris & Murphy, 1966; Hazelrigg, 1973). *Nonawareness* prevails among those members of society who fail to recognize or accept class divisions. *Class awareness* is the lowest level of class consciousness and involves recognition of the division of society into two or more groups. Because people may be aware of divisions but unwilling to locate themselves in that system, *class identification* is used to take the step of self-placement in a particular class and presupposes recognition of other classes. *Class solidarity* implies a sense of unity with and having the same values and interests as other members of the same class. Class solidarity also means sensitivity to other classes with divergent values and interests. *Class action* means taking, or being willing

Exhibit 6.1
Types of Subjective Awareness of Social Stratification

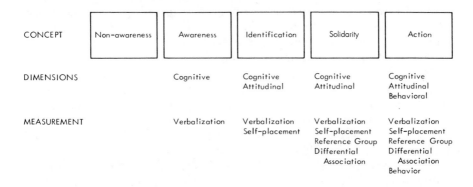

CONCEPT	Non-awareness	Awareness	Identification	Solidarity	Action
DIMENSIONS		Cognitive	Cognitive Attitudinal	Cognitive Attitudinal	Cognitive Attitudinal Behavioral
MEASUREMENT		Verbalization	Verbalization Self-placement	Verbalization Self-placement Reference Group Differential Association	Verbalization Self-placement Reference Group Differential Association Behavior

to take, some overt action to further the perceived interests of the class. This level of consciousness implies a degree of confrontation or conflict with other classes.

As Karl Marx observed in his use of the term *klasse an sich*, classes will be no more than aggregates of people if those distinctions do not shape the awareness, attitudes, and behavior of individuals. At some places in his writings he argued for the inevitability of class conflict,—that is, members of the emerging urban industrial proletariat would develop a collective consciousness and subsequently take action to overthrow the ruling bourgeoisie. Consequently, the logic of this model suggests a developmental process from awareness to class action, with one level being a condition for the development of the next level of consciousness. In practice, people's perspectives do not necessarily follow this pattern, and it is common for people to hold attitudes that might seem inconsistent. The United States is certainly not on the verge of armed class conflict, nor do Americans exhibit the same level of allegiance to trade unions or class-based political parties found in European nations, but that does not mean that Americans do not visualize society as divided into classes and express some feelings of solidarity with others at the same level.

CLASS AWARENESS

Systematic studies of sensitivity to class divisions date back to the 1940s (Centers, 1949). Any attempt to measure class awareness raises complex methodological problems. The major problem is that the very process of posing the question of classes can alert people to the issue, encouraging them to think about a matter not previously considered relevant. Or they may feel pressure to give a particular response because they believe that it is appropriate or socially acceptable. Some researchers have attempted to deal with this problem by determining if people will spontaneously raise the issue of classes (e.g., Leggett, 1968). Of course, the failure to volunteer class-based answers does not demonstrate that people are unaware of them, merely that they did not volunteer them.

With these limitations in mind there is consistent evidence that Americans see society as divided into social classes. Only a very small number of people—usually less than 2 or 3 percent—challenge the existence of a hierarchical division of society by asserting that the United States is a classless society. There is some indication that most people spontaneously visualize three classes: extremes of wealth and poverty and a broad intermediate group (MacKenzie, 1973: 117). There is apparently a strong tendency for Americans to think of themselves as "middle class." However, when prompted they are willing and able to accept finer distinctions within this broad intermediate class, namely, a basic division between a working class of blue-collar workers and a middle class of white-collar workers, and even an upper middle class of professional and managerial people. Very few people see a basic cleavage between just two classes.

A key issue in the examination of class consciousness is the criteria people use to define social class membership. On the surface it would appear that class is strictly an economic concept, because Americans tend to rely on words such as "rich," "millionaire," "poor," and "average" to describe members of different classes. Moreover, when forced to mention one single factor Americans will usually mention income. In contrast, occupation seems to play a much greater role in defining class in Canada and Britain (Butler & Stokes, 1974; Pammett, 1987; Bell & Robinson, 1980; Grabb & Lambert, 1982). However, more detailed analysis shows that class has a much more complex meaning. Class encompasses a number of specific factors, with lifestyles (73 percent), beliefs and attitudes (69 percent), occupation (68 percent), income (60 percent), education (59 percent) and family background (49 percent) all being rated as either "very important" or "somewhat important" in defining class position (Jackman & Jackman, 1983: 37). These factors may be interrelated, suggesting that people have a multidimensional, not a single, unidimensional, concept of class.

CLASS IDENTIFICATION

The vast majority of Americans are also willing to identify themselves as members of a specific social class (Centers, 1949; Schreiber & Nygreen, 1970; Jackman & Jackman, 1983). Most studies show that over 95 percent

Exhibit 6.2
Occupation and Class Identification

	Class Identification				
	Poor	Working	Middle	Upper Middle	Upper
Professional	<1%	17%	62%	20%	<1%
Managerial	<1	20	59	18	2
Sales	3	22	61	12	1
Clerical	7	43	41	9	0
Crafts workers	5	53	39	3	<1
Operatives	10	53	35	<1	1
Service	22	46	30	2	<1
Unskilled	17	51	30	1	0
Totals	8	37	43	8	1

Class identification is reported for those who responded to the following question: "People talk about social classes such as the poor, the working class, the middle class, the upper-middle class, and the upper class. Which of these classes would you say you belong in?" Source: Mary R. Jackman and Robert W. Jackman. *Class Awareness in the United States.* (Berkeley: University of California Press, 1983), Table 4.1, p. 73. Copyright © 1983 by the University of California Press.

can locate themselves in the stratification system (see Exhibit 6.2). Moreover, they also found that most people report strong attachment to their class. When asked about the intensity of their feelings, a full half reported feeling "very strongly" about their membership in that class. Another 28 percent reported "somewhat strong" feelings, and only one in five defined their attachment as "not too strong" (Jackman, 1979).

The data on class identification reported in Exhibit 6.2 are organized by occupation and show a correspondence between structural position and subjective identification, emphasizing the importance of work in shaping the broad outlines of the stratification system. A majority of professionals and managers think of themselves at the upper end of the stratification system, choosing the middle class or upper-middle-class label. Sales workers also tend to make the same distinctions. Clerical workers typically divide themselves into middle class or working class. A much clearer pattern is found in the blue-collar occupations, where a majority of crafts workers and factory workers place themselves in the working class, although about one third favor the middle-class designation. Some service workers and the unskilled are the most likely to identify with the poor.

As would be expected education and income modify class identification. People with less formal education and lower incomes will rate themselves at lower levels. This is apparent among that segment of blue-collar and service workers who identify with the poor and among the better educated and better paid clerical workers who identify with the middle class. Thus, increments of income and education cause people to locate themselves in a higher or lower class than other people at the same occupational level.

CLASS SOLIDARITY

The idea of class solidarity proceeds a step beyond self-identification and focuses on the extent to which people feel a sense of unity with other members of the same class, based on shared values and interests. Although there is some sense of compatibility with members of the same social class who are perceived as sharing similar values and lifestyles, this perspective does not widely extend to feelings that classes have *conflicting* economic and political interests. Rather, people are more likely to feel that classes have divergent but not incompatible interests. Thus, blue-collar workers might agree that they have different interests than managers but simultaneously feel that all classes are members of a "team" in which each makes an essential contribution (MacKenzie, 1973). It is uncommon for people to see different classes as "enemies" (Manis & Meltzer, 1954). This holds true despite the fact that there are strong feelings among the middle and lower levels of society that the political and economic system is tilted in favor of the wealthy. For example, surveys show that a majority of Americans believe owners and corporate executives have disproportionate influence on the government (Kluegel & Smith, 1986: 120).

It has been suggested that one of the major reasons that individuals do not develop a sense of solidarity with other members of their class is that potential class loyalties are overwhelmed by internal divisions based on income, race, ethnicity, and other factors that serve to divide rather than unite. Race appears to be among one of the most salient sources of diversity. One survey revealed only 19 percent of whites and 26 percent of blacks thought they shared "a lot" of common interests with members of the other race in the same social class (Colosanto & Williams, 1987).

CLASS ACTION

This form of class consciousness exists when overt action is taken in an attempt to further the interests of a class or to inhibit the interests of some other class. This form of behavior is rare in the United States, which is not surprising considering that few people see classes separated by divergent interests. Only small numbers of workers express interest in joining with others in picketing or other actions (Leggett, 1968). Labor unions and political parties have been the focus of class interests and have acted as institutionalized instruments of class action in some European nations but have not developed in that direction in the United States.

Labor Unions

The economic and political activities of manual workers in industrializing nations late in the nineteenth century represented attempts to develop broadly based working-class organizations, taking the form of open challenges to capitalism and attempts to unite *all* workers. In the United States the Western Federation of Miners was one of the groups that sought to "abolish the wage system" (Dubofsky, 1969). The Knights of Labor recruited at the class level, seeking to unite all working people—skilled and unskilled, women and men, white and black—except for liquor dealers, professional gamblers, bankers, and stockbrokers, under the slogan that "an injury to one is the concern of all" (Bailey, 1956: 538). At its peak in the 1880s the Knights claimed a membership of 1 million workers out of an urban labor force of 10 million. Broadly based blue-collar labor movements emerged in some European countries such as France (Hanagan, 1980) but not in the United States.

Many factors combined to undermine the labor union movement. Employers staunchly resisted the movement and the government often came to the aid of employers, for example, with federal troops used to quell railroad strikes in 1877 and again in 1894. Over the course of the first two decades of the twentieth century the Knights and other more radical unions such as the Western Federation of Miners, were superseded by the American Federation of Labor representing the skilled trades. The AFL took a more moderate and less confrontational stance and was able to win important concessions on wages, hours, and working conditions for members of specific occupations.

Unskilled and semiskilled factory workers were largely ignored by the AFL, in part because such jobs tended to be filled by racial and ethnic minorities, which separated them from crafts workers who were typically native-born (Mink, 1986). The devastating economic dislocation of the 1930s stimulated successful attempts to unionize whole industries—auto workers, steel workers—represented by the rival Congress of Industrial Organization. The unionization of these industries was not accomplished without strikes and violence, but the CIO did finally establish the right of unions to exist and collectively bargain for their members.

The AFL and CIO became one union in 1955, and organized labor today acts as an interest group in Washington (and the state capitals), lobbying for all workers' interests in such things as occupational safety, worker privacy, and minimum wage legislation and supporting pro-labor candidates for political office. Unions are able to exert some influence on the voting choices of its members, but it is very modest (Juravich & Shergold,

1988), and strikes are an effective weapon in increasing wages (Rubin, 1986).

At the end of the 1980s union membership was continuing a steady decline—standing at about 17 percent of the work force. Contracting membership reflects a number of factors, including an erosion of the traditional blue-collar industries such as steel and automobiles combined with limited success in unionizing white-collar and service workers. Unions represent but a small segment of the working class, and in the process of increasing the wages of this segment, have increased the economic discrepancy between the top and bottom of the working class (Form, 1985). Thus, although unions provide economic advantages for some workers, internal cleavages based on occupation, income, stability of employment, skill levels, race, and gender within the working class continue to divide it.

Political Parties

Political parties in some industrial democracies articulate the interests of specific classes. This is most evident in Western European nations that have parties, such as Labour (Britain) or Social Democrat (Germany), that expressly pursue working class interests. In contrast, the major American political parties have typically been loose coalitions rather than ideological groups. It is true that the Democratic party in the United States between the 1930s and the 1970s was able to solidify a high level of working-class support at the national level, and Democrats occupied the White House for most of those years. Party support was built on a coalition of blue-collar workers, religious, racial, and ethnic minorities in the aftermath of the great depression. These groups favored liberal economic policies and governmental intervention to buffer the effects of capitalism. Although attracting blue-collar workers, the party more than once chose members of the elite to be its national standard-bearer (e.g., John F. Kennedy) and has long depended on the financial support of wealthy southerners (Ferguson & Rogers, 1986).

A number of contemporary observers see the defection of large numbers of blue-collar workers to recent Republican presidential candidates, such as Ronald Reagan and George Bush, as signalling the demise of this coalition (Brown, 1991; Edsall & Edsall, 1991). The male, white working-class core of the party is apparently becoming disillusioned with what they perceive as undue attention to the other constituents of the party: the poor, women, and people of color. Thus, the common interests that once united the disadvantaged are being overwhelmed by divergent interests (e.g., tax relief, affirmative action) that tends to pit former political allies against each other.

CLASS CONSCIOUSNESS AND THE WORKING CLASS

Much attention has been devoted to class consciousness among blue-collar workers, in large part because of the major historical role assigned to this group by Karl Marx. It is clear that a certain configuration of characteristics is likely to increase working-class identification among manual workers. Union members and the youngest, least educated, lowest paid, most dissatisfied manual workers with the least discretion are the most likely to locate themselves in the working class (Zingraff & Schulman, 1984). The most obvious conclusion is that the most disadvantaged blue-collar workers identify with the working class while the more advantaged are more likely to place themselves in the middle class.

With respect to the working class, sociologists have long sought to understand why blue-collar workers fail to develop a sense of solidarity with the poor and lower level white-collar workers, who often encounter the same kinds of work experiences (a lack of discretion and responsibility), and why this group seldom presses for dramatic changes in the political economy despite the belief that the economic and political system is biased in favor of a wealthy minority.

Studies of male blue-collar workers in stable, well-paying jobs suggest that part of the answer may be found in the fact that they simultaneously perceive two hierarchies rather than one and locate themselves in both (MacKenzie, 1973; Halle, 1984). One identity is based on the characteristics of their work and leads them to divide the world into four classes—the rich, the poor, a broad middle class of white-collar workers, professionals, and managers, and the working class. Blue-collar workers perceive a definite and fundamental distinction between those who are working people and those who are not. One important feature is the attributes of the work—productive, manual, strenuous, difficult, and dangerous (Halle, 1984). The other feature is control and authority, or more precisely, the lack of it (Vanneman & Pampel, 1977). Thus their work and their class position are determined by the type of work they do and their subordination to the orders of organizational superiors. Managers certainly do not work, merely hiring others to work. Other white-collar workers are often characterized as doing nothing that is productive and meaningful—"working with their mouths" or "shuffling papers" or even doing nothing literally ("They just sit on their butts all day"). Thus, there is a sense of working-class identification, but it is clearly bounded, limited to those who engage in certain kinds of physical and manual work.

The concept of "working man" also includes considerations of class, color, and gender (Halle, 1984). The poor are not working people, for they are unable or unwilling to work. An emphasis on working-class tasks as strenuous, dirty, and dangerous has traditionally also made them "men's" tasks in the minds of many, just as clerical work is defined as "women's" work. The recent movement of larger numbers of women into blue-collar areas is contributing to a reevaluation of the concepts of both class and gender. A person's race or ethnicity is also important, apparently more important than any definition of social class. Therefore, blacks and Hispanics may do the same kind of work or have similar lifestyles but tend not to be accepted as members of the same class. People's race or ethnicity is powerful enough to divide them from other blue-collar workers.

Another blue-collar perspective on the class system is based on education, income, and material possessions. They have education comparable to that of white-collar workers and their income allows them to enjoy consumer goods and live in pleasant neighborhoods with white-collar families. Hence they also identify themselves as middle class, a very broad and amorphous group based largely on similar lifestyles. There is such diversity in this group that it is difficult to draw a line between the middle class and the rich at the top of the system and the poor at the bottom.

Halle's study also offers another insight. He suggests that confrontational class action does not develop because there is a strong commitment to America as a system of government superior to all others. Although there is widespread belief in corruption among politicians and control of the government by economic interests, this rarely translates into attraction for radical restructuring of society. For one thing, the basic system is believed to be sound, but has been subverted by the actions of people. Moreover, the lure of alternative political systems is dampened by the belief that reform could only be accomplished at the expense of individual liberty and freedom.

FAMILY, GENDER, AND CLASS CONSCIOUSNESS

The question of the formation of class consciousness is made more complex by the fact that many families include spouses occupying different class levels. As shown in Exhibit 6.3 somewhere between one half and two thirds of all employed husbands and wives are in occupations that would place them in different classes. The concentration of women in clerical and retail sales work is a major factor in accounting for this pattern.

There is some tendency for people to "borrow" selected characteristics from their spouse when locating themselves in the system, using the higher level attainments of the other and consequently raising their own class level. This process occurs among both women and men, but it appears to be most likely for married women not in the paid work force to rely on their husband's work, educational level, and income in defining their class placement. This is no doubt due in part to the fact that the role of unpaid homemaker is unclear in a class system centered on either occupation or economic lifestyle. Moreover, this way of thinking about class is grounded in the tradition of defining the male as the head of the household and

Exhibit 6.3
Class Location of Husbands and Wives, 1987

Occupation of Husband	Occupation of Wife								
	M	P	T	S	Cl	Cr	O	S	NE
Managerial	14	16	3	8	25	1	2	6	27
Professional	9	28	2	7	18	1	2	6	27
Technical	10	15	7	6	24	1	3	9	26
Sales	10	11	3	14	23	1	3	7	27
Clerical	8	9	4	7	28	1	6	10	26
Craft	6	7	2	9	22	3	9	12	30
Operative/unskilled	4	4	2	8	20	2	13	14	31
Service	7	7	2	8	20	2	5	19	31
Not employed	8	11	2	12	25	3	12	25	<1

Note: Data for married couples with earnings in 1987, excluding members of the armed forces. Rows do not add to 100 due to rounding.
Source: U. S. Bureau of the Census. Current Population Reports, P-60, No. 165. *Earnings of Married Couple Families, 1987*. Washington, DC: U.S. Government Printing Office, Table 2, p. 10.

implies that homemakers use the family as the unit of analysis in locating themselves in the stratification system.

The situation differs for married women in the paid work force. When employed, there is still a tendency toward "borrowing," but indications are that borrowing is losing its salience. Women in the 1980s, compared to women in the 1970s, are more likely to determine their class position on the basis of their own occupational and educational accomplishments than those of their husbands (Davis & Robinson, 1988). Several factors have apparently contributed to the increasing salience of women's own workplace experiences. The most obvious is that increasing numbers of women are in the paid labor force. In addition, the instability of marriage means that more women can anticipate having to support themselves from their own work at some point in their lives. Moreover, more women are moving into jobs that offer more rewards and challenges.

With respect to class placement there is also some indications that men and women have different concepts of class, at least in the distinction between working class and middle class (Robinson & Kelley, 1979; Simpson & Mutran, 1981; Vanneman & Cannon, 1987; Simpson, Stark & Jackman, 1988). The most important factors contributing to identification with the working class are employee status (as opposed to self-employed), being in a female-dominated job, and membership in a union; the lack of authority, which is so important in fostering working-class identification among men, is apparently somewhat less important for women. Rosen (1987: 72) suggests that women are not less sensitive to their subordination, merely more inclined to accommodate to it than to make it a major source of potential conflict.

CONCLUSION: Factors Mitigating Against Class Consciousness

Americans seem to recognize a hierarchy of classes and their position in it. It appears that no single factor defines class, but rather that class encompasses a structural dimension—type of work, authority or lack of it, an economic dimension (income), and a behavioral dimension (lifestyle). Although there is a sense of commonality with others in the same situation, it does not extend to strong feelings of discrepant interests or willingness to mobilize to pursue structural change or a redistribution of resources. Marx was sensitive to the failure of Americans to develop a sense of *klasse fur sich*. A number of factors have been offered to explain the absence of clearly articulated feelings of class consciousness in American society, especially among the less advantaged segments of society. The dominant ideology of opportunity played a role, but so too did a combination of social, organizational, economic, and political factors.

It is common to argue that American history has, in some important ways, been unique. Formed as a new nation in the eighteenth century, the United States lacked the feudal tradition of a hereditary aristocracy so common to many European nations (Bottomore, 1966). In addition, important political rights (suffrage) and the legal guarantees incorporated in the Bill of Rights were slowly extended to ever greater segments of the population. Industrialization produced widespread prosperity and made it possible for large numbers of people to enjoy a relatively high standard of living. Thus, it is argued that American society did not produce the widespread deprivation that would be likely to foster broadly based discontent. This approach has some validity, but there were more specific factors at work.

The organization of industrial work following the principles of Taylorism imposed strict discipline on workers and created artificial but powerful divisions among workers (Braverman, 1974). The detailed specialization and narrowing of jobs rendered workers easily replaceable and weakened their collective power. At the same time that these developments were occurring waves of immigrants swelled the population and created divisions that worked against feelings of solidarity among those similarly situated. The diversity of their cultural and religious heritages impeded communication and often produced hostility and antagonism. These antagonisms often had economic bases, for minorities often competed for the same jobs. Employers actively exploited ethnic divisions in battles against unions, using members of minority groups as strikebreakers (Foner, 1964). Women were similarly used this way (Baron, 1980). Consequently, the potential for solidarity based on common economic position was subverted by the disintegrating factors of race, ethnicity, and gender.

The dominant ideology of American culture is also a factor. The ideology emphasizes individualism, and most Americans seem to believe they are just about where they belong in the system considering their talents and efforts. Blue-collar workers explain their position in personal terms rather than in the workings of the economic system (Halle, 1986: 169). They are likely to cite their intellectual limitations or lack of effort in school, or that they lacked the boldness to set up their own business.

Another factor inhibiting the development of group consciousness is the characteristic belief in an open opportunity structure and the chance for individual mobility that permeates all levels of the society. Polls indicate a majority of Americans continue to believe there is plenty of opportunity for those who work hard. In addition, most feel that they have more opportunity than did their parents' generation. These beliefs are, to some extent, supported by their own experiences, for many are the children or grandchildren of immigrants who have been able to improve their relative position in society significantly.

ADDITIONAL READINGS

RICHARD P. COLEMAN and LEE RAINWATER. *Social Standing in America*. New York: Basic Books, 1978.

DOUGLAS M. EICHAR. *Occupations and Class Consciousness in America*. New York: Greenwood Press, 1989.

HERBERT GANS. *The Urban Villagers: Group and Class in the Life of Italian-Americans*. New York: Free Press, 1962.

RICHARD HAMILTON. *Class and Politics in the United States*. New York: John Wiley, 1972.

MARY R. JACKMAN and ROBERT W. JACKMAN. *Class Awareness in the United States*. Berkeley: University of California Press, 1983.

VICTORIA ANNE STEINITZ and ELLEN RACHEL SOLOMON. *Starting Out: Class and Community in the Lives of Working-Class Youths*. Philadelphia: Temple University Press, 1986.

REEVE VANNEMAN and LYNN WEBER CANNON. *The American Perception of Class*. Philadelphia: Temple University Press, 1987.

Part Three

Patterns of Inequality

Social class position has many consequences and implications, and among the most salient are economic, social, and political. Chapter 7 reviews broad patterns of economic inequality as well as some of the more subtle implications of financial inequalities. Chapter 8 explores social evaluations and judgments based on class ranging from occupational prestige to the dynamics of class, color, and gender in social relationships. Chapter 9 investigates the capacity to translate class into access to positions of power in the government and the ability of class-oriented groups and organizations to influence the state.

Chapter 7
The Dynamics of Economic Inequality

THE DISTRIBUTION OF WEALTH AND POVERTY

Early in this century B. C. Forbes (1918), founder of *Forbes* magazine, set out to identify the richest people in the United States. His research located 206 Americans with incomes of over a million dollars. Topping the list was John D. Rockefeller, with an annual income of $60 million and a total fortune estimated at $1.2 billion. Among the very rich, the 30 wealthiest controlled $3.68 billion, a figure estimated to represent nearly 2 percent of the total wealth of the nation. Contemporary research suggests there are today at least a million and one-half millionaires and 51 billionaires in America (Phillips, 1990: 239).

Topping the 1990 *Forbes* list of the 400 richest people was John Kluge, with a fortune estimated at 5.6 billion. Kluge started his career as a salesperson for snack foods, and subsequently turned to radio and television properties that yielded substantial profits. Over the years he has owned the Harlem Globetrotters, Ice Capades, Metromedia, and Ponderosa Steak Houses. He lives today on a 6,000-acre estate in Virginia with a private golf course designed by Arnold Palmer; he also has a castle and 80,000 acres of land in Scotland. His philanthropic activities include gifts of $50 million to Columbia University to encourage young scholars, especially minorities, to pursue careers in college teaching.

America's richest can be divided into two groups. One segment represents direct inherited wealth. Among them are the descendants of industrialists such as E. I. du Pont and John D. Rockefeller who amassed fortunes in the nineteenth century. There are, for example, ten members of the Du Pont family on the list, each with assets in the $300 million to $350 million range. The other group built their own fortunes. This includes such people as Estee Lauder ($500 million), Ernest and Julio Gallo ($350 million each), Ralph Lauren ($550 million), and Domino Pizza's Thomas Monaghan ($530 million). About 22 percent of these people inherited sizable amounts of money, which did give them a head start in building their own wealth. Donald Trump, for example, started his real estate empire with $200,000 from his father. Real estate, banking and finance, media and communications, and high tech manufacturing are the most common fields in which financial success was achieved.

Clearly there is a tiny segment of the population that enjoys resources sufficient to free them from ordinary worries about money. But there are also the disadvantaged—the poor and not so poor—for whom financial considerations are a matter of survival, touching on such fundamental matters as hunger and nutrition, housing, and medical care. For the broad middle-income group between these two extremes money sets effective limits on choices in homes, cars, clothing, leisure activities, and higher education for their children.

There are two different ways of estimating economic inequality in America, by annual income and by accumulated wealth.

Annual Income

One way of visualizing the scope of economic inequality is to calculate the *annual money income* of different segments of the population. This can be done by dividing the population into quintiles and calculating the percentage of all income earned by each. As shown in Exhibit 7.1 the lowest paid one fifth of American society earns less than 3 percent while the highest paid one fifth earn over 48 percent the total money income in any year. The 60 percent in the middle share the remainder. By using cumulative shares it can be seen that total income divides the working population in half, with the top 20 percent earning about half and 80 percent earning the other half.

Notable among the top quintile is a group of salaried corporate executives who form a part of the institutional elite and whose annual income places them among America's millionaires. A sampling of the highest paid executives reveals that at least 370 corporate executives earned a minimum of $1 million in total compensation (salary, bonus, stock

Exhibit 7.1
Distribution of Earnings, 1988

	Share of Earnings	Cumulative Share
Poorest fifth	2.1%	2.1%
Second	8.3	10.4
Middle	15.8	26.2
Fourth	25.2	51.4
Wealthiest fifth	48.6	100.0

Source: Paul Ryscavage and Peter Henle, "Earnings Inequality Accelerates in the 1980s." *Monthly Labor Review* 113 (December, 1990), Table 1.

options, golden parachutes) during 1989, including a dozen who earned
more than $10 million (Byrne, 1989). Included in this group are:

Frank G. Wells (Walt Disney)	$50,946,000
Paul Fireman (Reebok)	$14,606,000
Roberto C. Goizueta (Coca-Cola)	$10,717,000
Donald E. Petersen (Ford)	$ 7,147,000

American corporate executives are the best-paid in the world. One
survey of chief executives shows an average of compensation of $508,000
compared to $317,000 (in U.S dollars) in Japan, $286,000 in Britain,
$260,000 in Germany, and $148,000 in Sweden (Tooley, 1989). It is further
estimated that the discrepancy between top executives and other workers
has increased over the last several decades. In 1960 top executives earned
41 times the income of the average factory worker and 38 times that of a
schoolteacher, compared to 1988 when it was 72 times that of teachers and
93 times that of average factory workers (Elais, 1990: 12).

Accumulated Wealth

An alternative way of measuring economic inequality is to focus on
the distribution of the total private wealth in the society. *Private wealth*
represents the total assets in private hands, and includes cash, real estate,
stocks and bonds, and securities, personal property in the form of cars and
homes and furnishings, and the value of pension plans and life insurance.
The household is the unit of analysis in calculating private wealth because
resources are typically held jointly. For most Americans personal wealth
is made up of cash savings, the equity in their homes, and the value of their
cars and other personal possessions.

It is actually quite difficult to determine total wealth, for some monies
are effectively concealed, but there have been several recent attempts to
place a dollar value on total assets in America, and estimates range as high
as $10.6 trillion (U.S. Congress, 1986; Rose, 1986; Avery, Elliehausen &
Canner, 1984). American households can be divided in four major groups
(see Exhibit 7.2). At the bottom are about one third of the households, with
total assets of less than $10,000. One household in ten has zero or negative
assets. For some, this means that their debts exceed the value of anything
they own; for others, it means they own no home or car, nor do they have
any major material possessions. About one quarter of American households (26.8 percent) have a modest accumulation of assets, ranging between $10,000 and $50,000. These are the families who have been able to
put aside some savings, are in the process of paying for a house and car,
but obviously do not enjoy much long-term financial security. It is difficult

to imagine their ability to handle a major financial crisis such as coping with major medical bills. The next third are in a more comfortable position with assets ranging between $50,000 and $249,000. A small group (6 percent) has assets of over a quarter-million dollars.

The distribution of assets for minorities reveals even starker contrasts. Very small segments of black (0.6 percent) and Hispanic households (3.2 percent) have large accumulations of assets—$250,000 or more—that place them among the most advantaged members of society. But, at the other extreme, more than half of all black and Hispanic households have assets of less than $5,000. Measures of median wealth are even more revealing. Median assets for both groups stand at less than $5,000.

Exhibit 7.2
Distribution of Net Household Assets, United States, 1984

Net Worth	Percentage of All Households	White	Black	Hispanics
Zero, or negative	11.0%	8.4%	30.5%	23.9
$4,999 or less	15.3	14.0	23.9	26.3
$5,000–$9,999	6.4	6.3	6.8	7.6
$10,000–$24,999	12.4	12.2	14.0	11.4
$25,000–$49,999	14.4	15.0	11.7	9.5
$50,000–$99,999	19.2	20.7	9.3	13.1
$100,000–$249,000	15.3	16.9	3.3	5.1
$250,000–$499,000	4.0	4.4	0.5	2.1
$500,000–more	2.0	2.1	0.1	1.0
Median net worth		$39,135	$3,397	$4,913

Source: U. S. Bureau of the Census, Current Population Reports, Series P-70, No. 7. *Household Wealth and Asset Ownership, 1984.* (Washington, DC: Government Printing Office, 1986), pp. 5, 18-19.

The number of households with great wealth is small, but the amount of wealth concentrated in their hands is extraordinary. It is estimated that 10 percent of families own over 70 percent of the total wealth, including about half the value of all real estate, and over 90 percent of corporate stocks and bonds (U.S. Congress, 1986: 35). Within this 10 percent is an even smaller, more privileged group. The very wealthiest—the top half of 1 percent (about 420,000 households)—hold a minimum of $2.5 million each, and average $8.9 million in assets. Together, these "superrich" own 35 percent of the total private wealth in America. Moreover, it appears that the concentration of wealth is increasing, for the superrich controlled only 25 percent of the wealth in 1963.

MIDDLE-INCOME GROUPS

A large segment of people fall into a broad middle income category as shown by the size of median earnings (see Exhibit 7.3). And it must be remembered that the vast majority of this income is earned from wages and salaries (Ryscavage, 1986). Several aspects of this distribution deserve special mention. One is that the presence of a second earner raises family income by about $6,000. A second is that single-parent families—whether headed by men or women—average less than married couples, but households headed by women are at a $10,000 disadvantage. Finally, the interpretation of the data for single persons must take into account the fact that they tend to be younger workers, just starting out in the labor force.

Exhibit 7.3
Median Income in the United States, 1987

All families	$30,850
Married, two earners	40,420
Married, one earner	34,700
White	35,300
Black	27,180
Single parent, male	24,800
Single parent, female	14,620
Single, female	10,580
Single, male	16,700

Source: U.S. Bureau of the Census, 1989, *Money Income of Households, Families and Persons in the United States*, (Washington, DC: Government Printing Office, 1990). Table 40. p. 166.

Economic Stagnation in the Middle?

Middle-income families at or above the median may be able to develop a comfortable standard of living, including homeownership, consumer goods, health care, and providing education for their children. However, income trends over the recent past reveal patterns suggesting that the overall position of the middle-income groups did not change much during the 1980s, especially when inflation and tax rates are factored in. In 1977 the median family after-tax income was $25,518 (in 1987 dollars), but by 1987, it had actually declined to $23,508 (Phillips, 1990: 242). Measures of central tendency (means and medians) conceal changes occurring at the upper and lower edges of middle incomes. There is some indication that the gap between the top and bottom income groups is widening (U.S. Congress, 1986). Households in the four lowest income groups (those earning less $14,000) actually earned relatively less than comparable workers a decade earlier. In real terms this means that lower income households lost ground to inflation, earning wages that bought less than they would have ten years earlier. At the same time there was a significant increase in the earnings of the highest-paid one tenth of the population. The income of this group increased by 16 percent and the income of the highest 1 percent increased by a dramatic 49 percent (Phillips, 1990: 17).

A variety of demographic and economic factors have combined to create this situation (Levy, 1987). The changing configuration of the economy is a major factor, with higher paying middle-income jobs contracting and being replaced with jobs at the extremes. Hardest hit are stable, well-paying manufacturing work; it is, for example, estimated that 960,000 blue-collar factory jobs were permanently lost during the 1980s (Richman, 1988: 38). New jobs that were created included a large number of professional and technical jobs such as physical therapists and electrical engineers. However, there was also an increase in the number of low-paying service jobs such as cashier, waitress, and janitor. Hourly wage workers—meaning most lower and middle-income workers—were able to win only modest increases during this period. Many also lost cost-of-living adjustments that were popular during the 1970s. Tax rates have been adjusted downward, not harming lower income families but clearly benefiting higher income families.

Economic Inequality: The Gender Gap

Gender gap measures women's pay as a percentage of men's pay (usually computed on the basis of median annual wages). The relative income of women workers in the United States has long lagged behind that of men, a pattern frequently repeated in industrial societies (Swafford, 1978). Research on wage differentials in the early nineteenth century suggests that women in manufacturing earned about 30 cents for every dollar earned by men (Goldin & Sokoloff, 1982). More systematic data covering all workers have been available only for about three decades. These data suggest that women's earnings hovered at approximately 60 percent of men's throughout the 1960s and 1970s. Although there is a narrowing of the discrepancy between men's and women's earnings, women in the paid labor force still earn about 70 percent of what men do. Women fare relatively better in some occupations than others, and in some situations than others, but the overall pattern has been slow to change (see Exhibit 7.4).

The gender gap is the outcome of a combination of factors. Among the most significant is the uneven distribution of men and women among occupations. Women continue to be underrepresented in the better paid managerial and professional jobs and overrepresented in the lower paid clerical, service, and retail forms of work. It must be remembered that,

Exhibit 7.4
Trends in Median Earnings of Men and Women, 1960-1987

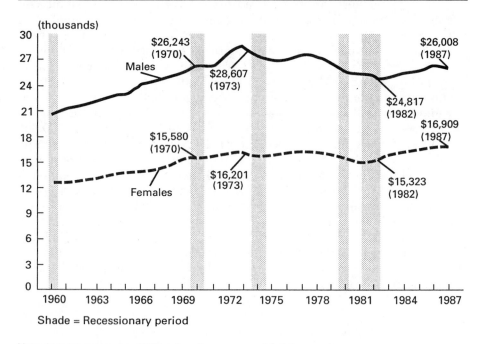

Shade = Recessionary period

Note: Income reported in 1987 dollars for year-round, full-time workers.
Source: U. S. Bureau of the Census. *Money Income of Households, Families and Persons, 1987.*
(Washington,DC: U.S. Government Printing Office, 1988). Figure 3.

despite the opening of occupational opportunities, approximately one third of all women workers are clerical workers of one kind or another. Clerical, service, and retail workers, regardless of their sex, tend to start at a low entry-level pay, and are less able to increase their wages because careers in these fields tend to be low-ceiling with few opportunities for advancement.

A number of other labor market factors must be considered in explaining the earnings gap. Women are less likely to be members of labor unions, and unionized workers tend to be better paid. Also, women work, on the average, fewer hours, have less work experience, and tend to have longer periods of unemployment. All these factors contribute to lower annual wages. Statistical analysis makes it possible to estimate the amount women would earn if they had comparable employment patterns, and controls for the effect of other factors such as skill and experience. Such studies always reveal that there is an "unexplained" difference—about one third of the earnings gap—that must be interpreted as the result of discrimination, both overt and unintentional, that produces lower pay and hinders opportunities for advancement.

Discrimination against women in the workplace, as elsewhere in society, has its origins in attitudes and beliefs prevalent in the larger society. One salient attitude is the question of whether or not women, especially those with young children, should be in the labor market. It is a question of both money and social roles. The traditional division of labor that prevailed during much of this century imposed responsibility for the family with women and responsibility for providing economic support with men. This can have negative consequences for women if it causes employers to doubt the appropriateness of working females. It could mean that men would be given preference for jobs and promotions on the ground that they must support families. The other dimension is parental, the belief that maternal employment detracts from time for the family and is a factor in the breakdown of the family. Studies during the 1980s confirm that many people believe that having a mother in the labor force is detrimental to their children (Greenberger et al., 1988).

Another form of bias relates to the correspondence between gender traits and occupational requirements. Simply put, traits attributed to women are assumed to be inconsistent with the traits necessary for success in the occupation. Such thinking generalizes to all members of a social category, ignoring individual differences and abilities. Moreover, it is often based on unverified assumptions about the traits needed to succeed in an occupation. Male police academy recruits, for example, preparing for the hazards of their work often equate their own personal safety with physical strength. Consequently, there is some reluctance to accept women as partners, despite the fact that the record shows that injury or death is seldom a matter of physical prowess, but rather a failure to follow established procedures (Charles, 1981; Remmington, 1981).

Economic Inequality: The Color Gap

Assessments of the economic picture for blacks entering the 1990s often conclude that there has been considerable economic progress for some segments of the African American population since the World War II era, but that significant black-white economic inequities persist, and that progress has slowed or even regressed in some areas in the last decade (e.g., Smith & Welch, 1986; National Urban League, 1989; Jaynes, 1989). Just five decades ago African Americans were concentrated at the bottom of the class structure in a handful of blue-collar occupations. One third of all males were engaged in agriculture, many as sharecroppers, and most women were in some form of domestic or service work. Income data for the period are not all that reliable, but suggest that men earned less than half what whites did. Educational attainment lagged far behind that of whites, and most young black children attended inferior, segregated schools.

By the 1990s there were, simultaneously, many indications of economic progress and many areas of stagnation. The average earnings of blacks have grown at a faster rate than those for whites, but continue to lag behind those of whites by any measure. The discrepancy is most pronounced among black men, who earn 65 percent of white males. Black women are approaching pay equity with white women (93 percent), but of course at a level well below that of men. Black household income stands at $20,742, only about 62 percent of the white household income of $33,526. Unemployment rates for blacks are twice the national average, and have remained at that level through economic cycles of prosperity and recession.

In any one year, approximately one third of black Americans are living below the poverty level, confirming that persistent inequalities remain. At the same time it is possible to point to measurable economic progress and the emergence of a black middle class. The number of black families with incomes of $50,000 or more doubled during the 1980s (O'Hare, 1989). In families with two working parents black incomes reach 85 percent of comparable white families. They have the same characteristics as other relatively affluent Americans: middle-aged, well-educated households combining the earnings of two or more workers.

These people represent a "new" black middle class, significantly different from the old black middle class, which may be found as early as the eighteenth century (Landry, 1987). The old middle class developed within a societal context of formal racial subordination and thus, although some small number of blacks might occupy middle-class status, they were never able to enjoy the same income or lifestyle as similarly placed whites (Frazier, 1957). Moreover, class position was often circumscribed by racial boundaries. Black teachers, doctors, ministers, journalists, and businesspersons usually served a black, not white, clientele.

POVERTY IN AMERICA

In 1964 President Lyndon Johnson declared "war on poverty," and in 1988 Jack Kemp accepted the position of secretary of housing and urban development saying, "I want to wage war on poverty." These two events, coming two decades apart, serve as a reminder of the persistence of poverty in America. The numbers of the people living in poverty fluctuate over time, and specific individuals escape poverty, but the conditions that produce poverty seem intractable because those who escape poverty are replaced by others.

In response to President Johnson's call to battle poverty the federal government developed a standard for defining poverty, and each year provides an enumeration of this group. The basic component in the calculation of the poverty threshold is the cost of a food budget that is nutritionally adequate, originally developed by the Department of Agriculture as a temporary emergency budget for use when a family was short of money, not one that would be satisfactory over long periods of time.

Poverty data based on the official government criteria were first tabulated for 1959. In that year nearly 40 million people were living in poverty (22.4 percent of the population). The numbers declined steadily during the 1960s, fluctuated around 20 to 25 million people during the 1970s, and increased again during the 1980s. In 1989 the poverty threshold for an individual was set at $6,311 and at $12,675 for a family of four. Using this criterion there were 30 million poor people in 1988, or approximately

Exhibit 7.5
Characteristics of People Living in Poverty, United States

Race
White	66%
Black	30
All other races	5

Age
Under 18	40%
18 to 24 years	12
25 to 54 years	30
55 to 64 years	7
65 and over	11

Residence
Central cities	41%
Other urban areas	29
Rural areas	27
Farms	3

Family status (adults)
Living alone or with nonrelatives	21%	
Males		(8)
Females		(13)
Living in families	79%	
Married couples		(35)
Male-headed, no wife present		(4)
Female-headed, no husband present		(40)

Employment status (adults)
Worked year-round, full-time	17%
Worked part of the year	33
Unemployed	50

Note: Percentages may not add to 100 percent due to rounding.
Source: U.S. Bureau of the Census, Current Population Reports, Series P-60, No. 157, *Money Income and Poverty Status of Families and Persons in the United States, 1987.* (Washington, DC: U.S. Government Printing Office, 1988).

13 percent of the total population. Over half, about 59 percent, of all poverty households received at least one form of noncash benefit—food stamps, free/subsidized school lunches, Medicaid, or subsidized housing.

The majority of the officially poor are white, but blacks, making up 12 percent of the population, are overrepresented (see Exhibit 7.5). Perhaps the most dramatic characteristic of this group is their age; half are either under 18 or over 65. It is also evident that although center-city poverty is the most visible, it is not exclusively an urban problem, but also touches small towns and rural areas. Most of the poor are members of families, but four in ten (44 percent) are in single-parent families— mostly headed by women. Finally, adult poverty is equally divided between those who worked at least some time during the previous year and those who were without jobs the entire year. Thus, working certainly does not guarantee that a person or a family will be able to rise out of poverty.

The Dynamics of Poverty

Vulnerability to poverty is not limited to a narrow segment of society, but rather touches many more people than is generally recognized. During the 1980s at least 30 million Americans lived below the poverty level every year. Two major life transitions are most likely to thrust people into this group—joblessness or a major family change caused by divorce, separation, or the death of a spouse. People do climb out of poverty—between 20 and 25 percent escape every year—but they are replaced by others who slip into poverty. Thus, poverty must be understood as a structural condition continually confronting large numbers of people. For some, poverty is a temporary condition, but for others, it is a long-term condition.

A study of people in poverty between 1969 and 1978 showed that about one person in four lived in a family that received some form of government economic assistance at least once during that ten-year period (Duncan, 1984). For about half of those (49 percent), poverty was of relatively short duration—two years or less out of ten, followed by movement above the poverty line. A second group experienced much longer periods of poverty ranging from more than two years up to eight out of ten years. For these people, the threat of poverty is a part of their normal existence, always there. A small group of the poor did experience long-term, persistent poverty. Persistent poverty was defined as being poor for eight of ten years, and made up somewhere between 2 and 3 percent of society. The majority of the persistently poor were in female-headed households, mostly black: the remainder were elderly men and women trapped by fixed incomes.

CASE STUDY:
The Chances of Escaping Poverty

In 1986, 23 percent of those living in poverty the year before were able to rise above the poverty level. The chances of escaping poverty are not equally distributed, as shown in Exhibit 7.6, and reveal some interesting patterns. Persons of color had a much lower chance of escaping poverty than whites. The young and the old were more likely to be mired in poverty than people in the 19 to 64 age group. And, as might be expected, employment is a major factor in understanding the dynamics of poverty. Over half (56.7 percent) of the adults who remained in poverty in both years did not work in either 1985 or 1986. Fifteen percent of those unemployed in both years escaped poverty, usually as a result of a change in family status or increased earnings by another family member. But the most significant exit rates were found among those who got better-paying jobs or who worked more hours.

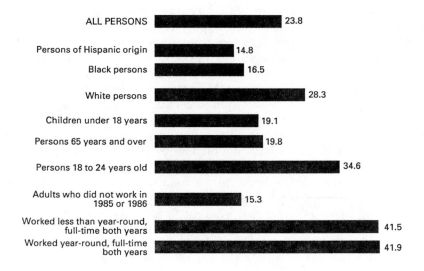

ALL PERSONS	23.8
Persons of Hispanic origin	14.8
Black persons	16.5
White persons	28.3
Children under 18 years	19.1
Persons 65 years and over	19.8
Persons 18 to 24 years old	34.6
Adults who did not work in 1985 or 1986	15.3
Worked less than year-round, full-time both years	41.5
Worked year-round, full-time both years	41.9

Source: U.S. Bureau of the Census, *Transitions in Income and Poverty Status, 1985-86*, Current Population Reports, Series P-70, No. 18. (Washington, DC: U.S. Government Printing Office, 1990), p. 14.

The United States does not have a monopoly on poverty; all the available data suggest it is a world-wide problem. An increasing flow of information from the Soviet Union suggests that poverty exists there on a large scale. Estimates run as high as 28 percent of the Soviet population below an official poverty level of $1,920 (Dentzer & Trimble, 1989). Admittedly, it is difficult to define poverty because things such as health care,

housing and education are heavily subsidized by the government. However, usual measures of living standards suggest a dismal existence for
many. Thirty million people drink water considered unsafe, 30 percent of
the hospitals have no indoor toilets, and one-quarter of the homes are
without hot water.

The Feminization of Poverty

The phrase *feminization of poverty* calls attention to the fact that an
increasing proportion of the poor is made up of families maintained by
women (Pearce, 1978). Many are single, divorced, and widowed women
without dependent children but ever-larger numbers of women without
partners are caring for young children. In 1986 there were 8.8 million women
with children under age 21 whose fathers were absent, and one third had
incomes below the poverty line (U.S. Bureau of the Census, 1987). Approximately 28 percent of white and 50 percent of both Hispanic and African
American single parent families were in poverty (Michael & Simon, 1988).

Female poverty represents the convergence of a number of factors
(Scott, 1984). Women's disadvantage in the labor force is one of the most
pervasive. Sex segregation concentrates job opportunities in the lower-paying service and clerical occupations. Moreover, technical obsolescence and
the loss of jobs to foreign competition in certain areas (e.g., textiles) have
a disproportionate impact on women's jobs.

The increasing instability of the family is another factor. Divorce
rates in the United States have doubled since 1960, and in a majority of
cases wives retain custody of any children. Divorced women suffer much
greater financial hardships than divorced men, especially women who were
full-time homemakers. It is estimated that the standard of living of former
husbands increases by 42 percent whereas former wives suffer a decline of
somewhere between 33 and 73 percent (Weitzman, 1985; Hoffman &
Duncan, 1988). This discrepancy can be traced to the fact that wives not
in the paid labor force during the duration of the marriage are at a
disadvantage in seeking work, whereas husbands enjoy the financial
benefits of work experience and seniority accumulated during marriage.
Those in the paid labor force, or who enter it after divorce, experience the
"earnings gap," which means that women will be earning approximately
two thirds of men.

The increasing proportion of children born to unmarried mothers is
another factor. A large percentage of children in the United States are born
to unmarried women. While most of these women will eventually marry,
they must assume major responsibility for child care for some period of
time. Moreover, many are teenagers, and the presence of children can
increase the chances of discontinuing their education, thus limiting their
futures and channeling them to lower-paying work.

Then, too, there is the matter of alimony and child-support payments. These programs were, in part, originally designed to alleviate the financial burdens on nonemployed spouses resulting from divorce. The average support payment stood at $2,710 in 1987 (U.S. Bureau of the Census, 1990a). Actually, support payments for women with dependent children were awarded in about 59 percent of the cases, and just over half received the full amount due them. Twenty-five percent got partial payments, and 24 percent got nothing from the absent father. Put another way, $10 billion in child-support payments was paid, but $14.6 billion was owed.

CLASS AND ECONOMIC INEQUALITY

The consequences of economic inequalities are evident in countless ways, reshaping lifestyles, affecting access to legal aid and health insurance, and contributing to persistent hunger. The 1980s also witnessed a resurgence in public awareness and concern for the plight of the homeless in America, a problem that is, at least in part, economic.

Lifestyles

The squeeze on middle-income groups has important social and demographic implications, placing increasing pressure on married women with young children to join the paid labor force to supplement family incomes. In addition, more people are moonlighting, taking second and third jobs. There is a rising trend in consumer debt, resulting in a dramatic increase in the number of people being forced into personal bankruptcy. The number of bankruptcies in 1989, 616,753, was more than double the number in 1980 (Kim, 1990). Finally, stagnating incomes and soaring housing prices mean that a smaller percentage of young people have the money to afford their own homes. One study estimates that 81 percent of all young adults aged 25 to 34 lack the down payment on a house, and even if parents helped them with the up-front money 60 percent do not earn enough to qualify for a mortgage (Karmin, 1990).

Health Insurance

The specter of illness threatens everyone, but the perils are most dramatic for the 33 million Americans (13 percent of the population) who are without medical insurance at any given time (Lewin, 1991). The uninsured must worry about how they will cope with an unexpected illness, and some must make hard choices. For example, a chronically ill woman in Maryland asked her doctor if it was more important to buy food or medicine, a pregnant Minnesota woman had to travel 84 miles to find a free clinic (Gold, 1989).

About one in eight of the uninsured earn less than $10,000 and are covered by government programs. However, the overwhelming proportion of the uninsured are employed people and their families (85 percent), and tend to be concentrated in the lower middle or working classes. Most are self-employed, small family farmers, or work for small retail or manufac- turing firms unable or unwilling to offer insurance to their employees, and workers are unable to buy private coverage because of prohibitive costs. Whether employed or not, younger people, and black (20.2 percent) and Hispanics (26.5 percent), are most likely to be without insurance.

CASE STUDY:
Legal Defense for the Indigent

The U.S. Supreme Court has repeatedly ruled that the threat of the death penalty puts a citizen at special risk, and consequently the legal system must be especially careful in capital cases. Therefore, states are obligated to provide legal aid for those too poor to afford an attorney. A study of the situation concludes that in some states "indigent defendants on trial for their lives are frequently represented by ill-trained, unprepared court-ap- pointed lawyers so grossly underpaid they literally cannot afford to do the job" (Coyle, Strasser & Lavelle, 1990: 30).

It is clear that the allocation of economic resources is a major part of the problem, either as a result of inattention or a disregard for the legal needs of the poor. For example, there may be unrealistically low limits on compensation for the lawyer's time, $1,000 for the entire case in one state. For another, judges routinely deny requests for monies for investigation and expert witnesses. Some states provide no pretrial training for lawyers preparing for capital cases, meaning that some embark upon cases with little or no experience with this special kind of case. The result is that the indigent are often represented by young and inexperienced lawyers with insufficient resources to mount an effective and credible defense.

Hunger In America

In 1969, President Richard Nixon set out to end hunger forever, commenting, "A child ill-fed is dulled in curiosity, and a worker ill-fed is less productive." Hunger did decline; yet, two decades later, hunger in America survives. The medical community defines *hunger* as a "chronic shortage of the nutrients necessary for growth and good health," and by that criterion millions of Americans may be hungry for some period every year, including 5.5 million children (Physician Task Force, 1985; Walmer, 1991). A lack of sufficient food endangers anyone, but for pregnant women, both mother and the child face special risks. Malnutrition in expectant mothers exposes the child to a whole range of deficiencies, not the least of which is low birth weight, and frail infants face an infant mortality rate 40 times higher than that of others (Brown, 1987).

Recurring problems of recession, inflation, and unemployment play an important part in the scope of hunger, and in some cases government policies at the state and national levels have contributed, either by producing it or failing to prevent hunger among those made poor by economic conditions. Programs designed to provide food or to supplement the diets of the poor often fail to reach them. There are some 30 million people living below the poverty level, but only two thirds receive food stamps. Critics argue the program is burdened by elaborate paperwork that hinders the application process, plus strict rules of eligibility may discourage or exclude applicants (Brown, 1987). Then, too, some potential recipients perceive a social stigma associated with accepting food allotments.

The Homeless: The New Street People

Although there is some debate over the actual number of those who regularly go without shelter, generally accepted estimates suggest that at least 600,000 and possibly more than a million persons are living in shelters or on the street on any given night (Wright, 1988). In addition, some homeless advocates claim that another 14 million are living on the edge, "one paycheck or one domestic argument from the streets." They are, in the words of one group of researchers, the poorest of the poor, for "not only do they lack material resources, but they lack human resources as well—friends or family who will take them in" (Piliavin, Sosin & Westerfelt, 1987–1988: 20).

What is striking about the new street people is their diversity—children and elderly, families and individuals, women and men. The homeless population is somewhat different in each place—a response to local social and economic conditions—but it is possible to sketch some broad patterns, although all figures are estimates (Wright, 1988; Snow et al., 1986). Husband-wife families form a part of the homeless population, probably 5 to 10 percent. These tend to be young, lower blue-collar families, typically thrown onto the streets by unemployment. Many have young children, although some have been able to place them with relatives or friends, an arrangement that saves the children the hardship of life in the shelters but separates them from their parents.

Between 10 and 20 percent of the homeless are children or youths under the age of 18. Most are members of family units, usually being cared for by a single parent (typically, a single mother). These young street people suffer unusually high rates of depression, anxiety, and reduced self-esteem. There are also some solitary adolescents (equal numbers of boys and girls) counted among these homeless children. They are typically "throwaways" (abandoned or evicted) or runaways fleeing abusive homes, often being reduced to crime or prostitution to survive. There are high rates of pregnancy and substance abuse among these youths.

Another large group, perhaps 20 to 30 percent, are adult women. The single largest segment of this group are women with children, the mothers of the youthful homeless. Some are battered women, evicted or seeking to escape from violent domestic arrangements, and others are unemployed or "working homeless" single parents. Still others are mentally impaired, and some have alcohol and drug abuse problems.

The remainder are men (50 to 60 percent), a few single-parent fathers but generally solitary males. Most are middle-aged or younger. There are very few older people, men or women, among the homeless, for two reasons: because they qualify for social security and other age-related benefits and because the mortality rate for the long-term homeless is so high that few survive to old age. Vietnam era veterans are over-represented, some suffering service-related disabilities.

Sources of Homelessness

The expansion of the homeless population is the result of the interplay among a number of social and economic forces. Among the most important are poverty and unemployment, increases in the incidence of troubled individuals or broken families, and the decline in the availability of low-income housing (Caton, 1989).

As would be expected, poverty and unemployment drive many people onto the streets. However, some of the homeless are the working poor, employed, but unable to find or afford housing. Another segment is driven to the streets and shelters by domestic circumstances. These are the female single parents and the teenagers. As the result of divorce or abandonment, or to escape domestic abuse, they find themselves having to cope alone. Research shows that those most likely to become homeless are socially isolated, lacking supportive social relationships with family or friends who might be able to aid them. For example, an unusual proportion had spent some period of foster care during their childhood (Piliavin, Sosin & Westerfelt, 1987–1988: 22).

One segment of the homeless—usually estimated between 15 and 20 percent of the total—has a history of mental illness (Snow, et al., 1986). Their plight represents an ironic twist in the evolution of the care of the mentally ill, a process called *deinstitutionalization* (Dear & Wolch, 1987). First, the assertion of patients' civil rights has made it virtually impossible for police, psychiatrists, or family members to hold people in hospitals against their will, unless they are very seriously impaired. Second, reforms in the treatment of chronic mental patients shifted the emphasis from institutional care to the idea of returning patients to the communities where they must live. Although a worthy idea, governments have failed to provide the necessary community-based outpatient facilities to help those released from institutions. Those not able to adapt successfully are left to fend for themselves on the streets.

Ultimately, the most direct problem is the lack of low-income housing. Many of the homeless are simply unable to locate affordable housing. Urban renewal has razed low-income housing and low-rent hotels, often to make way for middle-income homes, and neither government nor private efforts have kept pace with the demand for low-income housing. To cite but one example, the average rent for a single room in Chicago in 1985 was $195 per month, $27 more than the median monthly income of the homeless in that city (Rossi & Wright, 1987: 23). Thus, most homeless could not afford even the cheapest housing if they used all their money. And rents for low-income housing have been rising nationally, soaring by more than 30 percent from 1974 to 1985, even after being adjusted for inflation (Whitman, 1989b). This situation may deteriorate even further, for one projection of housing units estimates that 17.2 million households will need low-rent housing by the year 2003, but only 9.4 million units will be available (Barron, 1988). This is predicated on the assumption that the urban renaissance will continue and that the real impact of the mammoth federal budget cuts for subsidized low-income housing in the 1980s will be felt in the 1990s.

Responses to the Homeless

Americans exhibit contradictory and ambivalent attitudes toward the homeless. For example, in one study about one third of the population endorsed both self-induced causes (personal choice, aversion to work) and external or uncontrollable sources (bad luck, structural forces) (Lee et al., 1990). Indications of compassion and caring are unmistakable in efforts to alleviate the suffering. City governments, such as New York, Honolulu, Memphis, and Minneapolis, are devoting millions of dollars to the creation of affordable housing for the homeless (Minerbrook, 1989). In addition, much of the work being done on their behalf represents the efforts of charitable institutions and individuals. Nine out of ten shelters for the homeless are operated by community groups or churches, and at least 80,000 volunteers work in these shelters (Whitman, 1989a). Most Americans see homelessness as a serious problem, worry the problem is getting worse, and seem willing to pay higher taxes to help them (Toner, 1989).

In contrast, there is also a mean-spirited streak running through some segments of the population. Affluent suburbs in the United States and Europe have been accused of putting their homeless on buses to be transported to center cities (Barbanel, 1987), and one New England community dealt with street people by giving them one-way bus tickets to the West Coast (Johnson, 1988). In a Florida city a council member generated public outrage by suggesting poisoning garbage cans as a means of deterring people from foraging through them for food (Barbanel, 1987).

There is no single explanation of the sources of such negative responses to the deprived, but several factors seem to operate. At the deepest
level such negativity may reflect the pervasive effect of a dominant ideology
that locates responsibility for such problems in an individual's failings
rather than structural sources. At a more practical level it may be that the
unsightly street people are physically repulsive, violating middle-class
sensibilities or potentially threatening within the context of widespread
urban violence. In the courts it has become a clash between the public order
and the rights of the homeless to occupy public parks and abandoned
buildings, to sleep on the streets, to beg in the streets.

CONCLUSION: Favoring Greater Economic Equality

Economic resources are, by any criteria, unequally distributed across
society. The wealthiest 1 or 2 percent control a significant proportion of the
total assets. In contrast, approximately 13 percent of the population live
below the poverty level year after year. About one third (31 percent) of
Americans feel that current economic patterns are "fair" and about 9
percent are unsure, but most Americans express some reservations about
the current distribution of money and wealth. A full 60 percent feel that
money and wealth "should be more evenly distributed among a larger
percentage of the people" (Gallup Report, 1985: 25). As would be expected,
opinions on the fairness of the current system are shaped by class, race,
and gender. Women are somewhat less likely to endorse the fairness of the
current situation, as are minorities. And judgments of fairness are directly
related to the size of income, with half the people in families earning more
than $40,000 seeing the distribution of financial resources as fair and the
percentages declining to only 16 percent of those in the $10,000 or less
income bracket.

ADDITIONAL READINGS ON ECONOMIC INEQUALITY

CAROL L. CATON. *Without Dreams: The Homeless in America*. New York: Oxford
    University Press, 1989.
ROBERT W. JACKMAN. *Politics and Social Inequality: A Comparative Analysis*. New
    York: John Wiley, 1975.
MICHAEL B. KATZ. *The Undeserving Poor: From the War on Poverty to the War on
    Welfare*. New York: Pantheon, 1989.
FRANK LEVY. *Dollars and Dreams: The Changing American Income Distribution*.
    New York: Russell Sage, 1987.
WILLIAM P. O'HARE. *America's Welfare Population: Who Gets What?* Washington,
    DC: Population Reference Bureau, 1987.

JAMES T. PATTERSON. *America's Struggle Against Poverty, 1900–1985*. Cambridge, MA: Harvard University Press, 1986.

KEVIN PHILLIPS. *The Politics of Rich and Poor*. New York: Random House, 1990.

PETER H. ROSSI. *Down and Out in America: The Origins of Homelessness*. Chicago: University of Chicago Press, 1989.

RUTH SIDEL. *Women and Children Last: The Plight of Poor Women in Affluent America*. New York: Viking/Penguin, 1986.

PAUL E. ZOPF, JR. *American Women in Poverty*. Westport, CT: Greenwood, 1989.

Chapter 8
Social Evaluations and Social Relations

CLASS AND SOCIAL JUDGMENTS

Another more elusive major form of inequality is variously referred to as prestige, status, respect, social honor, or esteem. All such terms point to the fact that individuals and groups in a society tend to be ranked on scales of relative social superiority or inferiority. Some evaluations are based on personal performance, reflecting the traits a society values or devalues. Industrial societies, for example, often prize athletic prowess and musical ability. The subjective evaluation of others is important because people are sensitive to the judgments of those around them and prize the admiration and positive evaluation of others. Such evaluations are thus a subtle form of social control, encouraging and rewarding some accomplishments and deterring and penalizing others (Goode, 1978).

Consequential social evaluations are also based on position in the stratification system (occupation and class) and ascribed social characteristics (race, ethnicity, gender). There is some indication that a fundamental source of prestige in industrial societies is occupation, perhaps more powerful than any other single factor (Nock & Rossi, 1979). This is because occupation is used to anticipate a great deal of information about a person or family—income, education, ability, personal attributes. Such projections prevail despite the fact that they may very well be assumptions, stereotypes, or inappropriate generalizations.

Therefore, the relative prestige of occupations represents a general social evaluation of both the relative worth or desirability of different jobs and the persons who perform the work. Members of occupations, sensitive to their public status, devote themselves to improving (or protecting) the prestige of their work. For example, when the issue of lawyer advertising first reached the U.S. Supreme Court, opponents claimed that advertising would cause "commercialization, undermine the lawyer's sense of dignity and self-worth, and tarnish the dignified image of the profession" (*Bates* v. *State Bar of Arizona*, 1977). It also shows up in group attempts to upgrade their prestige by developing new titles for their work, as is evident in the evolution of "undertaker" to "mortician" to "funeral director."

The implications of social standing extend beyond the approbation of others. Social evaluations are also a factor in social relations. In a number of situations social interaction is separated by social class, with association concentrated among people at the same social level. This shows up in friendships and marriage patterns, as well as residential choices and membership in social clubs. Such behavior stands as a reminder that social prestige is ultimately a judgment of social superiority and inferiority and can be the basis of segregation along class lines.

In extreme cases people at the same class level will attempt to form closed communities, limiting all forms of social contact to others at the same level. Max Weber referred to them as "status communities," and his analysis included a discussion of the colonial aristocracy (including such people as George Washington) who formed exclusive clubs. The colonial aristocracy was later supplanted by a national upper class at the end of the nineteenth century, and some elements of this group survive in contemporary society.

OCCUPATIONAL PRESTIGE RANKINGS: Consensus and Stability

Systematic research on social prestige originated in the 1920s among vocational counselors seeking to determine the relative standing of different occupations, and sociologists have been systematically studying the concept since the 1940s. The resulting body of research confirms that occupations are ranked on relatively stable hierarchies of prestige. Rankings are subjective judgments, created by combining and averaging individual evaluations of the standing of occupations. Despite some individual variation, there is great consensus on the relative placement of most occupations, although it is true that some, such as homemaker and police officer, lack that consensus (Hope, 1982; Guppy & Goyder, 1984). People do tend to inflate the social standing of their own occupations, those that are similar to it, and those that seem realistic options for them. There is also some variation in the relative weight of different criteria, with, for example, economic rewards being a more salient criterion for people at the lower end of the stratification system and educational attainment being given more weight by those at the upper end.

Occupational Prestige: The United States

Exhibit 8.1 provides a sampling of occupational scores from a study conducted among the residents of Baltimore. These results, when combined with other research, reveal some broad general patterns. The very highest levels of the prestige hierarchy are dominated by upper-middle-

Exhibit 8:1
Social Class and Prestige: United States

Social Class	Representative Occupations	Score
Upper Middle	Physician	95.8
	Mayor	92.2
	Lawyer	90.1
	College professor	90.1
	Superintendent of schools	87.8
	Stockbroker	81.7
	Factory owner employing 2,000	81.7
	Electrical engineer	79.5
	Registered nurse	75.0
	Accountant	71.2
	High school teacher	70.2
	Elementary school teacher	65.4
	Office manager	68.3
	Hotel manager	64.1
	Circulation director, newspaper	63.5
	Social worker	63.2
Lower Middle	Private secretary	60.9
	Supervisor, warehouse	56.4
	Dental assistant	54.8
	Stenographer	52.6
	Office secretary	51.3
	Bookkeeper	50.0
	Telephone operator	46.2
	Salesperson, wholesale	46.2
	Keypunch operator	44.6
	Post office clerk	42.3
	Shoe store salesperson	35.9
	File clerk	34.0
Working class	Electrician	62.5
	Plumber	58.7
	Police officer	58.3
	Assembly-lline supervisor	53.8
	Carpenter	53.5
	Locomotive engineer	52.9
	Welder	46.8
	Auto mechanic	44.9
	Butcher	38.8
	Assembly-line worker	28.3
	Textile machine operator	27.9
	Delivery truck driver	26.9
	Coal miner	24.0
	Garbage collector	16.3
The Poor	Beautician	42.1
	Hairdresser	39.4
	Shirt maker	26.6
	Flour miller	25.0
	Waitress (F)/waiter (M)	22.1
	Box packer	15.1
	Laundry worker	14.7
	Salad maker in a hotel	13.8
	Janitor	12.5
	Yarn washer	11.8
	Maid (F)/household worker (M)	11.5
	Parking lot attendant	8.0

Note: The range of possible values is from 0 to 100.
Source: Christine E. Bose and Peter H. Rossi, "Gender and Jobs," *American Sociological Review*, 48 (June 1983), 327-328.

class occupations. Professionals (physician, lawyer, college professor) share the top of the scale with positions of local institutional power (mayor). Other studies show state governors, cabinet officers, members of Congress, and Supreme Court justices share the top of the prestige scale. The remainder of the upper middle class—technical professionals (scientist, engineer) and middle-level managers (superintendent of schools), generally place below them with scores ranging down from the 80s to the 60s.

Lower-middle-class clerical and sales workers tend to have scores ranging between the 50s and the 30s. The craft sector of working-class occupations tends to occupy the same range, but less skilled assemblers, machine operators, and truck drivers rate in the 20s. Garbage collector has very low prestige, but the unsavory nature of the work contributes to the lower score.

The lower end of the prestige hierarchy is anchored by service work and unskilled jobs. Employment as box packer, janitor, maid, laundry worker or parking lot attendant implies heavy manual labor, unpleasant working conditions, or low pay. None earns a score higher than 15. Only one direct service job—beautician— ranks above the others. This occupation is also noteworthy because it reveals that job titles can have some influence on evaluations. "Beautician" and "hairdresser" are different names for what is essentially the same job, but the former commands a few more points of prestige.

Occupational Prestige in Comparative Perspective

Studies of occupational prestige conducted in at least 60 countries reveal a great deal of similarity and consistency. Occupations tend to be ranked in a similar order in most societies, even in nations with markedly different religious, political, and cultural traditions. (Treiman, 1977).[1] (In statistical terms rank-order correlations are usually between .80 and .95.)

International comparisons from China, Brazil, and Czechoslovakia reveal the tendency toward consistency, as well as certain variations (see Exhibit 8.2). The first hierarchy is from Beijing, China and was conducted prior to the political turmoil of 1989. Professional work (physician and teacher) ranks at the top of the scale and garbage collector at the bottom. Craft workers and higher level clerical workers tend to rank above factory work or miners. Reporters and writers occupy a position higher than is usually found, and may be attributed to the fact that at the time of this

---

[1]There are conceptual and methodological considerations that caution against uncritically accepting this assertion. Occupations having similar titles may involve significant differences in tasks, responsibility, educational requirements, and income. One potential source of bias in many of these studies is that urban and educated respondents tend to be overrepresented.

Exhibit 8:2
Prestige Rankings in China, Brazil, and Czechoslovakia

Beijing, China	Bezerros, Brazil	Czechoslovakia
Physician	Cabinet member	Physician
Reporter	Priest	Collective farmenr
Teacher (high school)	Physician	Miner
Electrician	Lawyer	Teacher (high school)
Secretary	Farm owner	Mason
Mail carrier	Teacher	Cabinet minister
Textile worker	Auto repairer	Priest
Police officer	Police officer	Judge
Miner	Carpenter	Police officer
Garbage collector	Garbage collector	Sewage worker

Sources: Nan Lin and Wen Xie, "Occupational Prestige in Urban China," *American Journal of Sociology,* 93 (January 1988), Table 2, 804-805; Archibald O. Haller et al., "Variations in Occupational Prestige: Brazilian Data," *American Journal of Sociology,* 77 (March, 1972), 952-955; reprinted from *Social Forces,* 54 (December 1975), 355. "Occupational Prestige Hierarchies," by Roger Penn, copyright © The University of North Carolina Press.

research they enjoyed a special degree of freedom and autonomy (Lin & Xie, 1988).

The second prestige hierarchy is from an isolated rural area of Brazil (Haller, Holsinger & Saraiva, 1972). A majority of people are engaged in agriculture. The upper levels of the hierarchy are similar to those in China and the United States, with central government officials and professionals sharing high prestige. Priest does rate higher than in the United States, possibly reflecting the more central role of religion in less industrialized societies. Agriculture is the major livelihood and the farm owner ranks above white-collar work (bookkeeper), the lower professions (teacher, artist), and skilled manual work (auto repairer). Even the sharecropper, a very low status form of work in the United States, is, in Brazil, placed above carpenter and merchant and police officer. And garbage collector is, as in most cases, viewed as among the very least desirable occupations.

Czechoslovakia, under a communist government when this study was done, exhibits some sharp differences in occupational ranking (Penn, 1975). Government posts do not generally enjoy high prestige. Cabinet minister and judge are well down on the scale. In contrast, blue-collar work tends to fare better than in America. Miner and mason have very high status, seeming to confirm the dominant sociopolitical philosophy, which has sought to enhance the meaning of manual labor. The collective farmer, ranking second only to the physician, epitomizes the differences between capitalist and socialist ideologies. The related deemphasis of religion may help to account for the relatively modest position of priest in overall ranking.

The differences that do exist should not obscure the fact that there is some similarity to other ranking systems. Highly educated professionals are generally accorded high prestige. Physician tends to stand at the top of the hierarchy, and dirty work (sewer cleaner) is without much respect, as is true for both Western and less industrialized nations.

These examples suggest both the diversity and the commonalties found in occupational prestige around the world. Diversity may be rooted in the unique values, beliefs, or history of a society. This is manifest in the proletarian ideology of Czech society which serves to elevate manual labor, or the political history of Brazil, which places a military role at the pinnacle of prestige. Then, too, the level of industrial development is a factor. But underlying this diversity is some consistency.

The Basis of Prestige

The relative prestige accorded to occupations within a society appears to be influenced by two analytically distinct processes. Occupations earn prestige on the basis of a subjective evaluation process in which the perceived characteristics of the work are compared against some standards of desirability. Three considerations seem to be the most important: the requirements of the work, social and economic rewards, and the physical and social characteristics of the work (Marsh, 1971; Haug & Widdison, 1975; Adler & Kraus, 1985).

Once institutionalized, popular concepts of relative occupational prestige are transmitted early in the socialization process. Consequently, young children are able to reproduce adult prestige scores, despite the fact they have little accurate knowledge of the nature and rewards of the work being ranked (Tudor, 1971; Simmons & Rosenberg, 1971). An awareness of the prestige ascribed by others seems to exert a significant influence on subsequent personal judgments about prestige (Haug & Widdison, 1975; Feldman & Thielbar, 1972). The prestige hierarchy is thus a part of the cultural traditions of a society and helps to explain the stability of occupational ranking over time.

Perceived Prerequisites. Several of the qualifications for admission to a particular kind of work are considered in determining prestige. The level of intelligence, the complexity and difficulty of training, and the amount of education all correlate directly with prestige. This helps to account for the high ranking of the professions, all of which involve lengthy formal education. Moreover, as a general rule, professions that require graduate education or training (college professor, physician, scientist, lawyer) are placed above those requiring a bachelor's degree (teacher, architect, accountant). The fact that the crafts involve apprenticeships may contribute to their standing above those blue-collar jobs viewed as not requiring any extensive occupational training. Jobs of the poor perceived as not having any particular qualifications—unskilled and service—have the lowest prestige. The question of the scarcity of qualified personnel suggested by the functionalists may also be a factor. Although it is difficult to assess scarcity in any objective sense, it may help to account for the generally high prestige of occupations perceived as demanding rare and special attributes, such as the physical dexterity of the athlete, the analytic ability of the scientist, or the creative impulse of the artist.

Perceived Rewards. One consistent finding both in the United States and other countries is a very high correlation between income and occupational prestige (Treiman, 1977). Income, per se, confers prestige in the United States, for it has symbolic value as a rough guide for success. Income also has indirect value because it can be translated into a particular style of life. There are, of course, notable exceptions. Teacher and clergy have higher levels of prestige than could be predicted using income as the sole criterion, whereas butcher is lower than expected.

Perceived Structural Characteristics of the Work. Occupations earn prestige on the basis of the tasks involved, the social organization of the work, and working conditions. Cleanliness and safety are factors, as physically dirty or unsafe work tends to be devalued. Routine and repetitive work has less prestige than work that is interesting and creative. Level of responsibility and autonomy are also considerations. Jobs requiring the supervision, evaluation, and direction of subordinates place higher than those that are under the control of superiors or allow little individual discretion. Many authors would claim that power is a decisive factor in understanding prestige hierarchies, arguing that power is universally valued in all human societies (e.g., Lenski, 1966; Treiman, 1977: 21). This might explain the high ranking of roles in government in industrial societies since all such positions wield some power.

Some forms of work have lower prestige than would be expected on other criteria because they involve undesirable attributes, what Everett Hughes (1962) calls the *dirty work* of society. Dirty work is unpleasant, physically disgusting, or associated with things that are symbolically "unclean." For example, "The trade of butcher is a brutal and odious business," wrote Adam Smith in 1814, commenting on the work in the slaughterhouses and meat-packing plants of an earlier era. The conditions of work have improved, but it remains "dirty work" (Meara, 1974). The fact that garbage collector is everywhere a low-ranking occupation suggests that cleaning up human trash and residue is universally depreciated.

The functional tradition has generated a good deal of debate over the concept of the functional importance of jobs. It has been hypothesized that certain types of occupations are essential to the welfare and functioning of all societies (Davis & Moore, 1945). As functionalists see it, religion occupies a central role because it serves to integrate members of a society through a common value system, and scientific and technical occupations develop the techniques and hardware to achieve national goals such as the exploration of space or the eradication of disease. It is imperative that these roles be filled and that people are motivated to perform these essential services. Prestige and income are among the major rewards that can be used to motivate people, and thus prestige becomes one of the rewards attached to the more important positions in society. It is not at all clear that people utilize this abstract concept of functional importance in considering the prestige of occupations. They are, however, able to rate occupations along a continuum of "importance to society," and this is another factor that predicts the prestige of occupations.

CASE STUDY:
Manual Work and Mental Work

Both lower-middle-class and working-class positions have many of the same characteristics in common. Most are filled by employees who are required to follow proscribed routines and lack much discretion on the job. However, it is both conventional and appropriate to divide such workers into two prestige groups based on the type of work they do—manual (white-collar) or nonmanual (blue-collar) work. The labels white and blue collar work surfaced in the early stages of industrialization. One group worked in the factories and mills, as laborers, machine operators, or craft persons, and came to be identified by the sturdy dark clothing they wore. In contrast, those who worked in the offices performed services rather than being directly involved with production. Those who performed nonmanual tasks—recordkeeping, correspondence—wore distinctive white, which showed among other things that they did not soil their clothing doing their jobs. Thus, from the very beginning, clothing was a badge of social status.

Clothing was also an indication of social status at a more fundamental level, for it embodied some deep-seated beliefs about the relative value of different forms of work. The people who wore blue work shirts toiled with their hands, and Adriano Tilgher (1930) points out that Western societies have a long history of depreciating physical labor. Its origins may be traced to the ancient Greek idea that manual work was inferior and demeaning—something to be relegated to subordinate groups, slaves, and peasants—compared to the meaningful intellectual work of the mind. White collars are thus also a claim to greater importance and respectability. This distinction continues to have relevance for the way people think about different kinds of work, and themselves. White-collar workers tend to depreciate those who do physical labor, and blue collar workers are likely to ridicule clerical and sales workers, who they see as not working very hard or producing anything tangible or useful (LeMasters, 1975; Halle, 1984).

Members of the working class are acutely aware of their relatively lowly position in the status hierarchy. Blue-collar workers tend to view themselves as doing decent, important, and honest work, but they are very sensitive to the fact that their work does not carry the same social prestige as does white-collar work. There is not much question in their minds that office work carries more status than factory work. However, they are frustrated by a lack of respect for their work and by the derogatory stereotypes used to identify them.

Gender and Jobs. There is also the question of whether or not jobs typically identified as "women's work" have lower prestige because they are filled by females. Some research has shown that identification of a male or female incumbent of an occupation can affect the prestige score of specific jobs, but there is no clear overall pattern. In the study used in Exhibit 8.1, a woman advertising executive rated about 5 points higher than a man, and female washer repairers had an 11-point advantage. There was, however, no overall evidence of women incumbents depressing the scores of all jobs: for example, male welders rated 6 points above female welders (see also England, 1979). Other research does suggest that the presence of men or women in a job negatively affects scores if the job is sex-typed as being typical of the other sex, or if it is work assumed to require gender-related traits (Powell & Jacobs, 1984).

CLASS AND SOCIAL RELATIONSHIPS

The general term homophily is employed to describe a common, and relatively obvious, characteristic of social organization: the tendency for social relationships to develop among people who are in some way similar. For example, it is usual to find that friendships tend to be segregated on the basis of social qualities such as age, gender and ethnicity, or similar attitudes and beliefs. It is also apparent that people at the same class level are more likely to associate with other people at the same level than with people who rank above or below them in the stratification system. This pattern has long been documented in numerous social patterns, including friendships, place of residence, social clubs, and dating and marriage (Warner & Lunt, 1941; Laumann, 1966; Fischer, 1982).

Class-based association patterns are, in part, dictated by patterns of economic inequality. This would be evident in residential patterns where housing costs will contribute to the sorting of neighborhoods on the basis of income. In addition, formal and informal associations will be extensions of contacts in the workplace. For example, workers, whether teachers or construction workers, often participate in special-purpose social clubs or unions that bring them together off the job. Informally they may congregate or socialize after work and discuss the problems of their work. Thus, in a very real sense bars, clubs, and other social situations are extensions of the work setting.

However, the segregation of social relations along class lines also involves preferences for associating with members of one's same class (see Exhibit 8.3). For example, when asked to express neighborhood preferences, nine out of ten people give a class-based answer, and there is strong preference for a neighborhood composed of people of the same or higher class (Jackman & Jackman, 1983: 195). The expressed preference for living among people of the same class is strongest among the working and middle

Exhibit 8.3
Social Class and Neighborhood Preferences

	Preference for a Neighborhood with:	
Class	Own Class Only	Own/Higher Class
Poor	20.3%	68.3%
Working	52.5	35.1
Middle	57.3	13.2
Upper middle	40.5	5.5

Source: Mary R. Jackman and Robert W. Jackman, *Class Awareness in the United States.* (Berkeley: University of California Press, 1983), Table 9.1, p. 195. Copyright © 1983 by the University of California Press.

classes; not unexpectedly, it is weakest among the poor, who would probably rather escape areas of physical deterioration.

The same study showed that most parents indicated that they would prefer their children to marry someone of the same or higher social class. People often express such feelings very directly. Speculating on future marriage partners for a child, an upper-middle-class person comments, "What sort of a husband would a carpenter be.... My viewpoint would not jibe with a carpenter. Marriage is based on equals. I would want my daughter to marry in her own class. She would go to college and would want her husband to be educated. I would want to be able to mix with in-laws and converse with them" (Laumann, 1966: 29). This quote points to an underlying dimension of class and social relations—the common belief that members of different social classes have different perspectives and values. All other things being equal, many people simply feel more comfortable with others having similar styles of life. There is also an element of status enhancement, the desire to associate with social superiors.

CLASS AND CHARACTER JUDGMENTS

The dynamics of the dominant ideology (see Chapter 4) would suggest that members of the society would attribute generally negative character traits to members of the lower classes and more positive traits to higher classes, reasoning that location in the class structure is assumed to reflect individual abilities and effort. For example, research in the 1960s suggested that a majority of Americans held the poor individually responsible for their own plight, specifically as the result of a lack of thrift or effort (Feagin, 1972). People apparently tend to construct judgments about the character of people on the basis of class position. Americans are likely to believe that intelligence, competence, and responsibility increase at each higher class level (More & Suchner, 1976; Jackman & Senter, 1982). It may be assumed that such character judgments help to explain certain patterns of interaction, such as mock jury deliberations, where it is consistently found that people at the bottom of the stratification system—unskilled workers—have the least influence on deliberations, are viewed as least helpful, and are least likely to be chosen as foreperson (Berger, et al., 1977: 4).

Although such judgments identify specific traits, they do not necessarily solidify into rigid positive or negative stereotypes (Skafte, 1989). Higher class persons may be rated smarter and more intelligent, healthier, and happier than the poor, but they are also thought of as more selfish. The poor may be judged as less intelligent, more likely to steal, and have lower self-esteem, but also as hardworking, generous, and, with an ability to handle money wisely. In short, although the poor may be perceived as less able, such a concept does not extend to the notion that they are lazy and unmotivated. Rather it suggests recognition that social position shapes character rather than the notion that character determines position. This may be interpreted as further evidence of the weakening of the salience of the ideology of individualism and opportunity.

SOCIAL DISTANCE AND INTERGROUP CONTACTS

Studies of social relations among people of color often employ the concept of social distance, a technique developed by Emory Bogardus (1926). The Bogardus *social distance scale* evaluates willingness to accept minorities in social situations representing increasing degrees of social intimacy. Social distance scores are designed to tap underlying attitudes toward social relations among different groups. Scales are formed by asking if members of the group would be accepted

as residents in the country (scored as 7)
as visitors to the country (6)
as speaking acquaintances (5)
in the same work group (4)
into the neighborhood (3)
as very good friends (2)
as marriage partners (1)

Studies spanning several decades, usually tracking attitudes among college students, reveal relatively stable patterns of social distance among racial and ethnic groups (see Exhibit 8.4). These scores represent the answers of both males and females, but as a general rule females are more tolerant than males. Relative levels of acceptance toward members of these groups have fluctuated over time, generally increasing between the 1920s and the 1960s but apparently on the decline since then (Crull & Bruton, 1985).

The data indicate that Americans are consistently most accepting of Canadians, a close geographic neighbor with a long history of peaceful

Exhibit 8.4
Social Distance Scores

	1966	1975	1984
Canadians	1.15	1.69	2.07
Italians	1.51	1.91	2.18
Germans	1.54	1.89	2.19
Blacks	2.65	2.48	2.49
Native Americans	2.12	—	2.62
Jews	1.97	2.24	2.65
Chinese	2.34	2.77	3.12
Laotians	—	—	3.66
Russians	2.38	2.97	3.85
Arabs	—	3.25	3.91

Source: Sue R. Crull and Brent T. Bruton, "Possible Decline in Tolerance Toward Minorities: Social Distance on a Midwest Campus," *Sociology and Social Research*, 70 (October 1985), 61.

relations and sharing some common socio-cultural, linguistic, and political elements. In contrast, Arabs are the least accepted, a group separated by language, culture, ignorance and stereotypes. Arab Americans have long felt that other Americans do not understand Arab people or their culture (Applebome, 1990). Moreover, they worry that the Persian Gulf War will contribute to the perpetuation of stereotyping that pictures all Arabs as either greedy oil sheiks or fanatical terrorists.

It is commonly assumed that positive contacts among diverse groups will reduce intolerance and prejudice, an idea that is called the *contact hypothesis*. This reasoning postulates a self-perpetuating process of intolerance. Social distance judgments often reflect generalizations of broad social stereotypes prevailing in the larger culture. The isolation of groups from each other further strengthens the power of stereotypes because people are separated from interpersonal contacts that have some potential to disconfirm stereotypes. The overall picture is unclear, but there is some indication that the contact hypothesis has some validity. Close and positive relations with members of minority groups apparently contribute to lower social distance scores (Crull & Bruton, 1985).

SOCIAL DISTANCE IN PRACTICE

Social distance is one overt indication of intolerance among groups, but the underlying preference for maintaining the physical and social separation is also useful in attempting to unravel a very intriguing aspect of social relationships and intergroup contacts. It may be assumed that attitudes contribute to observed patterns of social segregation among groups. Segregation takes many forms, and residential segregation is among the oldest and most enduring. Patterns of residential segregation have a long history in the United States, ranging from government-mandated reservations for native Americans to the Chinatowns, little Italys, and barrios that flourish in urban communities. Residential segregation is a complex phenomenon, often influenced by the economic implications of social class, as minorities are often concentrated among the poor. However, exclusionary practices based on color have an independent effect and continue to play a role in residential segregation. In turn, residential segregation has educational and other consequences.

Residential Segregation

Perhaps the most visible form of residential segregation occurs within urban areas as increasing numbers of people of color settle in center cities while whites move toward the suburbs, a process called polarization.[2] Since 1960, an increasing proportion of minorities makes up the population of America's largest cities, with the most dramatic increases occurring in Detroit, Newark, and New York since 1960 (Winsberg, 1986). For example, in 1960 non-Hispanic whites composed 70 percent of the population of Detroit, but had declined to 33 percent in 1980.

Residential segregation is not limited to the inner cities, for it is also commonly repeated in suburban areas (Logan & Stearns, 1981). Interpretations that suggest residential segregation reflect a combination of financial considerations, and minorities' voluntary choices is not supported. Only a small portion of the racial segregation that occurs within suburban areas can be explained by black-white income differences (Stearns & Logan, 1986). Nor can it be explained by black preferences for black neighborhoods, for most would choose integrated neighborhoods (Streitweiser & Goodman, 1983). Rather, it is necessary to focus on the workings of a *dual housing market*, in which a variety of agencies, including realtors, lending institutions, and insurance companies, channel racial groups—both overtly and subtly—into separate areas and communities. These groups, reflecting the dominant social attitudes of their communities, serve to maintain residential segregation.

Blatant racial discrimination was prohibited by the Fair Housing Act of 1968, although enforcement has been uneven, as was made evident in 1989 when the *Atlanta Journal and Constitution* reported that a review of 10 million mortgage applications showed that people of color (Asians, American Indians, Hispanics, and African Americans) were all more likely to be rejected than were whites in most communities. Differences in income did not explain these rejection rates, for high-income blacks were rejected

[2]Polarization is only one of several alternative ways of measuring residential segregation, each of which measures a different aspect of the situation. See Massey and Denton (1988) for a discussion of this issue.

more often than low-income whites in 85 of the 100 largest cities (Glastris & Minerbrook, 1989).

This is explained in part by the survival of two practices prohibited by the Fair Housing Act, redlining and steering, that perpetuated residential segregation earlier in this century. *Redlining* refers to a reluctance to grant loans or insurance for property in minority neighborhoods. The term originated when banks physically drew red lines around such areas on community maps. The distribution of homeowners' insurance suggests that residents of white and suburban neighborhoods are favored over inner-city and minority communities (Squires & Velez, 1987; 1988). *Steering* indicates the tendency to direct potential home buyers into neighborhoods dominated by members of their own race. This is perpetuated by real estate agents who fail to show residences in white neighborhoods to black potential home buyers. There is evidence that some degree of steering occurs in as many as half the encounters with realtors in some cities, both North and South (Glaster, 1990).

CASE STUDY: EDUCATIONAL SEGREGATION-
A Progress Report

Separate schools for black and white children was official policy or informal fact in many areas prior to the 1954 Supreme Court ruling in *Brown* v. *Board of Education.* School segregation was the direct outcome of residential segregation in those places where it was not legally mandated. School desegregation plans were implemented across the country, but the continuing reality of residential segregation raises the question of the success of these actions in eliminating the racial and ethnic isolation of children in the schools. Research indicates that although segregation has declined it still persists, especially in the the Northeast (U.S. Commission on Civil Rights, 1987). There are, as shown in Exhibit 8.5, still a large proportion of children in schools with overwhelming numbers (96 to 100 percent) of classmates of the same race.

Exhibit 8.5
Segregation and Integration in the Public Schools

	Proportion of Public School Students with 96-100% of Classmates of the Same Racial/Ethnic Group	
	1968	1980
Whites	63.8%	44.0%
Blacks	55.7	20.5
Hispanics	6.4	7.5

Source: U.S. Commission on Civil Rights. *New Evidence on School Desegregation.* (Washington, DC: U.S. Government Printing Office, 1987), Tables 5, 6, and 7, pp. 15-17.

The persistence of segregation has important implications. Part of the middle-class American dream is that as families improve their financial status, they will be able to move to better neighborhoods, residential areas with better homes, schools, and recreational facilities. The predicament is that it is more difficult for African Americans and Hispanics than whites to escape low-income neighborhoods as their income rises (Massey, Cordran & Denton, 1987; Hwang et al., 1985). Consequently, people of color at the same income level as whites are more likely to live in neighborhoods with fewer resources and amenities for themselves and their children.

CONCLUSION: Class, Self-Concept, and Quality of Life

A person's "work is one of the things by which he is judged and certainly one of the more significant things by which he judges himself" (Hughes, 1958: 42). Occupational position clearly evokes a number of social judgments of superiority and inferiority, manifest in occupational prestige rankings, the generalized depreciation of blue-collar work, character traits attributed to people, and preferences relating to social relations and neighborhood choices. The existence of hierarchies of social inferiority and superiority based on social class position raises the possibility that location in the stratification system could influence the way people think about themselves and influence their overall levels of well-being.

Social scientists use the generic term self-concept to describe individuals' thoughts and feelings about themselves. Self-concepts are complex and include several dimensions (Gecas, 1982). One dimension is *self-esteem*, self-evaluations of social or moral worth. Self-esteem is shaped by many factors, but it does have a social dimension, forged in interaction with others who make and transmit valuative judgments (Rosenberg, 1989). The poor, often the most socially depreciated members of society, sometimes have the least positive self-concepts (Kaplan, 1971). Those in the least prestigious work typically seek to counter judgments of inferiority, reflected in the words of a grave digger:

> Not anybody can be a grave digger....You have to make a neat job....A human body is goin' into this grave. That's why you need skill when you're gonna dig a grave....It's like a trade. It's the same as a mechanic or a doctor....A grave digger is a very important person. (Terkel, 1972: 658-660)

Unfortunately, such claims that their work is good and useful and meaningful can neither erase nor neutralize broader social judgments.

Research on self-concepts has generally demonstrated that people at each higher class level tend to have more positive feelings about themselves, although the relationship is admittedly modest (Rosenberg & Pearlin, 1978; Faunce, 1989).

Class position is also associated with various indications of psychological well-being, including "happiness" and generalized "satisfaction with life" (Bracy, 1976). Such measures of quality of life may represent the interplay between the multitude of consequences of class—economic as well as social. For black Americans, feelings of psychological well-being are lower than for whites at every class level, suggesting the continuing significance of race despite economic and educational improvements over the last several decades (Thomas & Hughes, 1986).

ADDITIONAL READINGS

On Prestige

ROBERT H. FRANK. *Choosing the Right Pond: Human Behavior and the Quest for Status*. New York: Oxford University Press, 1985.

WILLIAM J. GOODE. *The Celebration of Heroes: Prestige as Social Control System*. Berkeley: University of California Press, 1978.

THEODORE P. GREENE. *America's Heroes: Changing Models of Success in American Magazines*. New York: Oxford University Press, 1970.

PAUL M. SIEGEL, ROBERT W. HODGE, and PETER H. ROSSI. *Occupational Prestige in the United States*. New York: Academic Press, 1971.

DONALD J. TREIMAN. *Occupational Prestige in Comparative Perspective*. New York: Academic Press, 1977.

On Social Relationships

JOSEPH BERGER, M. HAMIT FISEK, ROBERT Z. NORMAN, and MORRIS ZELDITCH, JR. *Status Characteristics and Social Interaction*. New York: Elsevier, 1977.

EDWARD O. LAUMANN. *Prestige and Association in an Urban Community*. Indianapolis, IN: Bobbs-Merrill, 1966.

On Conceptions Of Self

MELVIN L. KOHN and CARMI SCHOOLER. *Work and Personality*. Norwood, NJ: Ablex, 1983.

MORRIS ROSENBERG. *Conceiving the Self*. New York: Basic Books, 1979.

Chapter 9
The Shape of Political Power and Influence

THE DISTRIBUTION OF POWER AND INFLUENCE:
Concentrated or Dispersed?

A long-standing debate about the distribution of power and influence divides observers of contemporary American society. The growth of industrial societies concentrates unusual resources in certain organizations and institutions, education, industry, the state—especially central governments—and other areas. Several specific issues are involved, but all ultimately revolve around the question of whether inordinate power and influence converge in the hands of one group, or if they are more widely distributed at different levels of the stratification system.

One group of scholars emphasizes the concentration of power. They may, for example, argue that the society is dominated by members of a single more or less unified elite. The key elements of this perspective were laid out by C. Wright Mills (1956). Writing in the aftermath of World War II he argued that three institutional sectors—corporate, government, and military—had come to dominate society and vested singular power in the hands of those who directed those structures. Moreover, they did not reflect divergent hierarchies of power so much as a single elite where the interests of the corporate sector dominated. These people shared a common perspective because, he argued, they were overwhelmingly recruited from elite and upper-middle-class backgrounds. Not only did they share a common value system, but there was a constant interchange with people circulating among the military, industry, and the government. Mills referred to this group as the "power elite," and President Dwight Eisenhower used "military-industrial complex." Despite some differences in emphasis, elite theorists argue that the state is dominated and directed by a small segment of society.

A different view is offered by pluralists, who argue that power and influence are more widely distributed. For example, the government in democratic industrial societies is an autonomous entity, responding to countless different pressure groups—business, labor, agriculture, education—competing for influence. Pluralists typically emphasize the existence of organized and well-financed special interest groups, such as trade unions and professional associations, that pursue their own agendas, but argue that no one group is ever able to prevail in all cases and on all issues. Pluralists often accept that members of the elite class may have dominated politics in the early years of the republic, but insist that paths to success are increasingly open to merit and that no one class dominates all institutions.

Several issues have attracted attention in the study of the distribution of political power and influence. One is the relative ability of members of different classes to shape government policy and political decisions, either directly by control of the political apparatus or indirectly by influencing those who occupy positions of political power. The focus on the government recognizes the power of the state in those areas that have implications for unequal distribution—tax policy, social welfare, and the regulation of business. Another is the question of access to political power, and focuses on the roles that class, color, and gender play in access to public office, elective and appointive.

THE ELITE: Patterns of Power and Influence

Members of the elite have a vested interest in maintaining the overall social, economic, and political configuration that supports their advantaged position (Domhoff, 1972). Members of the economic and institutional elite compete with other groups to influence the state, and their endeavors have been documented in some detail. Activities include direct involvement and holding elective and appointive decision-making positions in government, as well as attempts to influence the selection of political candidates and influence policy decisions. Finally, influence is exercised through a number of informal social networks that grant access to political power.

Members of the elite class are apparently able to exert a good deal of influence over the direction of political institutions. This political influence is often exercised subtly and thus avoids public scrutiny. Many would argue that this is the only way in which the elite could operate and still maintain the legitimacy of the state. Although there may be no definitive conclusion, the power of the upper segments of the stratification system cannot be underestimated.

Active Involvement in Government

Historically, high-level government positions have been dominated by people from the upper levels of the stratification system. For example, one analysis of the presidency reveals that the vast majority (82 percent) of the men to hold that office, from George Washington to George Bush, had their origins in the upper levels of the stratification system, born to elite or privileged upper-middle-class families (Pessen, 1984). The exceptions are people such as Lincoln, Eisenhower, Nixon, and Fillmore, who came from working-class or lower-middle-class origins. And Andrew Johnson, elevated to the presidency on the assassination of Lincoln, is the only chief executive of truly modest origins to hold the office.

Once elected, presidents are likely to create administrations composed of people from the elite class. Studies of cabinet-level appointees from the 1890s on follow this pattern (Mintz, 1975). Well over half, and possibly two thirds of the appointments go to members of the elite on the basis of either inherited wealth or current position in the institutional elite, usually from the corporate sector. Elite domination of the legislative branch is less clear. In the U.S. Senate perhaps one in five is a representative of the elite and fewer still in the House of Representatives (Nagle, 1977).

Wealth associated with elite status allows people to pursue political office and represents one instance of translating economic resources directly into political power. The sheer cost of political campaigns is one factor, with Senate races easily costing hundreds of thousands of dollars and literally millions in larger states. Until recently, there were no limits on how much of their own money presidential candidates could invest, and there are still no effective state limits in most legislative campaigns.

Campaign Financing

Direct financing of political campaigns is one strategy for influencing public officials. Studies of presidential campaign financing show that wealthy individuals and families have been among the largest contributors during the entire twentieth century (Lundberg, 1937; Domhoff, 1967; Allen & Broyles, 1988). The goal of such contributions may be to bolster the candidacy of a favored individual during the struggle for nomination or election, or money can be distributed to all major candidates, thus guaranteeing that they will have supported the one candidate who is eventually victorious. Campaign contributors may hope to pursue a specific agenda, or they may merely wish to ensure later access to the candidate.

Corporate contributions to political candidates through political action committees (PACs) have been legal since the mid-1970s. In 1982 PACs distributed over $43 million to office seekers at all levels of government (Burris, 1987). Most of the money spent on congressional elections seems

to be determined by one very pragmatic consideration. Seventy-four percent went to incumbents, largely because incumbents consistently win
reelection by a wide margin.Ideologically, Republican candidates are favored by a ratio of 2–1.

Organized Interest Groups

More direct political activity is through organized pressure groups.
Corporate leaders form organized pressure groups to pursue specific agendas favorable to business. These groups may be able to promote policies
that are advantageous to the corporate sector but at the expense of the
broader public. For example, business groups have been able to convince
the government to erect a whole host of trade barriers that reduce competition and result in higher prices for products. One example is a 35-cent-
per-gallon tariff on imported frozen orange juice, in effect since the 1940s
and costing consumers $525 million in higher prices each year (Work,
1989). The total cost in higher prices of all such trade barriers may amount
to $80 billion annually.

There are also much more obscure but powerful business-sponsored
groups, such as the Business Roundtable, the Business Council, the
Council on Foreign Relations, and the National Planning Association,
which seek to shape foreign policy and social welfare programs and to
forestall antibusiness legislation (Useem, 1983). The Business Roundtable
exemplifies the inner workings of political influence. Composed of about
200 executives from some of the largest industrial corporations in the
United States, the group develops policy recommendations that are distributed to members of Congress and the executive branch, and individual
members personally lobby lawmakers. A small group known as the American Conference of Governmental Industrial Hygienists is another of these
groups (see the accompanying Case Study).

Informal Mechanisms of Influence

There is also a network of national clubs and resorts where the elite
socialize informally with members of the government (Domhoff, 1974).
Among the most well known is the Bohemian Grove, an exclusive camp in
northern California with a membership that includes corporate executives
(officers of 40 of the 50 largest) and bankers (20 of the largest 25). The
guest list at one of their meetings suggests that club meetings create the
opportunity for businesspeople to influence other powerful segments of the
society: several major university presidents, two members of the
president's cabinet, the chairman of the Joint Chiefs of Staff, the president
of United Press International, and the governor of California.

CASE STUDY:
OSHA, ACGIH, and PELs

The Occupational Safety and Health Administration (OSHA) was created in 1970 to formulate rules to protect workers from exposure to hazardous substances. Scientists estimate that 60,000 chemicals used in industry pose a threat to health. Among the most notoriously dangerous are known carcinogens such as asbestos and benzene. There are "permissible exposure limits" (PELs) for approximately 600 dangerous substances that define how much of a substance may be present in the air workers breathe. For example, the current standard for formaldehyde is one molecule per million molecules of air.

Permissible exposure limits for these 600 substances were most recently updated in 1989. Eleven different groups offered chemical exposure standards to OSHA. Ultimately the limits proposed by the American Conference of Governmental Industrial Hygienists (ACGIH) prevailed because they were "most suitable." The standards for 459 of the chemicals (79 percent) copied ACGIH guidelines exactly and in some cases adopted less stringent standards than the group recommended. In addition, OSHA declined to regulate another 42 chemicals that its own scientists felt should be regulated.

It thus appears that ACGIH was instrumental in establishing the levels of exposure for 30 million American workers. Despite its formal name the group is not a government agency but rather a private group. It is alleged that virtually every member of the small group that actually wrote the standards works for the companies that make or use the chemicals in the manufacturing process, either as paid consultants or employees on loan to ACGIH. The group holds no public meetings nor routinely makes its records public, and industry representatives are regularly consulted, but not trade union representatives. Consequently, it is suggested that employees of the major chemical companies wrote the standards for some of the chemicals their firms produce.

Critics fault the quality of the research the group does, and argue that it is inappropriate for a group with ties to chemical companies to establish standards for industry. Representatives of OSHA point out that they have an obligation to strike a balance between protecting workers and creating standards that are technically and financially feasible for the chemical industry. Thus, the chemical industry has had a major influence on the shape of regulations, but the workers exposed to them have not (Bauers & Wallick, 1989).

Finally, there is in Washington, D.C., a more subtle form of institutional elite influence on the government, known as the *revolving door*, which focuses on the interchange of personnel and information between industry and government The revolving door involves former members of the government moving into private industry and sometimes back into government. Critics cite the case of the late John Tower, who after serving as chairman of the Senate Armed Services Committee earned $750,000 from a consulting firm for defense contractors and was subsequently nominated (but withdrew) as secretary of defense (Waldman, 1989). Former government officials have vital insider information and a host of personal contacts that can prove useful in influencing the course of future government actions. It is also argued that the lure of potential high-paying jobs in the future could encourage government officials to be more cooperative with industry. Another very controversial organization is Kissinger Associates, one of a number of consulting firms of former high-ranking government officials who simultaneously advise corporate clients and the U.S. government (Gerth & Bartlett, 1989).

WHITE COLLAR AND BLUE COLLAR POLITICAL ACTIVITY

The broad middle class of white- and blue-collar workers also seeks to shape political policies by working for political candidates, contributing money, and joining organized interest groups. Some are active participants in government at the national, state, and local levels. Moreover, numerically this groups holds the balance of electoral power in elections. There are, however, important class differences within this broad category, and the most consistent finding is that almost all forms of political activity and participation decrease at each lower class level.

The Upper-Middle Class In Legislatures

A very large proportion of the people who hold seats in Congress are upper middle class, coming to the House or Senate from professional, business, or managerial careers. It has, for example, long been the case that members of a single upper-middle-class occupation—law—dominate Congress (Nagle, 1977). It seems that their position in local constituencies gives them a major advantage in the political arena. An upper-middle-class position grants them a whole host of advantages—time, income, social prestige, lifestyle, administrative experiences, and social contacts—that enable them to become active in local civic and political activities. Consequently, many eventually seek or are recruited into national public office. One consequence of this situation is that upper-middle-class interests receive special attention in Congress, as reflected in some elements of the tax laws, such as the ability to deduct second home mortgage interest or tax sheltered income.

Direct participation in the sense of holding political office is rare among members of the lower middle and working classes. Time and resources are a factor, but so too is the work situation. Working-class jobs seldom provide people with the opportunities to develop skills in directing and managing others.

Organized Interest Groups

A number of white- and blue-collar interest groups are active in the political sphere. Several of the wealthiest PACs are organized around upper-middle-class occupations. For example, medical, legal, and realtor

Exhibit 9.1
PAC Political Contributions, 1989

PAC	Spent	Cash on Hand
Teamsters	$3.6 million	$4.5 million
American Medical Assoc.	1.5	1.6
Realtors	2.7	2.2
National Education Assoc.	0.8	2.6
United Auto Workers	1.0	2.3
Auto Dealers	0.9	2.2
Assoc. of Trial Lawyers	1.2	0.9
AFSCME	1.3	0.6
AT & T	1.5	0.4

Source: Federal Election Commission, *Annual Report, 1990* (Washington, DC: U.S. Government Printing Office, 1991).

PACs each dispensed at least $1 million to candidates in 1989 (see Exhibit 9.1) and had another million dollar on hand for future campaigns (Kalette, 1990). Broader based class interests are also represented in the political process through unions that mount large PACs. Among them are the Teamsters, the United Auto Workers and the American Federation of State, County and Municipal Employees (white- and blue-collar government workers). The Teamsters is in fact the wealthiest single PAC, with $4.5 million on hand even after spending $3.6 million in 1989.

VOTING AND POLITICAL PARTICIPATION

The public exerts some influence over the course of government action by choosing among candidates for political office. Despite its powerful democratic traditions, the United States has a relatively low level of overall participation in the electoral process when compared to that in other industrial democracies. Voter turnout is typically less than 60 percent of all adults, lagging well behind Italy, Netherlands, Belgium, Australia, Sweden, Germany, and Norway, countries where voting averages are above 80 percent (Jackman, 1987).

Many factors influence voter turnout: class, education, income, and age. The data in Exhibit 9.2 report voting patterns in the 1988 presidential election, where only about 57 percent of adults over 18 went to the polls. There is a clear relationship between social class and voting, especially at the upper and lower reaches of the stratification system. The highest rates of participation are found among the upper middle class, with approximately three quarters of both managers and professionals casting votes. Turnout among the lower middle class ranges between 60 and 65 percent. Less than half of the working class turns out, and the lowest

Exhibit 9.2
Patterns of Voter Turnout, Presidential Election 1988

Percentage of Persons 18 and Older Who Voted		57.4%
Class/occupation		
Upper middle	Professional	78.2%
	Managerial	72.0
Lower middle	Technical	65.6
	Clerical	63.7
	Sales	60.5
Working	Craft	47.2
	Operative	40.3
The poor	Unskilled	38.2
	Service	47.6
	Domestic	40.7
	Unemployed	38.6
Sex		
Women		58.3
Men		56.4
Color		
White		59.1
Black		51.5
Hispanic		28.8

Source: U.S. Bureau of the Census, *Voting and Registration in the Election of November, 1988,* Current Population Reports, P-20, No. 440 (Washington, DC: U.S. Government Printing Office, 1989), Table 11, pp. 60–63.

levels are found among the poor. The service sector of the poor has the highest level of participation, similar to that of blue-collar operatives.

Voter turnout among African Americans (51 percent) still lags behind that of whites (59 percent). Such voting patterns reflect, in part, the concentration of blacks in the working class, which has a lower than average rate of participation among all groups. In contrast, Hispanics tend to have a very low overall level of voter turnout, as shown in the 1988 presidential election in which less than 30 percent voted. The low Hispanic vote is a complex phenomenon and has a number of sources (Conway, 1985). It must be remembered that approximately one third of the population is ineligible because they are not yet citizens. Hispanics are over-represented among the poor and the less skilled segments of the working class. Language is a barrier for others, distancing them from involvement in the process; and in some cases, literacy tests are conducted in English.

In addition, a high proportion of Hispanics are young, and political participation is consistently low among younger people in all groups.

Voter turnout is but one measure of involvement in the political
process. Others include keeping abreast of political matters, contributing
money, and becoming actively involved in political campaigns. All follow
the same general pattern found in voter turnout: The very lowest levels of
involvement tend to be found at the lowest levels of the stratification
system.

GENDER IN THE POLITICAL SPHERE

Some individual women have gained positions of significant political
power, but as a group women hold a relatively modest share of political
power. Less than 5 percent of the seats in Congress are held by women,
which is low compared to some other Western nations, such as Norway,
Sweden, and Denmark, where women occupy between one quarter and one
third of the seats in the national legislative body (Randall, 1987). Female
representation at the state and local levels is higher, with women holding
about 20 percent of the elective offices. This is underrepresentation by any
criteria, but when viewed in historical perspective, it might well be understood as the legacy of an earlier era in American politics. A longer term
perspective suggests a pattern of increasing access to elective and appointive office and a broadening of political influence.

The rarity of women in the political hierarchy until late in the
twentieth century reflected the convergence of a number of processes.
There was, for one, the social division of labor between home and work,
which extended to the political arena. As recently as 1972, a majority of
Americans felt that women should concentrate their energies on the home
and family and "leave running the country up to men" (Lipman-Bluman,
1984: 189). Then, too, women's class position worked to their disadvantage,
with relatively small numbers of women in the upper-middle-class occupations (business and the professions) that have been the traditional
recruiting ground for political candidates.

Women in the bureaucracies of political institutions suffered the
same discrimination that occurred in other spheres. For example, as
recently as 1985 just 3 percent of senior officials in the State Department
were women when the courts ruled that the State Department had a
history of discrimination against women by hiring smaller numbers and
giving them less visible and prestigious assignments and lower performance ratings, thus hindering their advancement toward high-level
policymaking positions (Gamarekian, 1989). The exclusion of women from
decision-making positions in public administration is not confined to the
United States. More women are embarking on careers in government all
over the world but continue to be concentrated at the lowest levels, a

situation that did not improve in any significant way during the 1980s (United Nations, 1991: 35).

Although access to formal political office may be obstructed, women have long played a major leadership role in grass-roots and local community organizations. These groups have targeted civil rights, environmental issues, industrial pollution, poverty, the declining quality of schools, peace, and the deterioration of neighborhoods (Lipman-Bluman, 1984). Two notable examples are the reforestation movement in Kenya, spearheaded by poor rural women, and the clean up of the toxic waste site at Love Canal, led by working class women (United Nations, 1991).

By the 1970s a number of groups such as the National Women's Political Caucus were formed to promote political participation. Women increased their involvement in party politics at the community and state levels and began seeking elective office in ever greater numbers. The combination of grass-roots experiences and success in lower level offices usually provides the seasoning and credibility necessary to seek higher political office. Thus, during the 1980s women were able to make significant progress in gaining access to positions of political power, both elected and appointive. Today women hold positions in Congress and the cabinet and in every state legislature, and they are governors and mayors.

The broadening of political sensitivity of women is also reflected in voting patterns (see Exhibit 9.2). Women are currently somewhat more likely to vote than are men, a trend that first appeared late in the 1970s. Prior to that point men were more likely to vote than were women. Women divided their vote almost equally between Bush and Dukakis in the 1988 presidential election, but generally tend to support the Democratic party. This is apparently partly influenced by the interaction of class and gender, with women more likely to hold jobs at the lower levels of the class system.

There is also some indication that gender is losing its saliency as a factor in choosing among candidates. Beginning in 1937 the Gallup organization posed this question, "If your party nominated a women for president, would you vote for her if she were qualified for the job?" At that point only 31 percent agreed, but the proportion has since soared to 80 percent. The idea that female gender traits render women less suitable for the demands of political office plays a role in explaining the origins of this belief, the notion that is a discrepancy between the assumed traits of women and the assumed skills required in politics (self-reliance, decision making). Definitions of a "good" president still favor masculine traits (Rosenwasser and Dean, 1988; Rosenwasser & Seale, 1989). Hence the socialization process would tend to discourage political activity and political careers, and those who were interested faced the opposition of party officials.

Obviously, polls and attitude surveys have limits, and the question of actual gender bias in the voting booth is much more difficult to measure. Comparing the success of women candidates against men is not easy because so many factors impinge on voters' decisions that it is difficult to apportion the exact influence of the sex of the candidates. Actually there are some indications that the sex of the candidate is not inevitably a major factor for most voters: men and women candidates are often evaluated in the same manner. Party preference is the major determinant of voting, but voters will cross party lines to vote for a candidate perceived as strong or against a weak candidate—whether woman or man (Zipp & Plutzer, 1985).

Once in positions of political influence, there is the different question of women's impact on public policy. Although the evidence is unclear, there is some indication that female officeholders have some impact on opening public employment to women (Saltzstein, 1986). A longitudinal evaluation of the situation in one state may portend the future (Saint-Germain, 1989). Women legislators in Arizona initiated more proposals than men having to do with "feminist" issues—promoting equality and improving the status of women, and as the proportion of women in the legislature increased, were more likely to be successful in having them enacted. However, their influence was clearly not confined to gender issues, for over time women contributed legislation in all areas of public policy and were somewhat more successful than male legislators in these neutral areas also. If this case is at all representative it suggests that increasing numbers of women in political office will have a discernible impact on the shape of public policy.

MINORITIES IN THE POLITICAL SPHERE

The 1960s are remembered for the violence produced by attempts to break down the barriers to black participation in government. Prohibitive poll taxes, stringent literacy tests, closed primaries, and outright intimidation were employed to deny the vote. Massive voter registration drives supported by the Voting Rights Acts of 1965 enfranchised hundreds of thousands of new voters. There has also been a shifting of public attitudes, with a majority of voters expressing a willingness to support a well-qualified black presidential candidate (Gallup Report, 1979). This has contributed to a significant increase in political representation among people of color at some levels. Between 1979 and 1990 black elected officials increased from 4,600 to 7,200 and Hispanic from about 1,500 to over 4,000 (Mydans, 1991). In 1990, 11 of the 20 largest cities in the United States were run by people of color. Minorities have been less successful in statewide elections (e.g., governors, senators). In the twentieth century there have been one black senator and one black governor, four Hispanic governors, and two Hispanic senators elected (Sonenshein, 1990).

Black candidates have been able to win elective office despite the fact that they are generally at a disadvantage in fund-raising. For example, in Democratic House of Representatives races in 1984, white challengers were able to amass an average of $399,298 compared to $117,866 for black challengers (Smith, 1988). A major part of the difference reflects the actions of PACs that contribute more money to whites than blacks.

Lower overall minority turnout has been noted, but that does not mean that these groups are not a significant political force, especially in those areas where they form a meaningful segment of the population. This is evident among the Hispanic population. The six states with the largest Hispanic populations—California, Texas, Florida, New York, Illinois, and New Jersey—had 173 of the 270 electoral votes needed to win the 1988 election (Valdivieso & Davis, 1988: 12). Consequently, both presidential candidates openly and aggressively attempted to appeal to Hispanic voters. The growth of the Latino population in these states has the potential to give them even greater political leverage into the 1990s.

The election of minority candidates to public office is of inestimable symbolic value, validating the increasing openness of the political system. However, a more salient issue is the practical effects of black voters and black representation on specific government policies. The overall evidence is unclear, but some research has focused on an issue of long-standing concern to African Americans—the structure and functioning of police departments. Some police departments, like many other organizations, once systematically discriminated against minority employment and were often socially distanced from minority communities. Moreover, incidents of white police mistreatment of black citizens continue to surface. Hence progress in this area would seem to be a vital component in fostering interracial tolerance.

A comprehensive review of police department activities suggests that certain kinds of innovations in policing practices are more likely to emerge in communities with black political involvement (Saltzstein, 1989). For example, cities with large black populations of potential voters are more likely to have community outreach programs (storefront offices, meetings with black community groups) and a policy of measured responses (mediation as opposed to arrest) to disturbances of the peace. Communities with black mayors make more progress with minority representation on the police force and in the institution of civilian review boards. Thus it appears that African American political strength in the form of votes or elected representation does have the potential under the right circumstances to translate into specific programs.

Party preference also reflects the interaction of class and ethnicity. Support for the Democratic party has been consistently stronger among those at the lower levels of the stratification system. Black Americans tend to identify as Democrats by a margin of eight to one. Hispanics nationwide also tend to support the Democratic candidate, with the exception of Cubans, many of whom are political refugees and favor the stronger anti-communist stance of the Republican party.

CONCLUSION: Class and Political Alienation

One of the more notable trends over the last several decades is the widespread erosion of public support and confidence in America's political system (Lipset & Schneider, 1983). Often broadly referred to as *political alienation*, it actually combines at least two separate dimensions (Mason, House & Martin, 1985). One is sometimes called *disaffection*, the belief that the government is uncaring, inattentive, and untrustworthy (Herring, 1989: 49–50). By way of comparison, in the mid-1960s two out of three Americans felt that the activities of government were directed toward "the benefit of all people," but this perception has fallen to the point where it is now endorsed by only about one in five. Similarly, while earlier a majority of the public (76 percent) expressed trust in government, more recent surveys indicate that only one quarter say they trust their government.

Disaffection focuses on feelings of trust, but there is also the more pragmatic issue of *efficacy*, beliefs about one's ability to influence or have an impact on the political process or activities of government. A lack of efficacy means a sense of powerlessness. Powerlessness is unmistakable in feelings that special interest groups have too much control or that political leaders are out of touch with the people.

The observed increases in political alienation are shaped by many factors, including some that touch all levels of the stratification system. Recurring public scandals (Watergate, Iran-Contra, savings and loan) have a broad negative impact on faith in government. Moreover, specific government actions produce patterns of dissatisfaction among different segments of the population (Herring, 1989). Reductions in social welfare spending increase feelings of political disaffection among the poor, and members of the elite and upper middle classes are alienated by reductions in government subsidies to industry (e.g., tax credits, grants of land or property). Political disaffection among the lower middle and working classes increases with corporate profits and levels of debt. Thus, government actions that bring benefits to one class are likely to engender dissatisfaction among other segments of society.

As would be expected, disaffection and efficacy tend to be linked, and the general pattern that emerges is that people at each lower level in the stratification system feel more alienated, with greater feelings of disaffection and lower perceptions of effectiveness (Verba, Nie & Kim, 1978). Class position shapes alienation in many subtle ways. More education means greater familiarity with the dynamics of the political process, and having more money to contribute to candidates increases a sense of involvement and direction It has also been suggested that the work of most people below the level of the upper middle class does not give them much experience with the exercise of power. The resulting lack of power in the economic sector may contribute to more general feelings of powerlessness in the political sector.

The irony is that political alienation is in part self-perpetuating in the sense that feelings of powerlessness can contribute to the failure to engage in the very activities—voting, political organization—that might have an impact and produce a feeling of having some control over the political process. Consequently, class position contributes to feelings of alienation and in turn reduces the effectiveness of the least advantaged classes. At the other extreme, a sense of control can stimulate even greater political effort, which in turn produces a greater effect on the political process (Herring, 1989: 99). This is evident in cities with black mayors (Bobo & Gilliam, 1990). In those communities the levels of political knowledge and political participation among blacks are higher than among blacks in other cities and higher than among whites at comparable class levels. This suggests that blacks in leadership positions instill a greater sense of efficacy and stimulate greater involvement.

ADDITIONAL READINGS

On Class and Politics

BENJAMIN I. PAGE. *Who Gets What from Government?* Berkeley: University of California Press, 1983.

MARK GREEN. *Who Runs Congress?* New York: Bantam, 1979.

CEDRIC HERRING. *Splitting the Middle: Political Alienation, Acquiescence, and Activism Among America's Middle Layers.* New York: Praeger, 1989.

JOSEPH KLING and PRUDENCE POSNER, eds. *Dilemmas of Activism: Class, Community, and the Politics of Local Mobilization.* Philadelphia: Temple University Press, 1990.

SEYMOUR MARTIN LIPSET and WILLIAM SCHNEIDER. *The Confidence Gap: Business, Labor, and Government in the Public Mind.* New York: Free Press, 1983.

MICHAEL USEEM. *The Inner Circle: Large Corporations and the Rise of Political Activity in the U.S and U.K.* New York: Oxford University Press, 1984.

On Gender and Politics

ROBERT Darcy, SUSAN WELCH, and JANET CLARK. *Women, Elections and Representation.* New York: Longman, 1987.

IRENE DIAMOND. *Sex Roles in the State House.* New Haven, CT: Yale University Press, 1977.

CYNTHIA FUCHS EPSTEIN and ROSE LAUB COSER, eds. *Access to Power: Cross-National Studies of Women and Elites.* London: Allen & Unwin, 1981.

VICKY RANDALL. *Women and Politics: An International Perspective.* Chicago: University of Chicago Press, 1987.

On Minorities and Politics

F. CHRIS GARCIA and RUDOLOPH O. DE LA GARZA. *The Chicano Political Experience.* North Scituate, MA: Duxbury Press, 1977.

ALBERT K. KARNIG and SUSAN WELCH. *Black Representation and Urban Policy.* Chicago: University of Chicago Press, 1980.

JOAN MOORE and HARRY PACHON. *Hispanics in the United States.* Englewood Cliffs, NJ: Prentice Hall, 1985.

Part Four

Inheritance
and Social Mobility

A key aspect of the dominant ideology of American society affirms that upward social mobility is based on individual effort and ability unfettered by modest social class origins, a perspective that has attracted and sustained generations of immigrants. Yet parental position in the stratification system is not irrelevant, influencing the educational and occupational attainments of children. This chapter explores the direct and subtle ways that class, color, and gender can facilitate or hinder movement across class lines.

Chapter 10
Patterns of Social Mobility

SOCIAL MOBILITY: Closed Versus Open Systems

Children invariably inherit their initial location in the stratification system from their parents. Each child begins life with economic resources, social rank, and lifestyles shaped by the class position of their parents. The study of social mobility focuses on experiences of individuals over the course of their lives. *Social mobility* is formally defined as the movement of individuals and groups from one level in the stratification system to another (either upward or downward). Mobility may be tracked in two different ways. One approach, *intergenerational mobility*, compares the social position of parents to that of their children. The other approach is *intragenerational mobility*, movement occurring during the life cycle of individuals.[1]

---

[1] There are a number of methodological and conceptual problems inherent in the study of intergenerational social mobility. Two problems deserve special mention, for the conventions followed in research sometimes limit the usefulness of the findings. One problem is defining the point in careers at which to measure social class position, for people experience intragenerational mobility during their own careers. One common way of handling this is to focus on parental class at the time the child is in the 14- to 18-year-old range, assuming that this is the age at which the most consequential educational and occupational paths are followed. Another issue is the question of determining the class position of the parental generation. Originally most research focused on pairs of individuals, for example, fathers to sons. This narrow approach tended to ignore daughters and the role of mothers in the socialization process, typically based either on the assumption that the husband was the "head of the household" and his occupation determined the class position of the family or that fewer married women occupied a long-term position in the paid labor market, obviously not true especially for women from the lower level of the stratification system. More recent studies are exploring four different combinations of individuals—fathers to sons and daughters, mothers to sons and daughters and the interaction among the different combinations.

Intergenerational Mobility

Stratification systems differ in the extent to which one generation's accomplishments and opportunities are determined by those of their parents. In the analysis of social mobility, it is useful to think of stratification systems falling along a continuum from open to closed.

Closed Systems

In several of the fundamental types of systems described in Chapter 3, parental position has fixed and permanent consequences for subsequent generations, confining them to the level of their birth. In caste systems, for example, group membership is hereditary, and it is virtually impossible for individuals to hope to succeed by their own efforts. Consequently, social class is an *ascribed* position and such arrangements are described as *closed* stratification systems. Closed systems are much more likely to be found in stable agricultural societies and tend to be threatened by the process of industrialization.

Closed systems are organized to perpetuate privilege. Structural barriers are erected through law or custom to ensure that higher level positions are closed to all except the children of the advantaged. Educational systems may be segregated along caste lines, denying lower level children access to the skills and credentials that might allow them to challenge for more advantageous positions. Such practical barriers are buttressed and legitimized by prevailing sociocultural ideas and beliefs. A common feature of closed systems are ideologies that posit some intrinsic divisions along class lines. Theories of genetic inferiority (e.g., racism) claim the existence of inherent biological differences among the classes that predispose members of groups for certain levels at birth. Aristocracies usually claim the right to rule on the basis of a combination of breeding (biological) and training (social) disparities. Rulers in medieval estate systems sometimes declared divine support for their power. Each of these ideologies supports the continuation of stable patterns of inequality through time and generations.

Open Systems

In a completely *open* system—admittedly an ideal type—there are no formal or ideological barriers to mobility, and people rise or fall (relative to their parents) on the basis of their own abilities and efforts. Social class position is thus an *achieved* status. In short, there is no causal link between the levels occupied by parents and children.

All democratic industrial class systems tend toward openness, and some mobility can be traced to the shifting economic patterns accompanying urbanization and industrialization (Hauser et al., 1975; Robinson,

1984; Slomczynski & Krauze, 1987). Broad demographic and technological changes typically stimulate restructuring of the underlying economic system, which in turn produces alterations in the stratification system by creating opportunities for movement between generations. In the early stages of industrialization the most profound transformation is the shift from agriculture to manufacturing and rural workers and small farm owners move into the urban working class. For many, considering the pay and working conditions in the urban factories, movement into the working class can be defined as collective downward mobility. Subsequent technological and organizational changes that create the clerical lower middle class provide opportunities for the children of working-class parents to improve their positions. Later the burgeoning of technologically based upper-middle-class occupations creates new channels of mobility. Advanced stages of industrialization in some nations bring the decline of the manufacturing sector, shrinking opportunities for stable working-class positions. Broad overall patterns will, of course, be modified by economic and political considerations.

These patterns are usually referred to as *structural mobility*, movement due to shifting class patterns and the consequent expanding and contracting of opportunities. Structural mobility is also called "forced mobility" to emphasize the notion that macroeconomic changes compel intergenerational movement. That is, the opening or closing of positions constrains children to take different positions than their parents. For example, the contraction of the agricultural sector means that some sons and daughters of rural parents must find employment in the urban labor market.

Industrialization also tends to be accompanied by the weakening of institutional barriers to social mobility, allowing people to experience what is called *circulation mobility*. Circulation mobility is explained by differences in education, opportunities, effort, ability, and luck. Among the most important factors facilitating circulation mobility is the evolution of educational systems open to children of disadvantaged classes, women, and people of color. This, plus the spread of political rights, have moved democratic industrial societies toward increasing opportunities for circulation mobility. Consequently, there is some indication of certain broad similarities in patterns of mobility in all advanced market industrial systems (Kerckhoff, Campbell & Winfield-Laird, 1985; Goldthorpe, Llewellyn & Payne, 1987).

The Crucial Role of Educational Credentials

Formal educational credentials play a decisive role in understanding both inheritance and social mobility, especially at the upper reaches of the stratification system. Inherited wealth among the elite carries with it inherent power, but passing on positions of power in the institutional elite increasingly requires the legitimation and validation of education. It is also readily apparent that virtually all upper-middle-class positions demand protracted formal education. Most of those lacking advanced formal education are effectively barred from access to these classes.

Intragenerational Mobility

Intragenerational mobility focuses on changes in class position that occur during the careers of individuals and groups. Intragenerational mobility is measured by movement upward, laterally or downward among jobs or careers. It is also affected by structural changes. Shifts in the economy close out opportunities for some while opening them for others. For a large number of people, downward mobility is precipitated by the loss of a job followed by reentry at a lower level in the system.

PATTERNS OF INTERGENERATIONAL MOBILITY

America is often thought of as the epitome of an open system, a society in which individual effort and ability rather than family background determine location in the stratification system. This is, of course, the basic tenet of the "dominant ideology," and it is relatively easy to find examples that verify this vision by citing the sons and daughters of immigrant parents who subsequently rise to the top of the political or corporate world. However, moving beyond such anecdotal evidence reveals a more complex picture. A broader, more comprehensive view of the total society suggests that the United States is both a fluid system with people circulating between levels, but also a stable system with a sizable share of children inheriting the same class level of their parents.

Fathers and Children

The occupational attainments of a sample of African American and white American males during the 1980s is summarized in Exhibit 10.1, with inheritance of social class position lying along the diagonal, highlighted for ease of analysis. The broad overall patterns in this study provide a useful context for the analysis of intergenerational mobility. The stability of the system is confirmed by the proportion of sons who remain at the same level as their fathers, but inheritance is clearly more pronounced at some levels than at others. The dynamic aspect of the stratification system is revealed by the number of sons who move relative to their fathers. Some mobility is upward with sons able to rise into higher level positions and some is downward, with sons falling relative to their fathers. Blacks generally do less well than whites, experiencing more downward mobility, less upward movement, and are more likely to remain in the lowest positions.

Exhibit 10.1
Patterns of Intergenerational Mobility among Males
in the United States: From Fathers to Sons

Father's Occupation	Son's Class Position				
	Upper White Collar	Lower White Collar	Upper Manual	Lower Manual	Farm
Upper White Collar					
White	59.3%	7.0%	14.2%	18.0%	1.5%
Black	37.0	9.3	16.7	37.0	.0
Lower White Collar					
White	48.1	10.8	15.2	25.3	.6
Black	42.1	15.8	21.1	21.1	.0
Upper Manual					
White	36.0	5.5	33.7	23.5	1.2
Black	18.2	8.0	33.0	40.7	.0
Lower Manual					
White	28.8	6.7	26.7	36.9	1.1
Black	17.9	12.1	19.6	50.4	.0
Farm					
White	24.9	4.6	22.1	25.8	17.1
Black	9.6	2.6	22.4	55.8	9.6
Totals					
White	40.4	6.3	23.3	25.4	4.9
Black	18.3	8.5	22.4	48.1	2.8

Source: Theodore J. Davis, Jr., "Social Mobility of African Americans in the 1980s: A Controversy Revisited." Unpublished paper, Department of Political Science, University of Delaware, 1991.

Variations at each level modify the overall patterns. Intergenerational inheritance is high among upper white-collar occupations, suggesting that parents can provide their children with important advantages in the competition for positions. Access to higher education is a factor but so too are more subtle attitudinal factors. Such advantages are certainly no guarantee of success because downward mobility also occurs. Black and white differences are pronounced at this level. African American sons are significantly less able to achieve the level of their fathers and dramatically more likely to experience downward mobility, with one third in lower manual jobs. The rate of movement from lower white collar positions is extraordinary with very few sons inheriting this position from their fathers. Approximately 40 percent are able to achieve managerial or professional positions and another 40 percent move downward into blue-collar or service occupations. The overall picture for blacks and whites is more similar at this level than at any other level. One in three African American and white sons occupy upper manual positions just as their fathers do. White males have more success (36 percent) in moving into upper white collar jobs than black males (18 percent) and blacks are also almost twice as likely to move downward. Approximately one third of white sons remain at the bottom of the stratification system, but a majority are able to improve on the position of their fathers with a large number achieving upper white-collar positions. The experiences of blacks is much more modest with one half continuing at the same level as their fathers.

The intergenerational experiences of African Americans reflect both progress and stagnation over the last three decades. Mobility opportunities for black Americans began to expand in the 1960s reflecting changes occurring in the larger society that began to weaken institutional barriers to social mobility (Hoult, 1984A; 1984B; Tickamyer & Blee, 1990). Prior to the era of emerging civil rights legislation, the significance of race overwhelmed all other considerations in determining the occupational attainments of blacks. It was a rigid and closed system (Featherman & Hauser, 1978). Most children of black parents could only look forward to inheriting positions at the lower reaches of the class structure. Even children of the small black middle class frequently experienced downward mobility. Consequently, parental social class was largely irrelevant because both educational and occupational attainments were capped by considerations of color.

The gradual opening of middle-class occupations has begun to render the system increasingly open to blacks, especially those with advanced educational credentials. However, African Americans as a group continue to face institutional barriers to mobility and continue to achieve more modest occupational attainments at each educational level than do whites. Although overall rates of mobility are lower, the impact of parental social class and gender seems to act in the same way that it does for whites, meaning that children of higher class blacks are advantaged over lower class blacks in both academic and occupational achievements.

The occupational destinations of daughters relative to fathers reveal both differences and similarities between male and female patterns (Tyree & Treas, 1974; Hauser et al., 1975; Chase, 1975; Rosenfeld, 1978; Beck, 1983; Stevens, 1986; Goldthorpe et al., 1987). Comparing employed sons and daughters shows similar overall patterns. Children at most levels show a tendency to inherit the position of their parents and a large proportion of mobility occurs between adjacent classes. The most notable difference between sons and daughters is that women experience more mobility and that downward mobility exceeds upward mobility. Larger numbers of upper white-collar daughters than sons end up in lower white-collar or service collar work. In very large part this is a function of sex-segregated occupational opportunities that causes a disproportionate number of women to be limited to positions at lower levels in the stratification system.

Mothers and Children

More recent research has also begun to examine the role of mothers in understanding the process of intergenerational mobility, but the findings are less consistent. There is some indication that fathers' occupation has a more pronounced impact on the subsequent attainments of children than mothers', in part because men tend to earn more and occupy higher-level positions and can pass these advantages on to their daughters as well as their sons (Boyd, 1982; Stevens, 1986). However, it is also clear that the employment status of mothers can be a decisive factor, stimulating higher occupational attainments among both white and African American daughters, but not among sons (Tickamyer & Blee, 1990). It is believed that the presence of an employed mother in the family provides daughters with a model of occupational attainment. Overall, this research suggests that children are most likely to inherit the class position of the same-sex parent, implying a stronger bond between fathers and sons and between mothers and daughters when occupational aspirations are formed. Much more research is needed to unravel the complex interaction among parental and offspring gender and social mobility.

INTERGENERATIONAL MOBILITY PROCESSES: Status Attainment

Attempts to understand patterns of social mobility focus on a set of background, attitudinal, cognitive, and educational factors that influence social class attainments. This body of research, known as the *status attainment* approach, emphasizes that level of formal educational attainment is the single most important factor in explaining occupational attainments, at least among white males. This research tradition follows a basic model that isolates some of the most important factors enhancing or impeding educational attainments and subsequent occupational attainments, as shown in Exhibit 10.2.

The basic reasoning has a clear logic to it, emphasized by proceeding from outcomes to sources:

1. Occupational attainments are strongly influenced by educational credentials.
2. Educational attainments are, in part, shaped by the level of educational and occupational aspirations.
3. Aspirations are raised by the support and encouragement of "significant others" (parents, teachers).
4. Encouragement and support increase with levels of academic performance.
5. Academic performance is directly related to mental ability; and academic ability is related to the social class of parents.

Exhibit 10.2
The Status Attainment Model

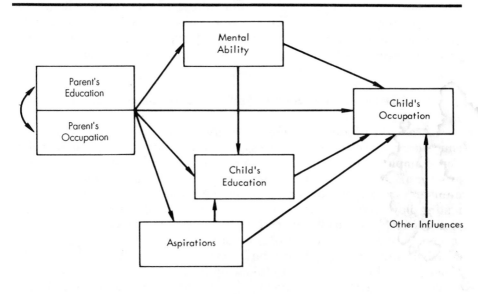

It must be emphasized that these relationships are more complex than suggested by this graphic representation. First, relationships can be interactive. For example, while higher educational aspirations can inspire higher attainments, rising scholastic attainments can encourage ever higher aspirations. Thus, continued academic success can stimulate a subsequent rise in aspirations, and likewise, repeated failure has the potential to dampen aspirations. Second, residual values (the impact of other factors) are large, meaning that other considerations beyond those contained in the model impinge upon the process.

As would be expected, in the long run educational attainments are decisive, especially higher education. Social class origins have very modest effects for those who complete college. However, social class background is very relevant in shaping educational credentials. Perhaps the most striking finding is that parental class is the single most important factor influencing children's ultimate occupational attainments by having an effect on each of the other factors, accounting for one half the variance by some estimates (Jencks et al., 1979: 214). Thus, parental class touches every dimension of the status attainment process.

There have been numerous challenges to the status attainment approach. The most crucial is that it ignores the structural context of aspirations and achievements (e.g., Knottnerus, 1987). Aspirations and attainments are limited by factors beyond the control of both parents and children. Moreover, attention to overall patterns often conceals the fact that people of color and women frequently earn lower returns on their educational and occupational attainments. The observed tendency for children of one generation to remain in the class of their parents raises the question of isolating the factors that limit opportunity and place some individuals at an advantage and others at some disadvantage.

Social Class and Academic Ability: Standardized Testing

Academic ability is an elusive concept, but for a variety of reasons educators have settled on batteries of standardized tests as measures of it. For example, public schools administer 105 million tests each year, an average of 2.5 tests per student per year (Leslie & Wingert, 1990: 56). These numbers are merely an indication of the major role that standardized testing plays in the educational system in the United States. Standardized tests are employed to allocate children among curricula within schools and to advise students and are a factor in college admissions. Perhaps the most decisive standardized tests are the Scholastic Aptitude Test (SAT) and the American College Test (ACT) taken by hundreds of thousands of high school seniors each year in the hope of gaining admission to the college of their choice. It is estimated that 90 percent all colleges and universities require SATs or ACTs as at least part of the admission process; and subsequent incarnations factor into access to graduate school (GREs) and professional schools (LSAT). To many observers, standardized tests stand as symbols of the structural barriers to educational opportunity that exist in the society. There are now, and have been for decades, pronounced differences in scores associated with class, race, and gender (Carmody, 1989).

Using either parental income or parental education as a measure of social class standing shows that average SAT scores increase dramatically at each higher level. To illustrate, the average score of students whose family income is $10,000 or less—families living in poverty—is 780, compared to scores of 996 for the children of parents in the $70,000 plus bracket. Considerations of gender and color are also associated with variations in average test scores. There is a gender gap, with males outscoring females by an average of 50 points; and although members of minority groups have made relatively large gains in recent years, all except Asian Americans continue to lag behind the white majority.

Such tests at best measure only certain types of abilities—verbal and mathematical skills—and ignore skills and abilities such as creativity, inventiveness, and imagination. In addition, critics have argued that these tests are biased against the lower classes, women, and minority groups (Weiss, 1989). Bias can affect outcomes in one of two ways. First, the very content of questions may be more familiar to males and affluent students exposed to more elaborate environments. Second, despite some misconceptions, the tests do not measure "innate intelligence" so much as they reflect the preparation and training of students. An executive of one testing agency acknowledges that college entrance examination scores "reflect the inequities that continue to exist in our society (and) disparities in academic preparation" (Ordovensky, 1989).

CASE STUDY:
Gender Questions

Men tend, on the average, to outperform women on standardized tests. There are consistent patterns within this overall discrepancy. Males perform better on questions dealing with sports and business, while females excel on those focusing on social relationships. Specific test questions illustrate this, with women likely to do better on Question 1 and men on Question 2 (Berger, 1989).

1. **Antonyms**

   IRK
   a) dilate
   b) inhibit
   c) reflect
   d) soothe
   e) confront

2. **Comparisons**

   DIVIDENDS:STOCKHOLDERS
   a) investments:corporations
   b) purchases:customers
   c) taxes:workers
   d) royalties:authors
   e) mortgages:homeowners

The correct answer to both questions is d.

Asian Americans and Test Scores

Asian Americans' college entrance test scores rival those of all other groups and consistently outrank others on the math section of the SATs, leading to Asian Americans being labeled the "model minority."[2] Asian American success has been traced to high levels of academic effort and in turn to cultural traditions. In a survey of San Francisco area high school students it was found that female Asian Americans spent an average of 12.3 hours per week doing homework, compared to 9.2 for blacks and 8.6

---

[2]It is important to note that immigration since the mid-1960s has brought large numbers of college-educated professional and technical Asian parents to the United States, and they are likely to value formal education and be able to provide their children with the financial and cultural advantages that all upper-middle-class families can (Hirschman & Wong, 1986). Moreover, this label overgeneralizes and conceals differences within this group (Hurh & Kim, 1989). As noted earlier the term Asian American includes peoples of diverse ethnic and national origins whose experiences are very often quite different. In addition, focusing on the successful within any group ignores the less fortunate, the aged, and the poor within that group.

for whites (Butterfield, 1986: 19). Comparable figures for males were 11.7 for Asian Americans, 6.3 for blacks and 8.0 for whites. Moreover, Asian American students had consistently better attendance records and cut classes less frequently.

It appears that Asian American parents at all economic and social class levels seek to instill a high level of dedication to educational attainment in their children. At a general level this reflects the influence of Asian culture, specifically Confucian philosophy, which emphasizes self-discipline, hard work, and humility. For example, in a comparison of Chinese, Japanese, and American parents, Asian Americans placed the strongest emphasis on the importance of hard work in school (Stevenson, 1982). They are likely to subscribe to the idea that anyone can do well if he or she studies hard. In contrast, Americans are more likely to attribute school success to natural talent, thus deemphasizing the importance of effort in the form of attendance and homework. Moreover, Asian culture emphasizes the importance of bringing honor to the family, and one way in which this can be done is through educational accomplishments. Still another aspect of this philosophy is its encouragement of personal humility. When ratings of intellectual ability are compared, American parents give their children the highest ratings, and the children typically rate themselves as above average. It may be that this creates a sense of complacency that reduces the levels of effort. In contrast, Japanese and Chinese are more likely to rate themselves average or below, thus instilling greater effort to achieve.

Class And Education

Despite the tradition of free and open public education in the United States, it is evident that not all school systems are created equal and that class, color, and gender are relevant throughout the educational process. The economics of class cannot be ignored, but so too are more subtle and invidious processes occurring within society and the educational system. These factors combine to help reproduce class levels through the generations.

Public Schools: The Funding Gap

The impact of social class emerges early in the education process in the form of inequality of resources in the schools. American public education systems traditionally have relied on property taxes to support a large proportion—currently about 40 percent—of their school budgets. Deteriorating property values in poorer areas, especially inner cities and rural areas, have contracted the tax base in many areas. The consequence is that poorer districts have less money to devote to the schools and less money means lower teacher salaries, larger class size, and fewer enrichment activities. For example, the wealthiest district in New Jersey had one personal computer for each 8 students compared to the poorest district where 58 children shared each machine (Hanley, 1990). In some cases the discrepancies in expenditures are dramatic, resulting in court intervention in many states. The Texas courts demanded a reexamination of funding procedures when it was shown that the 100 wealthiest districts in Texas spend an average of $7,233 per student compared to $2,978 among the poorest 100 (Suro, 1990: 28). The same problem has surfaced in many other states. It is evident that children of the poor are more likely to enter schools at a financial disadvantage compared to the children of the upper middle classes. Increasingly, sociologists are focusing on structural arrangements and social dynamics occurring within classrooms to help explain unequal educational outcomes.

Class and Tracking

The interaction of class and school attainments (aspirations and test scores) is nowhere better illustrated than in the dynamics of tracking. *Tracking* groups students into different curriculum programs on the basis of abilities and aspirations. Tracking was invented as a form of educational specialization to provide appropriate preparation for students heading for advanced education, while at the same time retaining potential dropouts by directing them toward viable vocational training. There are typically three routes or tracks, college prep, general and vocational or career. Although theoretically equal, track placement may have the potential to produce differential educational experiences that re-create inequality and privilege.

Children of color and those from poor and blue-collar origins are more likely to end up in the general or career track, and it is very likely that they will stay on those tracks (Oakes, 1985). One class-based factor in track assignment is that higher class students score better on the standardized tests where their background gives them an advantage. Another is that teachers sometimes have lower academic expectations for children of the poor (Baron, Tom & Cooper, 1985). Experiences on different tracks are often organized to virtually guarantee inequality of outcome. College prep tracks attract better teachers and enjoy an enriched curriculum where students are encouraged to grow and develop individual abilities. Career tracks tend to fill instructional time with experiences that are likely to depress ambition and attainment. For instance, honors English classes may be organized around discussions of *Romeo and Juliet* while lower tracks fill in blanks on pre-prepared worksheets. At one school vocational preparation in food service meant mopping floors in the cafeteria (Lightfoot, 1983).

One consequence is that test scores change, with scores declining among those on the lower tracks and improving on the college-bound track (Rosenbaum, 1975; Rowen and Miracle, 1983; Oakes, 1985). The same pattern is found in Britain, where schools are more openly organized to sponsor and encourage the success of different ability groups (Kerchoff, 1986). Perhaps the most disturbing consequence is the enduring label that accompanies the process of tracking. One lower track student reveals her feelings, "I felt good when I was with my class, but when they separated us, that changed...the way we thought about each other and turned us into enemies toward each other—because they said I was dumb and they were smart" (Rachin, 1989: 52).

The Social and Cultural Reproduction of Class

A number of authors have suggested that broader, even more subtle, social processes are at work to place some children at a disadvantage in the educational system. One of the most influential has been the French sociologist Pierre Bourdieu (1977), who focuses on *cultural capital*—the configuration of knowledge and experiences that members of different classes accumulate in the family during socialization.[3] Bourdieu contends that children of upper- and upper-middle-class parents read books, visit museums, attend concerts, and engage in other activities that make them more conversant with the ideas and values that are rewarded in most school systems. Consequently, their superior cultural literacy results in better grades in high school and college attainments at least among white males and females (DiMaggio, 1982; DiMaggio & Mohr, 1985). In contrast, children of the working class and the poor are more likely to lack this cultural capital, contributing to lower subsequent academic and occupational success.

The concept of cultural capital has also been extended beyond academic literacy to a configuration of social skills, work habits, and styles (Lamont & Lareau, 1988). The reasoning is that educational attainments— and grades more specifically—reflect *both* cognitive mastery of subject matter and the way in which students behave in the context of the classroom; appearance, cooperativeness, class participation, and effort are all aspects of this form of cultural capital rewarded in the schools. Research in this area is not consistent, although there is some evidence that poor children, Hispanics, and African Americans are perceived as having poorer work habits, and that such observations are associated with lower grades when controlling for performance on tests (Farkas et al., 1990).

Class and Higher Education

These factors combine to produce differential access to higher education, one of the prerequisites to upward mobility into the upper middle class. Not unexpectedly, the chances of a youth attending college are

---

[3]Empirical research on cultural capital has produced mixed results. The work of Robinson and Garnier (1985) in France and Katsillis and Rubinson (1990) in Greece has not supported Bourdieu's formulation.

directly related to social class. Full occupational data on the parents of college students are rare, requiring dependence on the level of economic resources of their family. As shown in Exhibit 10.3, an increasingly larger proportion of children in each higher income bracket is currently enrolled in some form of higher education. Children of black and Hispanic parents are less likely to be attending college, but among those that do the same overall association between class and education is repeated.

Even if there were no other factors at work, the sheer economic costs of higher education are prohibitive for some segments of society. It is estimated that a college education (in-state tuition and room and board at a *public* college) for a child born today will cost over $59,000 when he or she matriculates 18 years from now (Brenner, 1989). To accumulate that much money, parents would need to put aside $127 a month, every month, from the day the child was born until the start of college. The financial burden is even more dramatic at a *private* college, where it is estimated it will cost over $220,000, demanding a savings plan of $478 a month for 18 years. Clearly, such costs put education beyond the reach of many parents at the lower end of the class system. The vital role of higher education in future success has even spawned a relatively new occupation—the personal college counselor—an expensive luxury available only to more affluent parents, giving their children still another advantage (Kiernan, 1990). These private consultants work with individual students, offering a list of possible colleges (for a fee of $50), counseling—beginning as early as eighth grade—on course selection (fees ranging up to $2,000), helping to improve admissions test scores ($500 to $1,000), and coaching on how to conduct campus visits ($700).

Exhibit 10.3
Social Class and Higher Education,
Families with College-Age Children, 1986

Family Income	Children in College		
	White	Black	Hispanic
Under $10,000	13.3%	13.4%	10.4%
$10,000–$19,999	23.7	25.2	20.2
$20,000–$29,999	30.5	29.2	29.2
$30,000–$39,999	39.8	42.6	40.5
$40,000–$49,999	46.7	n/a	n/a
$50,000 and over	56.4	n/a	n/a
All families	36.6%	23.9%	21.9%

Note: Only families with college-age children are included.
Source: U.S. Bureau of the Census, *School Enrollment—Social and Economic Characteristics of Students.* (Washington, DC: U.S. Government Printing Office, 1988) Table 12, p. 43.

Various forms of financial aid are designed to lessen the impact of class, but they cannot eliminate it. Moreover, during the 1980s federal aid for students declined in absolute dollars, although the number of students increased, meaning more students were competing for fewer dollars of financial aid. Moreover, there has been a shift in the pattern of financial aid from grants to loans, which must be repaid. Many lower income students are reluctant to accumulate large debts to attend college. It should also be noted that the decline in the availability of student aid has a greater impact on minorities because average family income is well below that of whites.

Patterns of Higher Education Among African Americans

The civil rights movement opened college doors to capable black students in ever increasing numbers. Prior to the 1950s very few blacks were able to attend college, and those who did were often relegated to inferior or segregated schools. Moreover, most blacks ended up in preparation for a narrow number of careers, often teaching for women and the ministry for men, reflecting the limited career options available to them. In the fall of 1990 approximately 9.6 percent of the freshman class of American colleges and universities were black (Astin, 1991). Black women have traditionally been more likely to go on to college than black men. In part this can be traced to the family patterns where parents encouraged female education to protect their daughters from being relegated to careers as maids or the other menial jobs open to them. In contrast, male high school graduates were often attracted to the military or blue-collar work over advanced education. Today, black women outnumber black men on campuses by a ratio of 3 to 2.

African Americans who do enroll in college may find that white campuses are not congenial places for them, evidenced by a disturbing surge in overt racial incidents on college campuses (U.S. Commission on Civil Rights, 1990). This problem gained national attention in 1986 when a black cadet at the Citadel in Charleston, South Carolina, was awaked by hooded white students chanting his name. One estimate reports racial incidents on over 250 campuses since 1986. Consequently, many black students feel unwelcome, isolated, and alienated at predominately white schools.

Scientific Careers: The Critical Filter

The study of mathematics is called the "critical filter" in occupational selection, with a lack of math limiting subsequent math attainments and ultimately access to scientific and technical careers. Females and students of color were long much less likely to be taking advanced math courses and consequently were less likely to be prepared to embark on upper-middle-class scientific and technical career paths. Today the gap has narrowed in some of the scientific fields, but blacks, Hispanics, and women continue to be underrepresented.

Performance on any measure of math performance (grades, test scores, self-confidence in math) improves at each higher level in the class hierarchy, but is confounded by color and gender (Fleming & Malone, 1983). As a general rule, females do tend to get better grades in math and all subjects from the earliest school years on through high school (Stockard & Wood, 1984). Younger girls (under age 14) also outperform boys on both verbal and math standardized test scores, but male scores in math begin to outpace those of females in junior and senior high school (Sherman, 1980; Wentzel, 1988). This manifests itself in an advantage of about 50 points on SATs at the completion of high school. Moreover, high school–age girls express less interest and less confidence about their computer skills than boys (Krendl, Broihier & Fleetwood, 1989). Thus, women and men continue to perform differently in this area, suggesting the impact of sociocultural factors.

Very early boys are subtly and directly encouraged in the direction of scholastic performance in mathematics, often because math skills are presumed to be more consistent with conventional sex-typed masculine traits such as "analytic ability." This shows up in the fact that parents and counselors tend to be more supportive of males following math-based careers. For example, parents are more likely to purchase personal computers for sons than daughters and enrollments at computer camps favor boys by a margin of 3 to 1 (Kiesler et al., 1983).

There are also differential experiences in the context of the math classroom. Girls with high math aptitude are less likely to be assigned to "high ability" groups than boys (Hallinan & Sorensen, 1987). Teachers tend to initiate more academic contact with boys and to give more attention to male students than female students. In addition, males who give incorrect answers are usually exhorted to greater effort while females are praised simply for trying. The experiences of black children in the area of math are not as well researched, but parallels those based on gender in other contexts. Teachers tend to devote more attention to white children, sometimes give more praise, and are likely to grant only conditional praise for academic effort (e.g., "A good paper, for a change"), thus subtly suggesting a fundamental intellectual inferiority (Grant, 1984).

However, the inconsistency between grades and standardized test scores is perplexing (Kimball, 1989). It has been suggested that the higher grades earned by females may reflect the fact that social competencies as well as cognitive skills enter into the grading process. Females, on average, have an advantage in social competencies, being more cooperative and attentive and having more positive attitudes toward teachers. This leaves the decline in females' test scores to be explained. One interpretation is that it is due to the increasing salience of conventional gender roles that surfaces in later adolescence. This is the age at which conforming to culturally defined gender roles looms large and subtly encourages females to underemphasize competence at cross-gender skills such as math, it still being accepted as an area of male competence. The interaction between gender and math achievement is not fully understood, but the implications remain, especially among America's 2.4 million working engineers, where only about 5 percent are women and another 5 percent are minorities.

Class and Aspirations

One of the most complex variables in the whole equation is aspirations. Individual aspirations can be expected to contribute to educational and occupational attainments in a direct and straightforward manner. Those with higher aspirations should be motivated to greater effort and performance and consequently achieve more than the less motivated. There is evidence to support this interpretation, but the process is also interactive in that those who experience success develop higher aspirations (e.g., Haller et al., 1974). The status attainment literature shows that aspirations tend to be higher at each higher class level.

Several factors contribute to this situation. As would be anticipated, perceptions of opportunity are weaker at each lower level. Although Americans generally adhere to the dominant ideology of equality of opportunity, it is simultaneously recognized that class, color, and gender can impose handicaps. Few people at any level can ignore the advantages of the upper classes, with an overwhelming majority granting that the children of rich parents have a better than average chance of success (Kluegel & Smith, 1986: 49). Thus, children at lower levels are early confronted with intimations of an unequal opportunity structure. In addition, school experiences are a factor. Higher class children are likely to perform better on tests, further encouraging motivation and benefit from greater resources in the home and school, which encourages higher aspirations.

Unfortunately, the meaning of this finding is misleading for it often fails to consider relative levels of aspiration being studied (Empey, 1956). Aspirations are usually measured on an absolute scale. Youths are, for example, asked how many years of education they would like to attain, or to stipulate the careers they would like to pursue. Working-class and poor children are motivated to improve their situation, but simply have more modest absolute aspirations than children of white-collar parents. Thus, although their aspirations may be more limited than the goals of advantaged upper-middle-class youth, they are still imbued with a spirit of achievement that is strong relative to the place they are starting.

EDUCATIONAL PATHS INTO THE ELITE

The epitome of upward mobility is movement into the institutional elite, the top positions in business, education, and government. A review of the class origins of these men and women suggests that the stratification system is open to people of modest social origins but heavily weighted in favor of those from more advantaged class backgrounds. A significant proportion are children of elite parents and most who originate outside this class are recruited from the ranks of the upper middle class. The number of persons who started life in the lower middle or working class is small, and it is extremely rare for children of the poor to achieve such success.

Many of the advantages of the elite are articulated through a network of high status schools that simultaneously prepare these children for future positions of leadership and virtually guarantee that they will achieve them. For many children the first education step is enrollment in a narrow circle of exclusive boarding schools (Cookson & Persell, 1985). Prep schools such as Choate and St. Andrews provide a rigorous and sound academic preparation for future educational accomplishments and polish the social skills and values—the cultural capital of the elite—necessary for access to subsequent positions of power and influence. In addition, students are introduced to a network of other individuals who will also occupy such positions. The process continues with enrollment at a relatively small core of select undergraduate colleges—places such as Columbia, Harvard, Pennsylvania, Princeton, Stanford, and Yale (Useem & Karabel, 1986; Kingston & Lewis, 1990). There they continue to be surrounded by the other representatives of the upper classes.

Such schools are among the most exclusive and expensive, which narrows the pool of candidates, although they are increasingly open to the general population. Nonelite class children capable and fortunate enough to gain access to such schools dramatically increase their chances of upward mobility. One study of corporate executives showed that half had earned a B.A. from one of just eleven elite colleges (Useem and Karabel, 1986). It is at these schools that children of parents at lower levels in the stratification system can acquire the combination of skills, cultural capital, and social contacts that will help them later on.

SUMMARY: Class and Mobility

Both ascription and achievement play a role in determining an individual's class attainments. Opportunities for social mobility in democratic industrial societies depend heavily on educational credentials, which opens the system to individual achievement. However, social origins exert a powerful influence on educational attainments at every stage in the process, creating barriers for the children of lower classes, women, and minorities. The stratification system is open to merit and effort, but it appears that children at each higher level in the stratification system are at an advantage in academic competition. Their social backgrounds interact with the economic and social organization of school systems to produce higher levels of educational and occupational attainments. Children of the poor and the working class are at a disadvantage that appears to create artificial barriers to success. Finally, because the educational system is stratified, where a youth goes to school can be just as important—or more important—than years of schooling accumulated or ability. For example, research shows that the least able graduates (measured by standardized tests) of select colleges have a higher chance of economic success than the most able students from low-status schools (Kingston & Smart, 1990: 162).

INTRAGENERATIONAL MOBILITY

Parental class and other factors combine to influence the place in the class structure where people begin their careers. Obviously, not all people remain at that level for the rest of their careers. Intragenerational mobility focuses on the changes that occur over the course of careers. Over time some are able to move across class lines, from manual work into the lower middle class, for example, while others rise from the lower middle class into the ranks of the upper middle class.

Patterns of Career Mobility

There is a great deal of movement among jobs with at least 10 percent of the labor force changing jobs each year but most moves are horizontal within the same class. Consequently, the majority of men in industrial societies such as the United States, France, and Britain remain at the same class level (Hope, 1983; Winfield et al., 1989).[4] At all levels except the lower middle class, men are more likely to be immobile than to move into a different class during their careers (Stier & Grusky, 1990). One of the most salient factors inhibiting movement is the fact that people accumulate work experiences, seniority and expertise that are of limited benefit in other class positions.

The potential for career mobility is greatest for those who begin their working lives in the lower middle class. The internal opportunity structure

[4]Unfortunately, the lack of research on gender and color make it impossible to generalize beyond males.

with organizations helps to account for this pattern (Kanter, 1977; Rosenbaum, 1979). Positions in upper management are typically recruited from the ranks of lower management. The relative rarity of women and people of color at the higher tiers of organizational management suggests the presence of informal barriers that impose a "glass ceiling" on their achievement. For example, only 3 percent of top management at America's largest corporations in 1991 were female (Saltzman, 1991). It is a glass or transparent barrier because people have climbed high enough to see the top but are unable to reach it. This barrier has many dimensions: Women are often channeled into departments, such as human resources or public relations, that seldom lead to executive positions; male and female differences in communication styles may generate discomfort and misunderstandings; and the lack of child care facilities and parental leave may hinder the progress of women with young children.

Unemployment and Career Mobility

One event that does a have measurable effect on careers is job loss, although it must be remembered that divorce or the death of a spouse

Exhibit 10.4
Displaced Workers: Old Jobs and New

Occupation or Job Lost	Not Working	Reemployed		
		Downward Mobility	Unchanged	Upward Mobility
Upper middle				
Managerial	24.3%	46.7%	52.9%	—
Professional	27.1	42.8	57.2	—
Lower middle				
Technical	32.1	39.7	62.6	—
Clerical	45.9	22.3	61.8	15.8
Sales	33.3	24.6	59.6	15.7
Working				
Craft workers	38.4	17.3	71.0	11.6
Operatives	44.0	22.8	60.4	16.6
The Poor				
Service	49.0	—	61.4	38.6
Unskilled	58.0	—	35.0	65.0

Note: The 5.1 million workers included here had worked at least three years at their jobs, and were displaced for structural reasons. Because the data cover a maximum of five years, it is impossible to measure long-term mobility patterns.
Source: Paul O. Flaim and Ellen Sehal, "Displaced Workers of 1979–1982: How Well Have They Fared?" *Monthly Labor Review*, 108 (June 1985), Tables 3 and 12.

contribute to the downward mobility of large numbers of women. Each year hundreds of thousands of people are displaced from their jobs, usually for economic reasons such as layoffs or plant closings. Loss of work compels people to seek to reestablish their careers and an examination of the experiences of 5.1 million workers displaced during the 1980s (see Exhibit 10.4) reveals the implications of this event.

Some people had been unable to find new employment by the time this survey was conducted meaning that some had been without work for years. Joblessness means they must be counted among the ranks of the poor. Continued joblessness was concentrated among those who were among the poor before the onset of unemployment. The proportion of the poor still without work was twice that of the upper middle classes. About two thirds were still actively looking for work and the remaining one third had become discouraged and left the labor force. Considerations of color and gender were relevant at every point in the process (Kletzer, 1991). The risk of job loss is greater for people of color because they are more likely to be in more vulnerable manufacturing jobs. Displaced black workers experienced longer periods of unemployment and were less likely to be reemployed than whites. The same general pattern was repeated for women, longer periods of unemployment and less frequent reemployment.

A majority of people did find work after an average of 21.4 weeks of unemployment. This number conceals gender differences and differences between blue-collar and white-collar workers. Male white-collar workers were unemployed for an average of 10.4 weeks compared to 19.6 weeks for females. Male blue-collar workers were out of work for 26.0 weeks and blue-collar women suffered an average 40.4 weeks of joblessness. Although most people were able to find work, a significant proportion of reemployed workers suffered downward mobility. The potential for downward mobility was greatest among the upper middle class where four in ten were in lower-middle or working-class jobs or were even found among the poor. Technical workers were also especially vulnerable. Most people experienced no overall mobility, finding work at the same class level. There was some slippage within classes, as was the case with about 14 percent of displaced craft workers who were subsequently working as operatives or as truck drivers. Overall, one quarter accepted pay cuts equal to 20 percent of their previous wages. In some cases involuntary unemployment actually proved beneficial. Although the trauma of unemployment is typically very painful, some workers were freed from dead end jobs, and benefited from retraining programs that allowed them to secure better positions. This is evident among unskilled workers who moved into more stable blue-collar work. There was also some movement upward into the upper middle class from the lower middle class, for about 10 percent of technical workers who moved into professional and managerial work.

CONCLUSION: The Consequences of Downward Mobility

Downward mobility carries with it the potential for personal stress. It may require a downgrading of lifestyles, especially when it is accompanied by financial loss. Research suggests a link between downward mobility and various forms of personal adjustment, political orientations, mental illness, and even suicide (e.g., Wilensky & Edwards, 1949; Kessin, 1971; Lopreato & Chafetz, 1970). Moreover, it is not solely an individual experience for it impacts whole families, requiring spouses and children to reexamine lifestyles and long-term goals (Newman, 1988; Ehrenreich, 1989). At a broader level it has been suggested that Emile Durkheim's concept of anomie is relevant (Ellis & Lane, 1967). Individuals socialized into the standards and values of one class while growing up might experience feelings of isolation and normlessness as they adjust to life in a different social class. At a still broader level, there is the question of personal adjustment to relative "failure" in a society that celebrates success and achievement. This problem prevails despite the fact that the sources of downward mobility can often be traced to conditions beyond the control of the individual.

ADDITIONAL READINGS

On Intergenerational Mobility

OTIS D. DUNCAN and PETER M. BLAU. *The American Occupational Structure*. New York: John Wiley, 1967.

DAVID FEATHERMAN and ROBERT M. HAUSER. *Opportunity and Change*. New York: Academic Press, 1978.

JOHN H. GOLDTHORPE, CATRIONA LLEWELLYN and CLIVE PAYNE. *Social Mobility and Class Structure in Modern Britain*. New York: Oxford University Press, 1987.

PAUL WILLIAM KINGSTON and LIONEL S. LEWIS, eds. *The High Status Track: Studies of Elite Schools and Stratification*. Albany: State University of New York Press, 1990.

WILLIAM H. SEWELL and ROBERT M. HAUSER. *Education, Occupation and Earnings*. New York: Academic Press, 1975.

On Intragenerational Mobility

BARBARA EHRENREICH. *Fear of Falling*. New York: Pantheon, 1989.

STEVEN FINEMAN. *White Collar Unemployment: Impact and Stress*. New York: John Wiley, 1983.

PAULA LEVENTMAN. *Professionals Out of Work*. New York: Free Press, 1981.

KATHERINE S. NEWMAN. *Falling from Grace: The Experience of Downward Mobility in the American Middle Class*. New York, Free Press, 1988.

Bibliography

Adler, Isreal, and Vered Kraus. 1985. "Components of Occupational Prestige Evaluations," *Work and Occupations*, 12, 23–58.

Adler, Valerie. 1989. "Little Control=Lots of Stress," *Psychology Today* April, 18–19.

Akszentievics, Gyorgy. 1982. "International Comparative Survey on the Situation of Industrial Workers," Pp. 413–426 in Antal Boehm and Thomas Kolosi, eds., *Structure and Stratification in Hungary*, Budapest: Institute for Social Sciences.

Aldrich, Howard E., and Roger Waldinger. 1990. "Ethnicity and Entrepreneurship," *Annual Review of Sociology*, 16, 111–135.

Allen, Michael Patrick and Phillip Broyles. 1989. "Class Hegemony and Political Finance: Presidential Campaign Contributions of Wealthy Capitalist Families," *American Sociological Review*, 54, 275–287.

Alter, Jonathan. 1989. "Forbes's Publicity Machine," *Newsweek*, August 28, pp. 50–51.

Anderson, Charles H. 1974. *The Political Economy of Social Class*. Englewood Cliffs, NJ: Prentice Hall.

Anderson, Karen. 1988. "A History of Women's Work in the United States," in *Women Working*, Ann Helton Stromberg and Shirley Harkness, eds., pp. 25–41. Mountain View, CA: Mayfield.

Ansberry, Clare. 1988. "Dumping the Poor: Despite Federal Law, Hospitals Still Reject Sick Who Can't Pay," *Wall Street Journal*, November 29, pp. 1–11A.

Applebome, Peter. 1990. "Arabs in U.S. Feel Separated by Other Gulfs," *New York Times*, February 10, pp. 1–30.

Astin, Alexander W. 1991. *The American Freshman: Norms for Fall, 1990*. Los Angeles: American Council on Education.

Auerbach, Jerold S. 1976. *Unequal Justice*. New York: Oxford University Press.

Avery, R. G., G. Elliehausen, and G. Canner. 1984. "Survey of Consumer Finances, 1983," *Federal Reserve Bulletin*, 70, 857–868.

Bailey, Thomas A. 1956. *The American Pageant*. Boston: D. C. Heath.

Barbanel, Josh. 1987. "Societies and Their Homeless," *New York Times*, November 29, p. 8E.

Baron, Ava. 1980. "Women and the Making of the American Working Class: A Study in the Proletarianization of Printers," *Review of Radical Political Economics*, 14, 23–42.

Baron, James N. and William T. Bielby. 1984. "The Organization of Work in a Segmented Economy," *American Sociological Review*, 49, 454–473.

Baron, Reuben M., David Y. H. Tom and Harris M. Cooper. 1985. "Social Class, Race and Teacher Expectations," in *Teacher Expectancies*, Jerome B. Dusek, ed., pp. 251–269. Hillsdale, NJ: Lawrence Erlbaum Associates.

Barrera, Mario. 1979. *Race and Class in the Southwest*. Notre Dame, IN: University of Notre Dame Press.

Barron, James. 1988. "A Search for Solutions to the Housing Squeeze," *New York Times*, July 12, p. 5E.

Bates v. *State Bar of Arizona*. 1977. 433 U.S. 350.

Bauers, Bob, and Merritt Wallick. 1989. "Chemical Industry Wrote the Laws We Live By," *Wilmington [DE] News Journal*, June 11, pp. 1–19A.

Beck, S. H. 1983. "The Role of Other Family Members in Intergenerational Occupational Mobility," *Sociological Quarterly*, 24, 273–285.

Bell, Wendell, and Robert V. Robinson. 1980. "Cognitive Maps of Class and Racial Inequalities in England and the United States," *American Journal of Sociology*, 86, 320–349.

Bella, Andrea H. 1984. "Trends in Occupational Segregation by Sex and Race, 1960–1981," in *Sex Segregation in the Workplace: Trends, Explanations, Remedies*, Barbara F. Reskin, ed. Washington, DC: National Academy Press.

Bendix, Rinehard. 1962. *Max Weber: An Intellectual Portrait*. Garden City, NY: Doubleday.

Bennett, John E., and S. M. Bennett. 1975. "The Definition of Sex Role Stereotypes via the Adjective Check List," *Sex Roles*, 1, 327–337.

Bensman, Joseph, and Robert Lilienfeld. 1991. *Craft and Consciousness: Occupational Technique and the Development of World Images*. Hawthorne, NY: Aldine de Gruyter.

Bensman, Joseph, and Arthur J. Vidich. 1987. *American Society*. South Hadley, MA: Bergin & Garvey.

Berger, Joseph. 1989. "All in the Game," *New York Times Education Life*, August 6, pp. 23–24.

Berger, Joseph M., Hamit Fisek, Robert Z. Norman, and Morris Zelditch, Jr. 1977. *Status Characteristics and Social Interaction*. New York: Elsevier.

Berriman, Gerald. 1973. *Caste in the Modern World*. Morristown, NJ: General Learning Press.

Beteille, Andre. 1965. *Caste, Class and Power*. Berkeley: University of California Press.

Birmingham, Stephen. 1987. *America's Secret Aristocracy*. Boston: Little, Brown.

Blauner, Robert. 1972. *Racial Oppression in America*. New York: Harper & Row.

Bloch, Marc. 1961. *Feudal Society*. London: Routledge & Kegan Paul.

Blodgett, Nancy. 1986. "I Don't Think That Ladies Should Be Lawyers," *ABA Journal*, December 1, pp. 48–53.

Blood, Robert O., and D. M. Wolf. 1960. *Husbands and Wives: The Dynamics of Married Life*. New York: Free Press.

Bobo, Lawrence, and Franklin D. Gilliam, Jr. 1990. "Race, Sociopolitical Participation, and Black Empowerment," *American Political Science Review*, 84, 377–393.

Bogardus, Emory S. 1926. "Social Distance Between Groups," *Journal of Applied Sociology*, 10, 473–479.

Bose, Christine E. 1987. "Dual Spheres," in *Analyzing Gender: A Handbook of Social Science Research*, Beth B. Hess and Myra Marx Ferree, eds., pp. 267–285. Newbury Park, CA: Sage.

Bottomore, Tom. 1966. *Elites and Society*. New York: Basic Books.

Boulding, Elise. 1980. "The Labor of U.S. Farm Women: A Knowledge Gap, " *Work and Occupations*, 7, 261–290.

Bourdieu, Pierre. 1977. "Cultural Reproduction and Social Reproduction," in *Power and Ideology in Education*, J. Karabel and A. H. Halsey, eds., pp. 487–511. New York: Oxford University Press.

Boyd, Monica. 1982. "Sex Differences in the Canadian Educational Process," *Canadian Review of Sociology and Anthropology*, 19,1–28.

Boyd, Robert L. 1990. "Black and Asian Self-Employment in Large Metropolitan Areas: A Comparative Analysis," *Social Problems*, 37, 258–274.

Bracy, James H. 1976. "The Quality of Life of Black People," in *The Quality of American Life: Perceptions, Evaluations and Satisfactions*, Angus Campbell et al., eds., pp. 443–469. New York: Russell Sage.

Bradwell v. Illinois. 1873. 83 U.S. 16 Wall 141.

Braverman, Harry. 1974. *Labor and Monopoly Capitalism*. New York: Monthly Review Press.

Brenner, Lynn. 1989. "Making College Ends Meet," *New York Times Education Life*, November 5, pp. 39–44.

Brenner, O. C., Joseph Tomkiewicz, and Virginia Ellen Schein. 1989. "The Relationship Between Sex Role Stereotypes and Requisite Management Characteristics Revisited." *Academy of Management Journal*, 32, 662–669.

Brink, William, and Louis Harris. 1967. *Black and White*. New York: Simon & Schuster.

Brooks, Thomas R. 1971. *Toil and Trouble*. New York: Delacourt.

Brown, J. Larry. 1987. "Hunger in the U.S.," *Scientific American*, 256, 345–357.

Brown, Peter. 1991. *Minority Party: Why Democrats Face Defeat in 1992 and Beyond*. New York: Regnery Gateway.

Burris, Val. 1986. "The Discovery of the New Middle Class," *Theory and Society*, 15, 317–349.

———. 1987. "The Political Partisanship of American Business: A Study of Corporate Political Action Committees," *American Sociological Review*, 52, 732–744.

Business Week. 1991. *The Business Week 1000*. New York: McGraw-Hill.

Butler, D. E., and D. Stokes. 1974. *Political Change in Britain: Forces Shaping Electoral Choice*. London: Macmilan.

Butterfield, Fox. 1986. "Why Asians Are Going to the Head of the Class," *New York Times Education Supplement*, August 3, pp. 18–22.

Byrne, John A. 1989. "Is the Boss Getting Paid Too Much?" *Business Week*, May 1, pp. 46–52.

Caborn, Anne. 1988. "Britain's Richest 200," *Money Magazine* (March), 18–111.

Carmody, Deirdre. 1989. "Minority Students Gain on College Entrance Tests," *New York Times*, September 12, p. 16A.

Caton, Carol L. M. 1989. *Without Dreams: The Homeless of America*. New York: Oxford University Press.

Caven, Ruth. 1969. *The American Family*. New York: Crowell.

Centers, Richard. 1949. *The Psychology of Social Classes*. Princeton, NJ: Princeton University Press.

Chafetz, Janet Saltzman. 1984. *Sex and Advantage*. Totowa, NJ: Rowman & Allanheld.

Charles, Michael T. 1981. "The Performance and Socialization of Female Recruits in the Michigan State Police Training Academy," *Journal of Police Science and Administration*, 9, 209–223.

Chase, I. D. 1975. "A Comparison of Men's and Women's Intergenerational Mobility in the United States," *American Sociological Review*, 40, 483–505.

Cherry, Mike. 1974. *On High Steel: The Education of an Ironworker*. New York: Ballantine.

Chinoy, Eli. 1955. *Automobile Workers and the American Dream*. Garden City, NY: Doubleday.

Clancy, Paul. 1988. "Camel Companions," *USA Today*, December 28, p. 2A.

Clawson, Dan, Alan Neustadtl, and James Bearden. 1986. "The Logic of Business Unity: Corporate Contributions to the 1980 Congressional Elections," *American Sociological Review*, 51, 797–811.

Cobas, Jose A. 1986. "Paths to Self-Employment Among Immigrants: An Analysis of Four Interpretations," *Sociological Perspectives*, 29, 101–120.

Colasanto, Diane, and Linda Williams. 1987. "The Changing Dynamics of Race and Class," *Public Opinion*, 9, 50–53.

Collins, Randall. 1986a. *Weberian Sociological Theory*. New York: Cambridge University Press.

———. 1986b. *Max Weber: A Skeleton Key*. Beverley Hills, CA: Sage.

———, and Michael Makowsky. 1984. *The Discovery of Society*, 3rd ed. New York: Random House.

Conway, M. Margaret. 1985. *Political Participation in the United States*. Washington, DC: Congressional Quarterly.

Cookson, Peter W., Jr., and Caroline Hodges Persell. 1985. *Preparing for Power: America's Elite Boarding Schools*. New York: Basic Books.

Coyle, Marcia, Fred Strasser, and Marianne Lavelle. 1990. "Fatal Defense," *The National Law Journal*, 13 (June 11), 30–44.

Crull, Sue R., and Brent T. Bruton. 1985. "Possible Decline in Tolerance Toward Minorities: Social Distance on a Midwest Campus," *Sociology and Social Research*, 70, 57–61.

Cullen, John B. and Shelly M. Novick. 1979. "The Davis-Moore Theory of Stratification: A Further Examination and Extension," *American Journal of Sociology*, 84, 1424–1437.

D'Andrade, Roy G. 1966. "Sex Differences and Cultural Institutions," in *The Development of Sex Differences*, Elenore Maccoby ed, pp. 174–204. Stanford, CA: Stanford University Press.

Daniels, Arlene Kaplan. 1987. *Invisible Careers: Women Civic Leaders in the Volunteer World*. Chicago: University of Chicago Press.

Danziger, Sheldon. 1989. "Defining and Measuring the Underclass: Overview," *Focus*, 12, 1–5.

Davies, Christie. 1982. "Ethnic Jokes, Moral Values and Social Boundaries," *British Journal of Sociology*, 33, 383–403.

Davis, David B. 1966. *The Problem of Slavery in Western Culture*. Ithaca, NY: Cornell University Press.

Davis, Kingsley. 1953. "Reply to Tumin," *American Sociological Review*, 18, 394–397.

———, and Wilbert E. Moore. 1945. "Some Principles of Stratification," *American Sociological Review*, 10, 242–249.

Davis, Nancy, and Robert Robinson. 1988. "Class Identification of Men and Women in the 1970s and 1980s," *American Sociological Review*, 53, 103–112.

Davis, Theodore J., Jr., 1991. "Social Mobility of African Americans in the 1980s: A Controversy Revisited," Unpublished paper, Department of Political Science, University of Delaware.

Dear, Michael J., and Jennifer R. Wolch. 1987. *Landscapes of Despair: From Deinstitutionalization to Homelessness*. Princeton, NJ: Princeton University Press.

Deaux, Kay, and Mary E. Kite. 1987. "Thinking About Gender," in *Analyzing Gender: A Handbook of Social Science Research*, Beth B. Hess and Myra Marx Ferree, eds., pp. 92–116. Newbury Park, CA: Sage.

Deaux, Kay, and Lionel L. Lewis. 1984. "Structure of Gender Stereotypes: Interrelationships Among Components and Gender Label," *Journal of Personality and Social Psychology*, 46, 991–1004.

DeMott, Benjamin. 1990. *The Imperial Middle: Why Americans Can't Think Straight About Class*. New York: Morrow.

Dentzer, Susan, and Jeff Trimble. 1989. "The Soviet Economy in Shambles," *U.S. News & World Report* November 20, pp. 25–39.

DeParle, Jason. 1990. "What to Call the Poorest Poor?" *New York Times*, August 26, p. 4E.

Derrick, Jonathan. 1975. *Africa's Slaves Today.* New York: Schocken.

Desmond, Edward. 1990. "A Local Custom Called Cruelty," *Time*, May 28, p. 37.

DiMaggio, Paul. 1982. "Cultural Capital and School Success: The Impact of Status Culture Participation on the Grades of U.S. High School Students," *American Sociological Review*,47, 189–201.

———, and John Mohr. 1985. "Cultural Capital, Educational Attainment, and Marital Selection," *American Journal of Sociology*, 90, 1231–1261.

Domhoff, G. William. 1967. *Who Rules America?* Englewood Cliffs, NJ: Prentice Hall.

———. 1970. *The Higher Circles.* New York: Vintage.

———. 1974. *The Bohemian Grove and Other Retreats: A Study in Ruling Class Cohesiveness.* New York: Harper & Row.

———. 1983. *Who Rules America Now: A View for the Eighties.* Englewood Cliffs, NJ: Prentice Hall.

Dubofsky, Melvyn. 1969. *We Shall Be All: A History of the Industrial Workers of the World.* Chicago: Quadrangle.

Duncan, Greg J. 1984. *Years of Poverty, Years of Plenty.* Ann Arbor: Institute for Social Research, University of Michigan.

Dye, Thomas R. 1986. *Who's Running America: The Conservative Years.* Englewood Cliffs, NJ: Prentice Hall.

Earle, John R., and Catherine T. Harris. 1989. "College Students and Blue-Collar Workers: A Comparative Analysis of Sex-Role Attitudes," *Sociological Spectrum*, 9, 455–466.

E.C.L. 1987. "Class Differences: An Issue for 1988?" *Public Opinion* (May/June), 21–29.

Economist. 1978. "The State in the Market," 269 (December), 37–39.

Edsall, Thomas Byrne, and Mary D. Edsall. 1991. *Chain Reaction: The Impact of Race, Rights, and Taxes on American Politics.* New York: W. W. Norton

Ehrenreich, Barbara. 1989. *Fear of Falling.* New York: Pantheon.

———, and John Ehrenreich. 1979. "Professional-Managerial Class," in *Between Labor and Capital*, Pat Walker, ed., pp. 4–45. Boston: South End Press.

Ehrenreich, Barbara, and Deirdre English. 1979. *For Her Own Good.* Garden City, NY: Anchor Press.

Elias, Christoper. 1990. "Turning Up the Heat on the Top," *Insight*, July 23, pp. 8–15.

Ellis, Robert A., and W. Clayton Lane. 1967. "Social Mobility and Social Isolation." *American Sociological Review*, 32, 237–253.

Empey, LaMar T. 1956. "Social Class and Occupational Aspiration: A Comparison of Absolute and Relative Measurement," *American Sociological Review*, 21, 703–709.

Engels, Friedrich. 1972. *The Origin of the Family, Private Property, and the State.* New York: International Publishers.

England, Paula. 1979. "Women and Occupational Prestige: A Case of Vacuous Sex Equity," *Signs*, 5, 252–265.

Farkas, George, Robert P. Grobe, Daniel Sheehan, and Yuan Shuan. 1990. "Cultural Resources and School Success: Gender, Ethnicity, and Poverty Groups Within an Urban School District," *American Sociological Review*, 55, 127–142.

Faunce, William A. 1989. "Occupational Status-Assignment Systems: The Effect of Status on Self-Esteem," *American Journal of Sociology*, 95, 378–400.

Fausto-Sterling, Anne. 1986. *Myths of Gender: Biological Theories About Men and Women*. New York: Basic Books.

Feagin, Joe R. 1972. "Poverty: We Still Believe That God Helps Those Who Help Themselves," *Psychology Today* (November), 101–129.

———. 1975. *Subordinating the Poor*. Englewood Cliffs, NJ: Prentice Hall.

———. 1984. *Racial and Ethnic Relations*, 2nd ed. Englewood Cliffs, NJ: Prentice Hall.

Featherman, L. David and Robert M. Hauser. 1978. *Opportunity and Change*. New York: Academic Press.

Feldman, Saul D., and Gerald W. Thielbar. 1972. "Power, Privilege, and Prestige of Occupations," in *Issues in Social Inequality*, Gerald W. Thielbar and Saul D. Feldman, eds., pp. 227–241. Boston: Little, Brown.

Fendrich, Michael. 1984. "Wives' Employment and Husbands' Distress," *Journal of Marriage and the Family*, 46, 871–879.

Ferguson, Thomas, and Joel Rogers. 1986. *Right Turn: The Decline of the Democrats and the Future of American Politics*. NewYork: Hill and Wang.

Ferree, Myra Marx. 1985. "Between Two Worlds: German Feminist Approaches to Working-Class Women and Work," *Signs*, 10, 517–536.

Ferrell, David. 1990. "Too Much Still Isn't Enough," *Wilmington [DE] News Journal*, March 11, pp. 1–6J.

Fetterman, Mindy. 1989. "Working to Run Show 'On Own Terms,'" *USA Today*, June 21, pp. 1–2A.

Feuer, Lewis S. 1959. *Marx and Engels: Basic Writings on Politics and Philosophy*. Garden City, NY: Doubleday.

Finnegan, William. 1986. *Crossing the Line: A Year in the Land of Apartheid*. New York: Harper & Row.

Firebaugh, Glenn, and Kenneth E. Davis. 1988. "Trends in Anti-Black Prejudice, 1972–1984," *American Journal of Sociology*, 94, 251–272.

Fischer, Claude. 1982. *To Dwell Among Friends: Personal Networks in Town and City*. Chicago: University of Chicago Press.

Fleming, M. Lynette, and Mark R. Malone. 1983. "The Relationship of Student Characteristics and Student Performance in Science as Viewed by Meta-Analysis Research," *Journal of Research in Science Teaching*, 20, 621–628.

Foner, Philip S. 1964. *History of the Labor Movement in the United States*. New York: International Publishers.

Forbes, B. C. 1918. "America's 30 Richest Own $3.68 Billion." *Forbes*, 1, 1–5.

Ford, W. Scott. 1986. "Favorable Intergroup Contact May Not Reduce Prejudice: Inconclusive Journal Evidence, 1960–1984," *Sociology and Social Research*, 70, 256–258.

Form, William. 1985. *Divided We Stand: Working-Class Stratification in America*. Urbana: University of Illinois Press.

Franklin, Benjamin. 1961. *The Autobiography and Other Writings*. New York: New American Library.

Franklin, John Hope. 1974. *From Slavery to Freedom*, 4th ed. New York: Knopf.

Frazier, E. Franklin. 1957. *Black Bourgeoisie*. Glencoe, IL: Free Press.

Gallup Report. 1979. Princeton, NJ: Gallup Organization.

Gallup Report. 1985. Princeton, NJ: Gallup Organization.

Gamarekian, Barbara. 1989. "Women Gain, But Slowly, in the Foreign Service," *New York Times*, July 28, p. 6.

Gecas, Viktor. 1982. "The Self-Concept," *Annual Review of Sociology*, 8, 1–33.

Gerth, Jeff, and Sarah Bartlett. 1989. "Kissinger and Friends and Revolving Doors," *New York Times*, April 30, pp. 1–30.

Glaster, George. 1990. "Racial Steering by Real Estate Agents: Mechanisms and Motives," *Review of Black Political Economy*, 19, 39–62.

Glastris, Paul, and Scott Minerbrook. 1989. "A Housing Program That Really Works," *U.S. News & World Report*, February 27, pp. 26–27.

Glenn, Evelyn Nakano. 1987. *Issei, Nisei, War Bride: Three Generations of Japanese-American Women in Domestic Service*. Philadelphia: Temple University Press.

———, and Roslyn L. Feldberg. 1977. "Degraded and Deskilled: The Proletarianization of Clerical Work," *Social Problems*, 25, 52–63.

Gold, Allan R. 1989. "The Struggle to Make Do Without Health Insurance," *New York Times*, July 30, pp. 1–22.

Goldin, Claudia, and Kenneth Sokoloff. 1982. "Women, Children and Industrialization in the Early Republic," *Journal of Economic History*, 42, 741–747.

Goldthorpe, John H., Catriona Llewellyn, and Clive Payne. 1987. *Social Mobility and Class Structure in Modern Britain*.New York: Oxford University Press.

Goode, William J. 1978. *The Celebration of Heroes: Prestige as Social Control System*. Berkeley: University of California Press.

Goodwin, Leonard. 1972. *Do the Poor Want to Work?* Washington, DC: Brookings Institution.

Gordon, Leonard. 1986. "College Student Stereotypes of Blacks and Jews on Two Campuses: Four Studies Spanning 50 Years," *Sociology and Social Research*,70, 200–201.

Gordon, Milton. 1964. *Assimilation in American Life*. New York: Oxford University Press.

Gordon, Murray. 1987. *Slavery in the Arab World*. New York: New Amsterdam Books.

Grabb, Edward G. 1984. *Social Inequality: Classical and Contemporary Theorists*. New York: Holt, Rinehart and Winston.

———, and Ronald Lambert. 1982. "The Subjective Meanings of Social Class Among Canadians," *Canadian Journal of Sociology*, 7, 297–307.

Grant, Linda. 1984. "Black Females' Place in the Desegregated Classroom," *Sociology of Education*, 57, 98–110.

Greenberger, Ellen, Wendy A. Goldberg, Thomas J. Crawford, and Jean Granger. 1988. "Beliefs About the Consequences of Maternal Employment for Children," *Psychology of Women Quarterly*, 12, 35–59.

Guppy, Neil, and John C. Goyder. 1984. "Consensus on Occupational Prestige: A Reassessment of the Evidence," *Social Forces*, 62, 709–725.

Haas, Ain. 1983. "The Aftermath of Sweden's Codetermination Law," *Economic and Industrial Democracy*, 4, 19–46.

Haas, Linda. 1986. "Wives' Orientation Toward Breadwinning," *Journal of Family Issues*, 7, 358–381.

Halle, David. 1984. *America's Working Man*. Chicago: University of Chicago Press.

Haller, Archibald O., Donald B. Holsinger, and Hellico U. Saravia. 1972. "Variations in Occupational Prestige Hierarchies: Brazilian Data," *American Journal of Sociology*, 77, 941–956.

Haller, Archibald O., Luther B. Otto, Robert F. Meier, and George W. Ohlendorf. 1974. "Level of Occupational Aspiration: An Empirical Analysis," *American Sociological Review*, 39, 113–121.

Hallinan, Maureen T., and Aage B. Sorensen. 1987. "Ability Grouping and Sex Differences in Mathematics Achievement,"*Sociology of Education*, 60, 63–72.

Hanagan, Michael. 1980. *The Logic of Solidarity: Artisan and Industrial Workers in Three French Towns, 1871–1914*. Urbana: University of Illinois Press.

Hanawalt, Barbara A. 1986. *The Ties That Bound: Peasant Families in Medieval England*. New York: Oxford University Press.

Hanley, Robert. 1990. "The New Math of Rich and Poor," *New York Times*, June 10, p. 6E.

Haug, Marie R., and Harold A. Widdison. 1975. "Dimensions of Occupational Prestige," *Sociology of Work and Occupations*, 2, 3–27.

Hauser, Robert M., J. N. Koffel, H. P. Travis, and P. J. Dickinson. 1975. "Temporal Change in Occupational Mobility: Evidence for Men in the United States," *American Sociological Review*, 40, 585–598.

Hazelrigg, Lawrence E. 1973. "Aspects of the Measurement of Class Consciousness," in *Comparative Social Research: Methodological Problems and Strategies*. M. Armer and A. Grimshaw, eds., pp. 219–247. New York: John Wiley.

Herring, Cedric. 1989. *Splitting the Middle: Political Alienation, Acquiescence, and Activism Among America's Middle Layers*. New York: Praeger.

Hertz, Rosanna. 1986. *More Equal Than Others*. Berkeley: University of California Press.

Hiller, Dana V., and William W. Philliber. 1986. "The Division of Labor in Contemporary Marriage: Expectations, Perceptions, and Performance," *Social Problems*,33, 191–201.

Hirschman, Charles, and Morrison G. Wong. 1986. "The Extraordinary Educational Attainment of Asian-Americans: A Search for Historical Evidence and Explanations," *Social Forces*, 65, 1–27.

Hochschild, Arlie. 1989. *The Second Shift*. New York: Viking.

Hoffman, Saul D., and Greg J. Duncan. 1988. "What Are the Economic Consequences of Divorce?" *Demography*, 25, 641–644.

Holmberg, Allan. 1950. *Nomads of the Long Bow*. Washington, DC: Smithsonian Institution.

Hooks, Bell. 1984. *Feminist Theory from Margin to Center*. Boston: South End Press.

Hope, Keith. 1982. "A Liberal Theory of Prestige," *American Journal of Sociology*, 87, 1011–1031.

———. 1981. "Vertical and Nonvertical Mobility in Three Countries," *American Sociological Review*, 47, 99–113.

Hoult, Michael. 1984a. "Occupational Mobility of Black Men: 1962–1973," *American Sociological Review*, 49, 308–322.

———. 1984b. "Status, Autonomy, and Training in Occupational Mobility," *American Journal of Sociology*, 89, 967–989.

Huber, Joan, and William H. Form. 1973. *Income and Ideology*. New York: Free Press.

Hughes, Everett C. 1962. "Good People and Dirty Work," *Social Problems*, 10, 3–11.

———. 1958. *Men and Their Work*. New York: Free Press.

Hurh, Won Moo, and Kwang Chung Kim. 1989. "The 'Success' Image of Asian Americans: Its Validity, and Its Practical and Theoretical Implications," *Ethnic and Racial Studies*, 12, 512–538.

Hwang, Sean-Shong, Steven H. Murdock, Banoo Parpia, and Rita R. Ham. 1985. "The Effects of Race and Socioeconomic Status on Residential Segregation in Texas, 1970–1980," *Social Forces*, 63, 733–747.

Jackman, Mary R., and Robert W. Jackman. 1983. *Class Awareness in the United States*. Berkeley: University of California Press.

Jackman, Mary R., and Mary Scheuer Senter. 1982. "Different Therefore Unequal: Beliefs About Trait Differences Between Groups of Unequal Status," in *Research in Stratification and Mobility*, Donald J. Treiman and Robert V. Robinson, eds., vol. 2, pp. 123–134 Greenwich, CT: JAI Press.

Jackman, Robert W. 1979. *Politics and Social Equality: A Comparative Analysis*. New York: John Wiley.

———. 1987. "Political Institutions and Voter Turnout in Industrial Democracies," *American Political Science Review*, 81, 405–423.

Jacobs, Jerry A. 1989. *Revolving Doors: Sex Segregation and Women's Careers*. Stanford, CA: Stanford University Press.

James, David R. 1988. "The Transformation of the Southern Racial State: Class and Race Determinates of Local-State Structures," *American Sociological Review*, 53, 191–208.

Jaynes, Gerald, ed. 1989. *A Common Destiny: Blacks in American Society*. New York: National Academy Press.

Jencks, Christopher, et al. 1979. *Who Gets Ahead?* New York: Basic Books.

Jencks, Christopher, and Paul E. Peterson, eds. 1991. *The Urban Underclass*. Washington, DC: Brookings Institution.

Jensen, Joan M. 1980. "Cloth, Butter and Boarder: Women's Household Production for the Market," *Review of Radical Political Economics*, 12, 14–24.

Johnson, Sally. 1988. "Homeless Get Ticket to Leave," *New York Times*, November 20, p. 52.

Jolidon, Laurence, and Judy Keen. 1990. "Blacks Have Much Ground to Make Up," *USA Today*, February 13, p. 6A.

Jones, Dylan. 1990. "Joining the Nobility, for a Princely Sum," *USA Today*, July 19, pp. 1–2D.

Josi, Barbara R., ed. 1986. *Untouchable!* London: Zed Books.

Juravich, Tom, and Peter R. Shergold. 1988. "The Impact of Unions on the Voting Behavior of Their Members," *Industrial and Labor Relations Review*, 41, pp. 374–385.

Kahl, Joseph A. 1957. *The American Class Structure*. New York: Holt, Rinehart and Winston.

Kanamine, Linda. 1991. "Racism Still Thrives, Survey Says," *USA Today*, January 9, p. 6A.

Kanter, Rosabeth M. 1977. *Men and Women of the Corporation*. New York: Basic Books.

Kaplan, Howard B. 1971. "Social Class and Self-Derogation: A Conditional Relationship," *Sociometry*, 34, 41–64.

Karmin, Monroe W. 1990. "Solving the Affordability Problem," *U.S.News & World Report*, August 6, p. 41.

Katsillis, John, and Richard Rubinson. 1990. "Cultural Capital, Student Achievement, and Educational Reproduction: The Case of Greece," *American Sociological Review*, 55, 270–279.

Kemp, Alice Able, and Shelly Coverman. 1989. "Marginal Jobs or Marginal Workers: Identifying Sex Differences in Low-Skill Occupations," *Sociological Focus*, 22, 19–37.

Kerchoff, Alan C. 1986. "Effects of Ability Grouping in British Secondary Schools," *American Sociological Review*, 51, 842–858.

———, Richard T. Campbell, and Idee Winfield-Laird. 1985. "Social Mobility in Great Britain and the United States," *American Journal of Sociology*, 91, 281–308.

Kessin, Kenneth. 1971. "Social and Psychological Consequences of Intergenerational Occupational Mobility." *American Journal of Sociology*, 77, 1–18.

Kessler-Harris, Alice. 1982. *Out to Work*. New York: Oxford University Press.

Kiernan, Michael. 1990. "Calling in a Private College Counselor," *U.S. News & World Report*, January 8, pp. 64–65.

Kiesler, Sara, Lee Sproull, and Jacquelynne S. Eccles. 1983. "Second Class Citizens," *Psychology Today*, 17, 40–48.

Kim, James. 1990. "Erasing Debt Is First Step to Start Over,." *USA Today*, June 18, pp. 1–2B.

Kimball, Meredith M. 1989. "A New Perspective on Women's Math Achievement," *Psychological Bulletin*, 105, 198–214.

Kingston, Paul W. 1984. "The Maintenance of Educational Hierarchy: Recent Trends in Where Blacks Go to College," *College and University*, 14, 37–53.

————, and Lionel S. Lewis, eds. 1990. *The High Status Track: Studies of Elite Schools and Stratification*. Albany: State University of New York Press.

Kingston, Paul W., and John C. Smart. 1990. "The Economic Pay-Off of Prestigious Colleges." in *The High Status Track: Studies of Elite Schools and Stratification*, Paul W. Kingston and Lionel S. Lewis, eds. pp. 147–174. Albany: State University of New York Press.

Kletzer, Lori G. 1991. "Job Displacement, 1979–86: How Blacks Fared Relative to Whites," *Monthly Labor Review*, 114, 17–25.

Kluegel, James R. 1990. "Trends in Whites' Explanations of the Black-White Gap in Socioeconomic Status, 1977–1989," *American Sociological Review*,55, 512–525.

————, and Eliot R. Smith. 1986. *Beliefs About Inequality*. New York: Aldine De Gruyter.

Knottnerus, J. David. 1987. "Status Attainment Research and Its Image of Society," *American Sociological Review*, 52, 113–121.

Kohn, Melvin L. and Carmi Schooler. 1983. *Work and Personality: An Inquiry into the Impact of Social Stratification*. Norwood, NJ: Ablex.

————, and Kazimierz M. Slomczynski. 1990. *Social Structure and Self Direction: A Comparative Analysis of the United States and Poland*. Cambridge, MA: Basil Blackwell.

Kolchin, Peter. 1988. *Unfree Labor: American Slavery and Russian Serfdom*. New York: Oxford University Press.

Kolenda, Paula. 1985. *Caste in Contemporary India*. Prospect Heights, IL: Waveland Press.

Krendl, Kathy A., Mary C. Broihier, and Cynthia Fleetwood. 1989. "Children and Computers: Do Sex-Related Differences Persist?" *Journal of Communication*, 39, 85–93.

Lamont, Michele, and Annette Lareau. 1988. "Cultural Capital: Allusions, Gaps and Glissandos in Recent Theoretical Developments," *Sociological Theory*, 6, 153–168.

Landry, Bart. 1987. *The New Black Middle Class*. Chicago: University of Chicago Press.

Lane, David. 1976. *The Socialist Industrial State: Toward a Political Ideology of State Socialism*. Boulder, CO: Westview Press.

Lapidus, Gail W. 1978. *Women in Russia*. Berkeley: University of California Press.

Laumann, Edward O. 1966. *Prestige and Association in an Urban Community*. Indianapolis, IN: Bobbs-Merrill.

Lee, Barrett A., Sue Hinze Jones, and David W. Lewis. 1990. "Public Beliefs About the Causes of Homelessness," *Social Forces*, 69, 253–265.

Leggett, John C. 1968. *Class, Race, and Labor*. New York: Oxford University Press.

LeMasters, E. E. 1975. *Blue-Collar Aristocrats*. Madison: University of Wisconsin Press.

Lenski, Gerhard E. 1966. *Power and Privilege: A Theory of Stratification*. New York: McGraw-Hill.

————, and Jean Lenski. 1987. *Human Societies*, 5th ed. New York: McGraw-Hill.

Leslie, Connie, and Pat Wingert. 1990. "Not as Easy as A, B or C," *Newsweek*, January 8, pp. 56–58.

Levy, Frank. 1987. *Dollars and Dreams*. New York: Russell Sage.

Lewin, Tamar. 1991. "High Medical Costs Hurt Growing Numbers in U.S.," *New York Times*, April 28, pp. 1–29.

Light, Ivan. 1972. *Ethnic Enterprise in America*. Berkeley: University of California Press.

Lightfoot, Sarah Lawrence. 1983. *The Good High School*. New York: Basic Books.

Lin, Nan, and Wen Xie. 1988. "Occupational Prestige in Urban China," *American Journal of Sociology*, 93, 793–832.

Lindgren, Ethel J. 1938. "An Example of Culture Contact Without Conflict: Reindeer Tungus and Cossacks of Northern Manchuria," *American Anthropologist*, 40, 605–621.

Lipman-Bluman, Jean. 1984. *Gender Roles and Power*. Englewood Cliffs, NJ: Prentice Hall.

Lipset, Seymour Martin, and William Schneider. 1983. *The Confidence Gap: Business, Labor, and Government in the Public Mind*. New York: Free Press.

Lockwood, David. 1958. *The Blackcoated Worker*. London: Allen & Unwin.

Logan, John R., and Linda B. Stearns. 1981. "Suburban Residential Segregation as a Non-Ecological Process," *Social Forces*, 60, 61–73.

Lopreato, Joseph, and Janet S. Chafetz. 1970. "The Political Orientation of Skidders: A Middle Range Theory," *American Sociological Review*, 35, 440–451.

Lundberg, Ferdinand 1937. *America's Sixty Families*. New York: Vanguard Press.

Maccoby, Eleanor E., and Carol N. Jacklin. 1974. *The Psychology of Sex Differences*. Stanford, CA: Stanford University Press.

McKee, J. P., and A. C. Sherriffs. 1957. "The Differential Evaluation of Males and Females," *Journal of Personality*, 25, 356–371.

MacKenzie, Gavin. 1973. *The Aristocracy of Labor*. New York: Cambridge University Press.

MacLeod, Jay. 1987. *Ain't No Making It*. Boulder, CO: Westview Press.

Mahar, Pauline Moller. 1959. "A Multiple Scaling Technique for Caste Ranking," *Man in India*, 39, pp. 127–147.

Manis, Jerome G., and Bernard M. Meltzer. 1954. "Attitudes of Textile Workers to Class Structure," *American Journal of Sociology*, 60, 30–35.

Marsh, Robert M. 1971. "The Explanation of Occupational Prestige Hierarchies," *Social Forces*, 50, 214–222.

Marshall, L. 1965. "The Kung Bushmen of the Kalahari Desert," in *Peoples of Africa*, Jack Gibbs, ed., pp. 257–258 New York: Holt.

Marx, Karl and Friedrich Engels. 1959. *Marx and Engels: Basic Writings on Politics and Philosophy*, Lewis Feuer, ed., Garden City, NY: Doubleday.

———. 1964. *Selected Writings*. T. B. Bottomore, ed., New York: McGraw-Hill.

Mason, William M., James S. House, and Steven S. Martin. 1985. "On the Dimensions of Political Alienation in America," *Sociological Methodology*, 14, 111–151.

Massey, Douglas S., Gretchen A. Condran, and Nancy A. Denton. 1987. "The Effect of Residential Segregation on Black Social and Economic Well-Being," *Social Forces*, 66, 29–56.

Massey, Douglas S., and Nancy A. Denton. 1988. "The Dimensions of Residential Segregation," *Social Forces*, 67, 281–311.

Mead, Lawrence. 1989. "The Logic of Workfare: The Underclass and Work Policy," *Annals of the American Academy of Political and Social Science*, 501, 156–169.

Meara, Hannah. 1974. "Honor in Dirty Work: The Case of American Meat Cutters and Turkish Butchers," *Sociology of Work and Occupations*, 1, 259–283.

Michel, Lawrence, and David Simon. 1988. *The State of Working America*. Washington, DC: Economic Policy Institute.

Midlarsky, Manus I. 1988. "Rulers and the Ruled: Patterned Inequality and the Onset of Mass Political Violence," *American Political Science Review*, 82, 491–509.

Milkman, Ruth. 1983. "Female Factory Labor Industrial Structure: Control and Conflict Over 'Women's Work' in Auto and Electrical Manufacturing," *Politics and Society*, 12, 159–203.

Millican, Anthony. 1988. "Attacks Tied to Bigotry Up, Report Says," *USA Today*, January 13, p. 3A.

Mills, C. Wright. 1951. *White Collar*. New York: Oxford University Press.

———. 1956. *The Power Elite*. New York: Oxford University Press.

Minerbrook, Scott. 1989. "The Big-City Push to Fill the Housing Gap for the Poor," *U.S. News & World Report*, August 28, pp. 28–29.

Mink, Gwendolyn. 1986. *Old Labor and New Immigrants in American Political Development*. Ithaca, NY: Cornell University Press.

Mintz, Beth. 1975. "The President's Cabinet, 1897–1972: A Continuation of the Power Structure Debate," *Insurgent Sociologist*, 5, 131–148.

More, Douglas M., and Robert W. Suchner. 1976. "Occupational Status, Prestige, and Stereotypes," *Sociology of Work and Occupations*, 3, 169–186.

Morris, Richard T., and Raymond J. Murphy. 1966. "A Paradigm for the Study of Class Consciousness," *Sociology and Social Research*, 50, 298–313.

Morrison, Donna R., and Daniel T. Lichter. 1988. "Family Migration and Female Employment: The Problem of Underemployment Among Migrant Married Women," *Journal of Marriage and the Family*, 50, 161–172.

Mydans, Seth. 1991. "California Expects Hispanic Voters to Transform Politics," *New York Times*, January 27, p. 4E.

Myrdal, Gunnar. 1944. *Challenge to Affluence*. New York: Pantheon.

Nagle, John. 1977. *Systems and Succession: The Social Basis of Political Elite Recruitment*. Austin: University of Texas Press.

Nash, Manning. 1962. "Race and the Ideology of Race," *Current Anthropology*, 3, 285–288.

National Urban League. 1989. *The State of Black America, 1989*. New York: National Urban League.

Newman, Katherine S. 1988. *Falling from Grace: The Experience of Downward Mobility in the American Middle Class*. New York: Free Press.

New York Times. 1988. "Philanthropy for the 21st Century," July 12, p. 4F.

New York Times. 1991. "Most Blacks Are Found to Favor Term 'Black,'" January 29, p. 19A.

Nisbet, Robert A. 1970. *The Social Bond*. New York: Knopf.

Nock, Steven L., and Peter H. Rossi. 1979. "Household Types and Social Standing," *Social Forces*, 57, 1325–1345.

Noel, Donald L. 1968. "How Ethnic Inequality Begins," *Social Problems*, 16, 157–172.

Nottingham, Elizabeth K. 1954. *Religion and Society*. New York: Random House.

Oakes, Jeannie. 1982. *Keeping Track: How Schools Structure Inequality*. Santa Monica, CA: Rand Corporation.

———. 1985. "The Reproduction of Inequality: The Content of Secondary School Tracking," *The Urban Review*, 14, 107–120.

O'Hare, William. 1989. "In the Black," *American Demographics*, 11 (November), 25–29.

———, Kelvin M. Pollard, Taynia L. Mann, and Mary M. Kent. 1991. *African Americans in the 1990s*. Washington, DC: Population Reference Bureau.

Ordovensky, Pat. 1989. "Minorities Gain, but Gaps Remain." *USA Today*, September 12, p. 5D.

Ostrander, Susan. 1984. *Women of the Upper Class*. Philadelphia: Temple University Press.

Palmer, Phyllis. 1989. *Domesticity and Dirt: Housewives and Domestic Service in the United States, 1920–1945*. Philadelphia: Temple University Press.

Pammett, Jon H. 1987. "Class Voting and Class Consciousness in Canada," *Canadian Review of Sociology and Anthropology*, 2, 269–290.

Parsons, Talcott. 1940. "An Analytic Approach to the Theory of Social Stratification," *American Journal of Sociology*, 45, 841–862.

———. 1949. "Social Classes and Class Conflict in Light of Recent Sociological Theory," *American Economic Review*, 39, 16–26.

———. 1953. "A Revised Analytic Approach to the Theory of Social Stratification," in *Class, Status and Party*, Rinehard Bendix and Seymour Martin Lipset, eds., pp. 395–415 New York: Free Press.

Pear, Robert. 1991. "A Double Dose of Pain for the Poor," *New York Times*, April 7, pp. 1–5E.

Pearce, Diana. 1978. "The Feminization of Poverty: Women, Work, and Welfare," *Urban and Social Change Review*, 12, 28–36.

Pease, John, William H. Form, and Joan Huber Rytina. 1970. "Ideological Currents in American Stratification," *American Sociologist*, 5, 127–137.

Penn, Roger. 1975. "Occupational Prestige Hierarchies: A Great Empirical Invariant," *Social Forces*, 54, 352–364.

Pessen, Edward. 1984. *The Log Cabin Myth*. New Haven, CT: Yale University Press.

Peterson, Richard A., John T. Schmidman, and Kirk W. Elifson. 1982. "Entrepreneurship or Autonomy? Truckers and Cabbies," in *Varieties of Work*, Phyllis L. Stewart and Murieal G. Cantor, eds., pp.181–198. Beverley Hills, CA: Sage.

Phillips, Kevin. 1990. *The Politics of Rich and Poor*. New York: Random House.

Physician Task Force. 1985. *Hunger in America: The Growing Epidemic*. Middletown, CT: Wesleyan University Press.

Piliavin, Irving, Michael Sosin, and Herb Westerfelt. 1987–88. "Tracking the Homeless," *Focus*, 10, 20–24.

Pope John Paul II. 1988. *Mulieris Dignitatem*. Washington, DC: NC News Services.

Poulantzas, Nicos. 1975. *Political Power and Social Classes*. London: New Left Books.

Powell, Brian, and Jerry A. Jacobs. 1984. "The Prestige Gap: Differential Evaluations of Male and Female Workers," *Work and Occupations*, 11, 283–308.

Rachin, Jill. 1989. "The Label That Sticks," *U.S. News & World Report*, July 3, pp. 51–52.

Randall, Vicky. 1987. *Women and Politics: An International Perspective*. Chicago: University of Chicago Press.

Remmington, Patricia A. 1981. *Policing*. Lanham, MD: University Press.

Richman, Louis S. 1988. "Are You Better Off Than in 1980?" *Fortune*, October 10, pp. 38–44

Ricketts, Erol R., and Isabel Sawhill. 1988. "Defining and Measuring the Underclass," *Journal of Policy Analysis and Management*, 7, 316–325.

Riding, Alan. 1989. "The Struggle for Land in Latin America," *New York Times*, March 26, pp. 1–2E.

Robinson, Robert V. 1983. "Explaining Perceptions of Class and Racial Inequality in England and the United States," *British Journal of Sociology*, 4, 344–366.

———. 1984. "Structural Change and Class Mobility in Capitalist Societies," *Social Forces*, 64

———, and M. Garnier. 1985. "Class Reproduction Among Men and Women in France: Reproduction Theory on Its Home Ground," *American Journal of Sociology*, 91, 250–280.

Robinson, Robert V., and Jonathan Kelley. 1979. "Class as Conceived by Marx and Dahrendorf: Effects on Income Inequality, Class Consciousness, and Class Conflict in the United States and Great Britain," *American Sociological Review*, 44, 38–58.

Rose, Stephen J. 1986. *The American Profile Poster*. New York: Pantheon Books.

Rosen, Ellen I. 1987. *Bitter Choices: Blue-Collar Women in and out of Work*. Chicago: University of Chicago Press.

Rosenbaum, James E. 1975. "The Stratification of the Socialization Process," *American Sociological Review*, 40, 48–54.

———. 1979. "Organizational Career Mobility," *American Journal of Sociology*, 85, 21–48.

Rosenberg, Morris. 1989. "Self-Concept Research: A Historical Overview," *Social Forces*, 68, 34–44.

———, and Leonard I. Pearlin. 1978. "Social Class and Self-Esteem Among Children and Adults," *American Journal of Sociology*, 84, 53–77.

Rosenfeld, Rachel A. 1979. "Women's Intergenerational Mobility," *American Sociological Review*, 43, 36–46.

Rosenwasser, Shirley Miller, and Norma G. Dean. 1989. "Gender Role and Political Office," *Psychology of Women Quarterly*, 13, 77–85.

———, and Jana Seale. 1989. "Attitudes Toward a Hypothetical Male or Female Presidential Candidate," *Political Psychology*, 9, 591–598.

Rossi, Peter H., and James D. Wright. 1987. "The Determinants of Homelessness," *Health Affairs*, 6, 19–32.

Rossides, Daniel W. 1990. *Social Stratification*. Englewood Cliffs, NJ: Prentice Hall.

Rowen, Brian, and Andrew W. Miracle Jr. 1983. "Systems of Ability Grouping and the Stratification of Achievement on Elementary Schools," *Sociology of Education*, 56, 133–144.

Rubin, Beth. 1986. "Class Struggle American Style: Unions, Strikes and Wages," *American Sociological Review*, 51, 618–633.

Rubin, Lillian. 1976. *Worlds of Pain: Life in the Working Class Family*. New York: Basic Books.

Rundel, Rhonda. 1987. "New Efforts to Fight Heart Disease Are Aimed at Blue-Collar Workers," *Wall Street Journal*, March 16, p. 25.

Ryscavage, Paul. 1986. "Reconciling Divergent Trends in Real Income," *Monthly Labor Review*, 109, 24–29.

Saint-Germain, Michelle A. 1989. "Does Their Difference Make a Difference? The Impact of Women on Public Policy in the Arizona Legislature," *Social Science Quarterly*, 70, 956–968.

Saltzman, Amy. 1991. "Trouble at the Top," *U.S. News & World Report*, June 17, pp. 40–48.

Saltzstein, Grace Hall. 1986. "Female Mayors and Women in Municipal Jobs." *American Journal of Political Science* 30: 140–164.

———. 1989. "Black Mayors and Police Policies," *Journal of Politics*, 51, 525–544.

Sandefur, Gary D., and Arthur Sakamoto. 1988. "American Indian Household Structure and Income," *Demography*, 25, 71–80.

Sawhill, Isabel. 1989. "The Underclass: An Overview," *The Public Interest*, 96, 3–15.

Sawyer, Robert. 1986. *Slavery in the Twentieth Century*. London: Routledge & Kegan Paul.

Schreiber, E. M., and G. T. Nygreen. 1970. "Subjective Social Class in America, 1945–1968," *Social Forces*, 48, 348–356.

Schein, Virginia Ellen. 1973. "The Relationship Between Sex Role Stereotypes and Requisite Management Characteristics," *Journal of Applied Psychology*, 57, 95–100.

Schuman, Howard, Charlotte Steeh, and Lawrence Bobo. 1988. *Racial Attitudes in America*. Cambridge, MA: Harvard University Press.

Schuster, Rachel. 1987. "NFL: Pressure Builds to Hire Black Coaches," *USA Today*, December 4, p. 9C.

Scott, Hilda. 1984. *Working Your Way to the Bottom: The Feminization of Poverty*. London: Pandora Press.

Sharda, Bam Dev, and Barry E. Nangle. 1981. "Marital Effects on Occupational Attainment," *Journal of Family Issues*, 2, 148–163.

Sherman, J. 1980. "Mathematics, Spatial Visualization and Related Factors: Changes in Girls and Boys, Grades 8–11," *Journal of Educational Psychology*, 72, 476–482.

Shibutani, Tamotsu, and Kian M. Kwan. 1965. *Ethnic Stratification: A Comparative Approach*. New York: Macmillan.

Shostak, Arthur B. 1969. *Blue Collar Life*, New York: Random House.

Simmons, Roberta G., and Morris Rosenberg. 1971. "Functions of Children's Perceptions of the Stratification System," *American Sociological Review*, 36, 235–249.

Simpson, Ida Harper, and Elizabeth Mutran. 1981. "Women's Social Consciousness: Sex or Worker Identity?" *Research in the Sociology of Work*, 1, 335–350.

———, Davis Stark, and Robert A. Jackman. 1988. "Class Identification Processes of Married, Working Men and Women," *American Sociological Review*, 53, 284–293.

Sio, Arnold A. 1965. "Interpretations of Slavery: The Slave Status in the Americas," *Comparative Studies in Society and History*, 7, 289–308.

Skafte, Dianne. 1989. "The Effect of Perceived Wealth and Poverty on Adolescents' Character Judgments," *Journal of Social Psychology*, 129, 93–99.

Slomczynski, Kazimierz M., and Tadeusz K. Krauze. 1987. "Cross-National Similarity in Social Mobility Patterns," *American Sociological Review*, 52, 598–611.

Smith, James P., and Finis R. Welch. 1986. *Closing the Gap: Forty Years of Economic Progress for Blacks*. Santa Monica, CA: Rand Corporation.

Smith, M. Dwayne, and Lynne J. Fisher. 1982. "Sex-Role Attitudes and Social Class: A Reanalysis and Clarification," *Journal of Comparative Family Studies*, 13, 11–88.

Smith, Robert C. 1988. "Financing Black Politics: A Study of Congressional Elections," *Review of Black Political Economy*, 17, 5–30.

Snow, David A., Susan G. Baker, Leon Anderson and Michael Martin. 1986. "The Myth of Pervasive Mental Illness Among the Homeless," *Social Problems*, 33, 408–417.

Sonenshein, Raphael J. 1990. "Can Black Candidates Win Statewide Elections?" *Political Science Quarterly*, 105, 219–241.

Sperling, Dan. 1989. "Affluent See PCs to VCRs as 'Necessities,'" *USA Today*, February 27, p. 1A.

Squires, Gregory D., and William Velez. 1987. "Insurance Redlining and the Transformation of an Urban Metropolis," *Urban Affairs Quarterly*, 23, 63–83.

———. 1988. "Insurance Redlining and the Process of Discrimination," *Review of Black Political Economy*, 16, 63–75.

Srinivas, M. N. 1966. *Social Change in Modern India*. Bombay: Allied.

Stanley, Sandra C., Janet G. Hunt and Larry L. Hunt. 1986. "The Relative Deprivation of Husbands in Dual-Earner Households," *Journal of Family Issues*, 7, 3–20.

Staples, Clifford L., Michael L. Schwalbe, and Victor Gecas. 1984. "Social Class, Occupational Conditions, and Efficacy-Based Self-Esteem," *Sociological Perspectives*, 27, 85–109.

Stearns, Linda Brewster, and John R. Logan. 1986. "The Racial Structuring of the Housing Market and Segregation in Suburban Areas, *Social Forces*, 65, 28–42.

Stevens, Gillian. 1986. "Sex-Differentiated Patterns of Intergenerational Occupational Mobility," *Journal of Marriage and the Family*, 48, 153–163.

Stevenson, Harold W. 1982. *School Experiences and Performances of Asian-Pacific American High School Students*. Washington, DC: U.S. Department of Education.

Stewart, Sally Ann, and William Dunn. 1989. "Beverly Hills: A Town Apart," *USA Today*, January 27, p. 3A

Stier, Haya, and David B. Grusky. 1990. "An Overlapping Persistence Model of Career Mobility," *American Sociological Review*, 55, 736–756.

Stockard, J., and W. Wood. 1984. "The Myth of Female Underachievement: A Reexamination of Sex Differences in Academic Underachievement," *American Educational Research Journal*, 21, 825–838.

Stolzenberg, Ross M. 1990. "Ethnicity, Geography, and Occupational Attainment of Hispanic Men in the United States," *American Sociological Review*, 55, 143–154.

Stone, Lawrence. 1965. "Class Divisions in England, 1540–1640." in *European Social Class: Stability and Change*, Bernard Barber and Elinor Barber, eds., New York: Macmillan.

Streitweiser, Mary, and John Goodman. 1983. "A Survey of Recent Research on Race and Residential Location," *Population Research and Policy Review*, 2, 253–283.

Sullivan, Teresa A. 1978. *Marginal Workers, Marginal Jobs*. Austin: University of Texas Press.

Sumner, William Graham. 1914. *The Challenge of Facts and Other Essays*. New Haven, CT: Yale University Press.

Suro, Roberto. 1990. "Courts Ordering Financing Changes in Public Schools," *New York Times*, March 11, pp. 1–28.

Swafford, Michael. 1978. "Sex Differences in Soviet Earnings." *American Sociological Review*, 43, 657–673.

Taylor, John. 1989. *Circus of Ambition*. New York: Warner.

Taylor, Robert Joseph, Linda M. Chatters, M. Belinda Tucker, and Edith Lewis. 1990. "Developments in Research on Black Families: A Decade Review," *Journal of Marriage and the Family*, 52, 993–1014.

Terkel, Studs. 1972. *Working*. New York: Random House.

Thomas, Melvin E., and Michael Hughes. 1986. "The Continuing Significance of Race: A Study of Race, Class, and Quality of Life in America, 1972–1985," *American Sociological Review*, 51, 830–841.

Thompson, Linda, and Alexis J. Warner. 1989. "Gender in Families: Women and Men in Marriage, Work and Parenthood," *Journal of Marriage and the Family*, 51, 845–871.

Tickamyer, Ann R., and Kathleen M. Blee. 1990. "The Racial Convergence Thesis in Women's Intergenerational Occupational Mobility," *Social Science Quarterly*, 71, 711–728.

Tilgher, Adriano. 1930. *Homo Faber: Work Through the Ages*. New York: Harcourt, Brace & World.

Time. 1983. September 8, p. 48.

Toner, Robin. 1989. "Americans Favor Aid for Homeless," *New York Times*, January 22, pp. 1–21.

Tooley, Jo Ann. 1989. "Surprise, It's Nice to Be a CEO," *U.S. News & World Report*, January 16, p. 70.

Treiman, Donald J. 1977. *Occupational Prestige in Comparative Perspective*. New York: Academic Press.

Trost, Cathy. 1988. "Men, Too, Wrestle with Career-Family Stress," *Wall Street Journal*, November 1, p. 1B.

Tudor, Jeanette F. 1971. "The Development of Class Awareness Among Children," *Social Forces*, 49, 470–476.

Tumin, Melvin M. 1953. "Some Principles of Stratification: A Critical Analysis," *American Sociological Review*, 18, 387–393.

Turner, Frederick Jackson. 1920. *The Frontier in American History*. New York: Holt.

Tyree, Andrea, and Judith Treas. 1974. "The Occupational and Marital Mobility of Women," *American Sociological Review*, 39, 293–302.

United Nations. 1981. *Statistical Yearbook, 1980*. New York.

———. 1991. *The World's Women, 1970–1990: Trends and Statistics*. New York.

U.S. Bureau of the Census. 1986. Current Population Reports, Series P–70, No. 7. *Household Wealth and Asset Ownership: 1984*. Washington, DC: U.S. Government Printing Office.

———. 1987. Current Population Reports, Series P–60, No. 155. *Receipt of Selected Noncash Benefits: 1986*. Washington, DC: U.S. Government Printing Office.

———. 1989a. Current Population Reports, Series P–60, No. 162. *Poverty in the United States, 1988*. Washington, DC: U.S. Government Printing Office.

———. 1989b. Current Population Reports, Series P–25, No. 431. *The Hispanic Population in the United States*. Washington, DC: U.S. Government Printing Office.

———. 1990a. Current Population Reports, Series P–23, No. 152. *Child Support and Alimony: 1988*. Washington, DC: U.S. Government Printing Office.

———. 1990b. Current Population Reports, Series P–70, No. 18. *Transitions in Income and Poverty Status, 1985–86*. Washington, DC: U.S. Government Printing Office.

U.S. Commission on Civil Rights. 1986. *Recent Activities Against Citizens of Asian Descent*. Washington, DC: U.S. Government Printing Office.

———. 1990. *Bigotry and Violence on American College Campuses*. Washington, DC: U.S. Government Printing Office.

———. 1987. *New Evidence on School Desegregation*. Washington, DC: U.S. Government Printing Office.

U.S. Congress. 1986. Joint Economic Committee. *The Concentration of Wealth in the United States*. Washington, DC: U.S. Government Printing Office.

U.S. Department of Justice. 1988. *Criminal Victimization in the United States, 1986*. Washington, DC: U.S. Government Printing Office.

Useem, Michael. 1983. *The Inner Circle: Large Corporations and the Rise of Business Activity in the U.S. and U.K.* New York: Oxford University Press.

———, and Jerome Karabel. 1986. "Pathways to Top Corporate Management," *American Sociological Review*, 51, 184–200.

Valdivieso, Rafael, and Cary Davis. 1988. *U.S. Hispanics: Challenging Issues for the 1990s*. Washington, DC: Population Reference Bureau.

Vanfossen, Beth E. 1977. "Sexual Stratification and Sex Role Socialization," *Journal of Marriage and the Family*, 39, 563–574.

Vanneman, Reeve, and Diane Cannon. 1987. *The American Perception of Class*. Philadelphia: Temple University Press.

Vanneman, Reeve, and Fred C. Pampel. 1977. "The American Perception of Class and Status," *American Sociological Review*, 42, 422–437.

Veblen, Thorstein. 1899. *The Theory of the Leisure Class*. New York: Macmillan.

Vega, William A. 1990. "Hispanic Families in the 1980s: A Decade of Research," *Journal of Marriage and the Family*, 52, 1015–1024.

Verba, Sidney, Norman H. Nie and Jae-on Kim. 1978. *Participation and Political Equality: A Seven-Nation Comparison*. New York: Cambridge University Press.

Voslensky, Michael. 1984. *Nomenklatura: The Soviet Ruling Class*. Garden City, NY: Doubleday.

Voydanoff, Patricia. 1988. "Work Role Characteristics, Family Structure Demands, and Work/Family Conflict," *Journal of Marriage and the Family*, 50, 749–761.

Waldman, Steven. 1989. "The Revolving Door," *Newsweek*, February 6, pp. 16–18.

Walmer, Tracy. 1991. "1 Out of 8 U.S. Kids Is Hungry," *USA Today*, March 27, p. 1A.

Warner, W. Lloyd and Paul Lunt. 1941. *The Social Life of a Modern Community*. New Haven, CT: Yale University Press.

———, Marcia Meeker, and Kenneth Eells. 1949. *Social Class in America: A Manual of Procedure for the Measurement of Social Status*. Chicago: Science Research Associates.

Weber, Max. 1946. *Theory of Social and Economic Organization*. A. M. Henderson and Talcott Parsons, trans. New York: Free Press.

Weikart, David P., ed. 1985. *Changed Lives*. Ypsilanti, MI: High Scope Press.

Weiss, John. 1989. *Standing Up to the SAT*. New York: Arco.

Weiss, Michael J. 1988. *The Clustering of America*. New York: Harper & Row.

Weitzman, Lenore. 1985. *The Divorce Revolution: The Unexpected Social and Economic Consequences for Women and Children in America*. New York: Free Press.

Wentzel, Kathryn R. 1988. "Gender Differences in Math and English Achievement: A Longitudinal Study," *Sex Roles*, 18, 691–699.

Whitman, David. 1989a. "Shattering Myths About the Homeless," *U.S. News & World Report*, March 20 pp. 26–28.

———. 1989b. "Behind the Housing Crisis," *U.S. News & World Report*, October 16, pp. 28–32.

Wilensky, Harold, and Hugh Edwards. 1949. "The Skidder: Ideological Adjustment of Downward Mobile Workers," *American Sociological Review*, 14, 215–231.

Wiley, Norbert. 1967. "America's Unique Class Politics: The Interplay of Labor, Credit and Commodity Markets," *American Sociological Review*, 3,: 529–541.

Williams, J. Allen, Jr., and Suzanne T. Ortega. 1990. "Dimensions of Ethnic Assimilation: An Empirical Appraisal of Gordon's Typology," *Social Science Quarterly*, 71, 697–710.

Williams, John E., and Deborah L. Best. 1990. *Measuring Sex Stereotypes: A Multination Study*. Newbury Park, CA: Sage.

Wilson, Jean Gaddy. 1989. *Taking Stock: Women in the Media Before the 21st Century*. Columbia: University of Missouri, New Direction for News Institute.

Wilson, William Julius. 1987. *The Truly Disadvantaged*. Chicago: University of Chicago Press.

———. 1989. "The Underclass: Issues, Perspectives, and Public Policy," *Annals of the American Academy of Political and Social Science*, 501, 182–192.

Winfield, Idee, Richard T. Campbell, Alan C. Kerchhoff, Diane D. Everett, and Jerry M. Trott. 1989. "Career Processes in Great Britain and the United States," *Social Forces*, 68, 284–308.

Winsberg, Morton D. 1986. "Geographic Polarization of Whites and Minorities in Large U.S. Cities: 1960–1980." *Population Today*, 14 (March), 6–7.

Wirth, Louis. 1945. "The Problem of Minority Groups." in *The Science of Man in the World Crisis*, Ralph Linton, ed., pp. 347–372. New York: Columbia University Press.

Work, Clemens P. 1989. "Uncle Sam as Unfair Trader," *U.S. News & World Report*, June 12, pp. 42–44.

Wright, Erik Olin. 1976. *Class, Crisis and the State*. London: New Left Books.

———. 1985. *Classes*. London: New Left Books.

———, 1989. The Debate on Classes. London: Verso.

———, and Bill Martin. 1987. "The Transformation of the American Class Structure, 1960–1980." *American Journal of Sociology*, 93, 1–29.

Wright, James D. 1988. "The Worthy and Unworthy Homeless," *Society*, 25, 64–69.

Zingraff, Rhonda, and Michael D. Schulman. 1984. "Social Bases of Class Consciousness," *Social Forces*, 63, 98–116.

Zipp, John F., and Eric Plutzer. 1985. "Gender Differences in Voting for Female Candidates: Evidence from the 1982 Election," *Public Opinion Quarterly*, 49, 179–197.

Zussman, Robert. 1985. *Mechanisms of the Middle Class: Work and Politics Among American Engineers*. Berkeley: University of California Press.

Author Index

Subject Index